Kafka's Blues

Figurations of Racial Blackness in the Construction of an Aesthetic

✦

Mark Christian Thompson

NORTHWESTERN UNIVERSITY PRESS
EVANSTON, ILLINOIS

Northwestern University Press
www.nupress.northwestern.edu

Printed in the United States of America

10 9 8 7 6 5 4 3 2 1

Library of Congress Cataloging-in-Publication Data

Names: Thompson, Mark Christian, 1970– author.
Title: Kafka's blues : figurations of racial blackness in the construction of an aesthetic / Mark Christian Thompson.
Description: Evanston, Illinois : Northwestern University Press, 2016. | Includes bibliographical references and index.
Identifiers: LCCN 2016014072 | ISBN 9780810132856 (pbk. : alk. paper) | ISBN 9780810132863 (cloth : alk. paper) | ISBN 9780810132870 (e-book)
Subjects: LCSH: Kafka, Franz, 1883–1924—Criticism and interpretation. | German literature—Czech Republic—Prague—History and criticism. | Blacks—Race identity—In literature. | Race in literature.
Classification: LCC PT2621.A26 Z9318 2016 | DDC 833/.912—dc23
LC record available at http://lccn.loc.gov/2016014072

For my daughter, Madeleine Anna Thompson,

September 14, 2011

CONTENTS

Kafka's Blues

ABBREVIATIONS

Throughout the text and notes, the following abbreviations are used to cite the works of Franz Kafka:

AH — *Amerika (The Man Who Disappeared).* Translated by Michael Hofmann. New York: New Directions, 2004.

AM — *Amerika.* Translated by Willa and Edwin Muir. New York: Schocken Books, 1996.

B — *Briefe 1902–1924.* Edited by Max Brod. Frankfurt: Fischer, 1958.

BF — *Briefe an Felice und andere Korrespondenz aus der Verlobungszeit.* Edited by Erich Heller and Jürgen Born. Frankfurt: Fischer, 1967.

BM — *Briefe an Milena.* Edited by Jürgen Born and Michael Müller. Frankfurt: Fischer, 1983.

BV — *Brief an den Vater.* Frankfurt: Fischer, 2011.

C — *The Complete Stories.* Edited by Nahum N. Glatzer. New York: Schocken Books, 1995.

D — *Drucke zu Lebzeiten: Kritische Ausgabe.* Edited by Wolf Kittler, Hans-Gerd Koch, and Gerhard Neumann. Frankfurt: Fischer, 1994.

J — *The Diaries.* Translated by Joseph Kresh and Martin Greenberg. New York: Schocken Books, 1975.

KA — *Kritische Ausgabe.* Edited by Jürgen Born, Gerhard Neumann, Sir Malcolm Pasley, and Jost Schillemeit. Frankfurt: Fischer, 1994.

L — *Letters to Friends, Family, and Editors.* Translated by Richard and Clara Winston. New York: Schocken Books, 1977.

LF — *Letters to Felice.* Edited by Erich Heller and Jürgen Born.Translated by James Stern and Elisabeth Duckworth. New York: Schocken Books, 1973.

LM — *Letters to Milena.* Translated by Philip Boehm. New York: Schocken Books, 1990.

LTF — "Letter to His Father." In *Kafka's "The Metamorphosis" and Other Writings*, edited by Helmuth Kiesel, translated by Ernst Kaiser and Eithne Wilkins, 175–229. New York: Continuum, 2002.

N — *Nachgelassene Schriften und Fragmente: Kritische Ausgabe.* Edited by Jürgen Born, Gerhard Neumann, Malcolm Pasley, and Jost Schillemeit. 2 vols. Frankfurt: Fischer, 1992–93.

T — *Tagebücher.* Edited by Hans-Gerd Koch, Michael Müller, and Malcolm Pasley. Frankfurt: Fischer, 1990.

V — *Der Verschollene (Amerika).* Edited by Jürgen Born, Gerhard Neumann, Sir Malcolm Pasley, and Jost Schillemeit. Frankfurt: Fischer, 1994.

Kafka's Blues

INTRODUCTION

This book shows that many of Kafka's major works engage in a coherent, sustained meditation on racial blackness and in several instances metaphorically portray bodily transformation from white European into what Kafka refers to as the "Negro"—a term that he used in English. Kafka's thinking of racial blackness is integral to his work in terms of thematic progression and aesthetic form. Indeed, this book demonstrates that the creation of a work of art is, for Kafka, impossible without passage through a contextual and corporeal state of being "Negro." Kafka represents this passage in various ways—from reflections on New World slavery and black music, to evolutionary recapitulation theory and ethnography, to biblical allusion.

Examining figures of racial blackness in Kafka places this study in close proximity to the recently developed postcolonial critical paradigm in Kafka studies. While this study does not practice postcolonial criticism sensu stricto, it shares with the growing body of postcolonial work in Kafka studies concerns over exoticism, racial alienation, and the cultural displacement and deterritorialization of the minoritized, subaltern subject. Postcolonial-inflected readings in Kafka studies tend to take Deleuze and Guattari's *Kafka: Pour une littérature mineure* (1975) as the starting point. The conceptual and historical premises and lexicon of Deleuze and Guattari's text, such as deterritorialization, have by no means gone unchallenged in the field. Kafka scholars as important as Stanley Corngold undercut Deleuze and Guattari's value for a postcolonial reading of Kafka, and to a larger extent the postcolonial endeavor within Kafka studies, by pointedly reminding us that, as Corngold writes, "Kafka's relation to the traditions of his literary community is no different in principle from that of other German and European writers who turned for inspiration to non-European sources (thus Goethe to Persian poetry, Schopenhauer to Sanskrit literature, Yeats and Brecht to [Japanese] Nō [theater], Pound to Chinese ideograms" (Corngold 1994, 95–96).

Works such as Susanne Zantop's *Colonial Fantasies: Conquest, Family, and Nation in Precolonial Germany, 1770–1870* (1997), and Russell Berman's *Enlightenment or Empire: Colonial Discourse in German Culture* (1998), while not directly concerned with Kafka or Deleuze and Guatarri, act as a corrective to this view. The intellectual climate and aesthetic engagement both in and outside the colonial metropole involved a far more wide-ranging and complex dialectic of colonizer and colonized that, in Kafka's case, differs from mere exoticist fascination and appropriation. For while it is true that

Kafka, as a German-speaking Jew living in Prague beholden to Vienna as subject of the Dual Monarchy, was not subject to the same juridical treatment and social stigmatization as, say, an Indian under the British Raj, postcolonial theory has nevertheless offered Kafka scholars indispensable, powerful tools for understanding Kafka's exoticized and exoticizing, alienated, marginalized linguistic and cultural predicament. Kafka's relation to citizenship, state, and minority status is not that of Goethe.

Deleuze and Guattari's text, as well as the postcolonial discursive practices partly derived from it, thus remain valuable as vital hermeneutic models from which to derive a method of close reading that aligns well with the critical issues raised by Kafka's body of work. As Réda Bensmaïa writes, "The concept of minor literature permits a reversal: instead of Kafka's work being related to some preexistent category or literary genre, it will henceforth serve as a *rallying point* or *model* for certain texts and 'bi-lingual' writing practices that, until now, had to pass through a long purgatory before even being read, much less recognized" (foreword, Deleuze and Guattari 1975, xiv). Starting either in direct relation or with some amount of reference to this rallying point offered by Deleuze and Guattari, major works of recent Kafka scholars such as John Zilcosky, Rolf J. Goebel, Gerhard Neumann, and others have established postcolonial approaches to Kafka as a preeminent, compelling collective force with which scholars of any critical disposition must reckon.[1] This study adds to the growing list of works in Kafka studies interested in how exoticism and minority culture intervene in the creation of Kafka's oeuvre.

Part of the postcolonial project within Kafka studies necessitates to some extent a cultural-historical accounting of Kafka's literary output. This in turn complements another recent trend in Kafka studies—namely, the critical practice of reading his texts through their cultural-material circumstances and seeing them as historically contingent. Works of Kafka cultural studies such as Scott Spector's *Prague Territories: National Conflict and Cultural Innovation in Franz Kafka's Fin-de-Siècle* (2000), Mark Anderson's *Kafka's Clothes: Ornament and Aestheticism in the Habsburg Fin de Siècle* (1992), sociological-contextual surveys such as the multieditor volume *Kafka und Prag: Literatur-, kultur-, sozial- und sprachhistorische Kontexte* (2012), and recent turns to Kafka's office writings, while not taking an explicit postcolonial view of matters, situate Kafka's works in their immediate historical-material surroundings and in this way generate formidable interpretive reading models.[2] These critics have helped to expand Kafka studies away from the previously centrifugal forces of rigorously yet exclusively theoretical-philosophical modes of interpretation and predominately biography-informed readings of his texts. This is not to say that these critical endeavors were faulty or unproductive but that the act of reading Kafka as embedded in and determined by a certain time and place, beholden to material objects and cultural artifacts, has offered us a complementary yet different view of his oeuvre with regard to the conditions of its inception. The cultural-material epistemes of each text and the body of work as a whole continue to make their presence felt in Kafka's work as they create and modify the epistemological conditions for the moment of close reading and philosophical reflection.

Of course, postcolonial and cultural studies as critical practices and main interpretive frames for reading Kafka do not preclude close reading or more traditional, theoretical and biographical modes of understanding. They coexist with and enrich these approaches. As a case in point, this study uses the methodologies of close reading and biography, as well as the postcolonial and cultural critical procedures of Kafka studies, and does so for two specific reasons. First, the tropes and themes it traces—namely, racial blackness in all its variants—have no firmly established archive in Kafka studies. The closest we have come to this is the excellent body of work surrounding Kafka's use of "Negro" in *Der Verschollene* (written between 1911 and 1914, published 1927). This is not a reproach but a sign of the second reason—namely, that racial blackness in Kafka is deeply buried. In order to exhume it while at the same time establishing its archive, it is necessary to use all available means. Biography and theory here are essential to postcolonial critique and cultural-critical investigation, and no one discursive approach is privileged, on the whole, over another.

Furthermore, this book also looks to thematic and theoretical aspects of African American literary studies, and black studies more generally, to present certain claims that have no comprehensive precedent in Kafka studies. American studies and the wider arena of Anglo-American modernist studies also serve this purpose. Obviously, questions of primitivism and exoticism in fin-de-siècle literature transcend national literary barriers and narrowly construed determinations of ethnic cultural expressivity. European primitivism, for example, is just as much an issue in African American and American literature as it is in studies of European modernism; and the influence of jazz on aesthetic culture is just as much an issue for European modernism as it is in African American and American studies. The difference between approaches comes in the differing ways in which individual artists and collective movements addressed an issue. Jean Toomer, James Weldon Johnson, and W. E. B. Du Bois responded to primitivism in a way other than that of Alfred Döblin, Gottfried Benn, and Emil Nolde. Nevertheless, artists of any background of the time and place of primitivism share the instigation of the encounter.

Kafka's reaction to primitivism is somewhat unique in that he does not write a text containing formally primitivist elements, as in the cases of, say, Gertrude Stein's "Melanctha" (1909) and Guillaume Apollinaire's *Alcools* (1913); nor does he reproduce the black dialect we find in Eliot's and Pound's more unguarded moments.[3] Kafka's "primitivism" is not the literary stylistic approximation of African art of Picasso and Matisse, and he does not include specifically African or Africanized characters in his texts, as do a host of authors including Peter Altenberg and Robert Musil. One could not even go so far as to say that "In der Strafkolonie" (written 1914, published 1919) is an exercise in primitivism, despite its setting. What we find at work in Kafka are aspects of primitivism that are not formal or characterological but tropological and taxonomic. Kafka is concerned with exoticism and degeneration, primitivist tropes that determine a text without breaking bread with an overall primitivist aesthetic. In this sense, it is the ethnocultural primitivism of works as disparate as Freud's *Totem und Tabu* (1913), Max Nordau's *Entartung* (1892), and Otto Weininger's *Geschlecht und Charakter* (1903) that authorizes Kafka to use certain of its composing elements without committing to the whole, and not those of Hermann Bahr, Carl Einstein, and Der Blaue Reiter.

Thus we find in Kafka a presentation of cultural figural blackness without any deep concern for black lived and historical experience. This is not to say that Kafka was unaware of or ignored the reality of New World slavery and postreconstruction lynching but that racial blackness in Kafka is a pervasive metaphor and mechanism for imagining how one becomes an artist. In this sense, in his work Kafka has displaced primitivism from the work of art to the art worker, which is why his primitivist discourse is more in the order of that of a cultural critic rather than an artist. That said, Kafka's artist figures are not purely primitives, wild men, or "savages"; they are themselves always already exotic beings caught in a process of becoming an artist that carries them through a stage of racial blackness on the way to the unknown poised before black figuration.

We know that Kafka gave significant if not detailed thought both to black art and to the artists who produce it. For in a journal entry of December 15, 1910, Kafka observes that "Kein Wort fast, das ich schreibe, paßt zum andren, ich höre, wie sich die Konsonanten blechern aneinanderreiben, und die Vokale singen dazu wie Ausstellungsneger" (*T* 130) (Almost every word I write jars against the next, I hear the consonants rub leadenly against each other and the vowels sing an accompaniment like Negroes in a minstrel show [*J* 29]). Kafka's writing produces a literary text that emits a calculated cacophony, one that clangs as the consonants rub together and as the vowels carol like performing *Völkerschau* blacks (generally translated as "human zoo"). The word *Ausstellungsneger* (literally, "exhibition nigger" or "exhibition Negro") is translated here as "Negroes in a minstrel show." While the translation by Joseph Kresh and Martin Greenberg is not accurate, one understands their choice. The concept of an "exhibition Negro" is far less well known in North America, despite the fact that such *Völkerschauen* took place there. Furthermore, while not ideal, Kresh may have felt that "Negroes in a minstrel show" was less offensive than "exhibition Negro," as it avoided the topic of *Völkerschauen* while retaining the idea not of minstrelsy construed as whites in blackface but of black performers with some modicum of black autonomy.[4] Indeed, for such troupes, most of their audience was black (Toll 1974, 227).[5] It should also be noted that minstrel shows of both sorts, including the well-known black minstrel theater Callender's Consolidated Colored Minstrels (also known as Callender's Georgia Minstrels), were exported to Europe as early as the mid-nineteenth century, where they drew wide interest. Given their enduring popularity, it is unlikely that Kafka did not know what a black minstrel show was. Thus, we have a case where the wrong translation does something at least partially right. Be that as it may, Kafka is referring here to Africans in *Völkerschauen*. In order to avoid the same problem the translator faced, I refer to *Ausstellungsneger* in German, thus steering clear of cumbersome phrases such as "exhibition nigger" and "exhibition Negro" or some such variant. It should be understood, however, that when I do use "minstrel," "minstrelsy," and any of their permutations, I mean (unless I state otherwise) only Africans and peoples of African descent in *Völkerschauen* and black minstrel shows.

While employing his musical *Ausstellungsneger* as simile for his art, Kafka insists that the sense of his writing is drowned out by the sheer weight of its—to the European ear—blistering dissonance, or what Tricia Rose has referred to in a different context as "black noise."[6] Indeed, the Negro signifies for Kafka impenetrable meaning conveyed through black noise performed under the label of music. This starting point for a type of exoticism in Kafka's work was easily available to him in his immediate surroundings in the form of the popular, previously mentioned *Völkerschau*. Impresarios, the most famous of whom was Carl Hagenbeck, coaxed, cajoled, or kidnapped Africans in order to display them for profit in their "natural" habitats either in or as a zoo in European and American cities.[7] Such a spectacle was widely known and visited at the turn of the century, Vienna being one of the *Völkerschau*'s most frequent destinations.[8]

These shows served many purposes. Aside from the sheer thrill of exoticist-colonial spectacle, they generated colonial propaganda as entertainment, justifying the colonial enterprise by displaying the power and ability of the colonizer to produce such shows along with a content that presented the subaltern as inferior and in need of colonial uplift. Human zoos—as well as panopticons such as Castan's in Berlin, which also provided *Völkerschauen*, in wax—racialized the human body by producing embodied examples of perceived human difference.[9] Colonial subjects were no longer seen exclusively in photographs or read about in newspapers, travelogues, novels, and so on; they lived and breathed in colonial fantasies made real before the audience's very eyes. For the spectator, here was an African in flesh and blood, living as an African would in his or her "native" village. The audience was given not a reminder but the creation of the living black body as irrevocably and inherently inferior other at the heart of European and American metropoles. Generating and placing this other in the context of a zoo and often alongside animals associated the two in the viewer's mind, reinforcing the common colonial-racist stereotype that blacks were located closer to animals on the evolutionary scale than to humans. The juxtaposition of black with animal became entertainment and indelible proof of white power.

The *Völkerschau* was also an ethnographic showcase, highlighting scientific-racial stereotypes of blacks that persist to the present day. Taking a cue from Henry Maine's evolutionary account of the development of law in societies in *Ancient Law* (1861), as well as from Cesare Lombroso's ideas of criminal atavism, peoples of African descent displayed in *Völkerschauen* were shown to be congenitally criminal in that they were already and necessarily in captivity and if let loose would succumb to their base instinct for destruction. One need only think of Freud's ethnological conception of the unconscious in *Totem und Tabu* to see the perceived danger blacks posed, criminal and sexual, to fin-de-siècle society. The Hottentot Venus and the scantily clad or naked, prodigiously phallic African male, chosen by the zoo for certain exaggerated anatomical properties, were determined to be "deviant bodies" because of them.[10] Furthermore, blacks were often idle and bored during the "performances," confirming for the audience that they were incorrigibly lazy, since what the spectator saw must have been the "performers'" usual, authentic activity, which conformed to scientific and ethnographic "fact." This aspect of black "character" was also strongly emphasized in minstrel shows. When the "natives" did "perform," the "shows," as accurate portraits of life in African tribal society, often showcased music and dance, giving credence for the audience to the idea that blacks were inherently musical, a stereotype also reinforced by minstrel shows.

Such was only a portion of the racism of the day. Salient to note is that, where most spectators saw these black traits in a negative light in need of correction via Christianity, colonial rule, and slavery, Kafka understood them as positive qualities to be appropriated not for the work of art but as the artist. Unlike Picasso in the Trocadéro stealing styles from tribal artifacts taken hopelessly out of context, Kafka's identification was first and foremost with the "performer's" body and then with his or her product. And while his appropriation was also hopelessly out of context, the average fin-de-siècle observer would have rejected such a claim. Of course, Kafka did not question that blacks did congenitally possess scientifically and ethnographically identified attributes of perversion, criminality, and laziness, potentially making his perception of them no less racist than that of his contemporaries. But he nevertheless used what he saw in order to describe a problem in ethnographic procedure and attempt to reach a positive solution to what appeared to him as the aporias of racism. I am not "forgiving" Kafka for his metaphorical and metonymic use of blacks understood only schematically and firmly embedded in a much wider, more complicated, historically nuanced ethnographical-racist discursive field. I am positing that what Kafka did with what he saw in *Völkerschauen* and elsewhere regarding blacks was innovative enough beyond the run-of-the-mill cultural and aesthetic primitivism of his day to open a space for questioning scientific and ethnographic racism.

"Race" also and obviously meant for Kafka "Jewishness." Indeed, some of the qualities attributed to blacks whose negative attributes Kafka inverted, most notably sexual danger, were assigned to Jews as well. This was due in part to a common African origin theory between blacks and Jews, popularly expressed in Weininger's *Geschlecht und Charakter*. Weininger believed that Jews "possess[ed] a certain anthropological relationship with both Negroes and Mongolians" (Gilman 1995, 108). This hidden link was often revealed in *Mischlinge*. As Sander Gilman has pointed out, the *Mischling*, the child of a union between Jew and non-Jew, "is the end product of the process of Jewish degeneration that produces children that reveal the hidden sexual difference of the Jews, their 'blackness' " (Gilman 1995, 14). Expressing widely experienced "white" fears of atavism—the resurgence of a primitive racial trait in offspring—and degeneration, or reverse societal evolution instigated by the "superior race" mixing with "inferior races" and inferior races "breeding" rampantly among themselves, sexual deviancy and threat are the most pronounced traits shared between blacks and Jews. For, "[the Hottentot Venus] represents a literary reworking of the *Mischling*'s atavism. It also evokes the German Jew's willingness, even eagerness, because of his or her sexual difference, to cross racial lines" (Gilman 1995, 15).

In his thinking on the relationship between blacks and Jews, Kafka was also deeply influenced by Arthur Holitscher's description of shared cultural links between African Americans and Jews living in close proximity in New York. In particular, Holitscher was interested in what he saw as the interplay between black music and Jewish theater. For Holitscher, what was making its way across the Atlantic and into European music was, although African American inspired, in part Jewish in origin. In formulating this opinion, Holitscher posits a close relationship between Russian Jews and blacks in America, such that their cultural products can be at times confused for and easily assimilated by one another. Holitscher cites New York as the site for extensive cultural intermixing and experimentation between blacks and Jews. An example of this process as it manifested in Europe would be Löwy's Yiddish theater, which plays such a decisive role in Kafka's artistic development. As Anthony Notthey has pointed out, the theaters that Löwy visited in formulating his own aesthetic displayed theatrical productions heavily influenced by Yiddish theater troupes first established in New York, in the very environment Holitscher describes (Northey 1977, 448).[11] What Kafka witnesses while watching Löwy's troupe perform would have been filtered in part by his reading of Holitscher and the idea that, though not ragtime, some elements of the performance were appropriations of black culture. Indeed, a running tension and conceit throughout Holitscher's *Amerika, Heute und Morgen* is that cultural aspects of New York's Jews and African Americans were interchangeable.

Kafka had already found in Holitscher's travelogue compelling evidence of African American attitudes toward Jews that indicated an in situ conflation of the two. Holitscher writes, "Der Neger lebt in den großen Städten, in den kleineren sowie auf dem Lande in richtigen Ghettos, unter seinesgleichen" (The Negro lives segregated in real ghettoes in the big cities, the small, and the little villages) (Holitscher 1919, 363). In his reference to living in *richtigen Ghettos*, meaning ghettos like those of the Jews in Europe, Holitscher gives the impression of an urban landscape that creates a common bond between Jews and blacks in terms of diasporic social space, in that the majority culture in both instances oppresses the two minorities in the exact same way of spatial confinement. Indeed, "Das Ghetto auf der Ostseite Newyorks, mit seinem unerhörten Schmutz, asiatischen Gewimmel und Gerüchen, ist im großen ganzen der Wohnort der eben erst Hereingekommenen, dann der 'jüdischen Indianer und Neger,' wie ich jene Elemente nennen möchte." (The ghetto of New York's East Side, replete with its unbelievable dirt, Asian swarms, and odors, is in large part home to those who first settled here, then "Jewish [or "Jewified"] Indians and Negroes," as I like to call this element) (Holitscher 1919, 347).

Holitscher transforms both the American Indian and the Negro into adjectival Jews. For Holitscher, blacks and Jews are in the same boat to such an extent that he cannot but notice what he believes to be their shared common ancestry. And, according to Holitscher, he is not alone in this assumption. African Americans believe as he does: "'We are in the same boat!' sagte mir mein Freund, der junge Neger aus der 53. Straße. "'Unsere Schicksale haben ja viel Ähnlichkeit miteinander. Und dann kommen wir ja beide aus Afrika, die Juden und wir Neger!'" ("We are in the same boat!" said my friend, a young Negro from Fifty-Third street. "Our destinies have a lot in common. After all, we both come from Africa, Jew and Negro!") (Holitscher 1919, 365).

Although Holitscher would then go on to say, "Nun, natürlich ist dieser Philosemitismus cum grano salis zu nehmen" (Now, naturally this "Philosemitism" is to be taken with a grain of salt), it is only because blacks in America are predominantly Christian. Otherwise, Holitscher at no time casts serious doubt on what he calls, in terms of racial composition, cultural expression, and societal standing, "Philosemitismus" (Holitscher 1919, 365).

This testimony would have backed up antisemitic opinion of the day that blacks and Jews were genealogically and culturally related and so equally degenerate to the point of being, to the racist eye, the same.[12] In other words, blacks and Jews may look different and practice different religions, but that's as far as their *essential* differences go. In a letter to Milena of August 4, 1920, Kafka identifies this common racist attitude. Discussing how her father might compare him to her husband, Kafka writes, "zwischen Deinem Mann und mir ist vor Deinem Vater gar kein Unterschied, für den Europäer haben wir das gleiche Negergesicht" (*BM* 182) (Your father sees no difference between your husband and me. For the European, we all have the same Negro face [*LM* 136]).[13] Echoing the view that the Negro is recognized in the depersonalized

Jewish face, Kafka moves from the particular to the general. It is not just a matter of how Milena's father will react but also that no European cannot or is essentially unwilling to tell the difference between the faces of blacks and Jews. And it was Milena who went both outside of and beyond *Mischling* and shared origin theories when she stated flat out that Jews were "the Negroes of Europe" (Gilman 1995, 109).

This book, however, does not propose to trace pressure points between antisemitic discourse and antiblack racism. There are any number of works dealing with Kafka and his relation to Judaism in all its forms, and Sander Gilman has done much to present this aspect of Kafka's oeuvre in its cultural setting and debates. This book sees Kafka's initial interest in black culture as inspired by what he perceived to be the common interests of two minority cultures. But it insists that Kafka's appropriation of black culture quickly became for itself and for the presentation of an aesthetic under its own terms. The reason for this is because Kafka was looking for a racialized figurative human model that precisely did not have assimilation open to it. This is not to say that Kafka either wanted or did not want to assimilate but that the exigencies of his aesthetic engagement demanded a figure who could not be accounted for within the dominant culture, who was too low on the human evolutionary scale even to produce *Mischlinge* that would give proof of atavistic return. In this sense, Kafka is not looking for a mediated return to a primitive state but the unalloyed primitive itself that is too far removed from the highest level of the racial hierarchy to function in any way in society.

Indeed, it is this book's thesis that Kafka's works enact outside the embryonic state and in reverse the recapitulation theory popularized by evolution theorist Ernst Haeckel (a theory Kafka, like his contemporaries, knew from university) premised first and foremost upon the idea that Africans were located at the bottom of the human hierarchy. Haeckel's recapitulation theory postulated that the development of the human embryo traversed the various evolutionary stages of man, or as Haeckel famously put it, "ontogeny recapitulates phylogeny." Recapitulation theory was itself bound to ideas of human difference and stadial-evolutionary race and was an important element in the scientific racism of Kafka's day, including versions of the theory found in social Darwinism and psychology. Noted English social Darwinist and proponent of scientific racism Herbert Spencer popularized the idea in psychological discourse that individual human mental development passes through all the stages of human evolution, a notion that Freud would appropriate and reimagine along psychoanalytic lines.[14] And while the extent to which Freud influenced Kafka's writings is debatable, it is important to remember that *Totem und Tabu* first appeared in 1913, shortly after Kafka had his literary breakthrough with "Das Urteil" (written September 22–23, 1912, published 1913). My point is not that Kafka would take directly from Freud in order to construct his aesthetic of recapitulation but that Freud forms a part of general, popular theories of recapitulative human development, biological and psychological, current in Kafka's intellectual milieu. Kafka synthesizes the basic premises of these connected "scientific" ideas and has his characters degenerate, or enact what I am calling recapitulative transformation, passing through the Negro state on the way to becoming animal and, ultimately, uncreated.

It is important to note another recapitulation theory under whose influence Kafka may have been working—one that I will consider here only in passing. In Christian doctrine, recapitulation theory signifies Christ's reversal of eschatological human development from and conditioned by Adam's sin. Proposed first by Irenaeus, Christian recapitulation theory claims that Christ resets progressive human development by passing through each stage of being human and human history within the guiding light of salvation (Richardson et al. 1903, 4.6.1). In essence, Christ recapitulates humanity in himself, redeeming the whole of human history seen as individual development and as a progressive, "evolutionary" eschatology. "Evolution" here does not, of course, denote Darwin's use of the term but connotes directed, perfectible, and perfecting spiritual mutability. Furthermore, it was not unusual for Kafka to use specifically Christian tropes, themes, and settings, one glaring example of which would be the Samsa family, which *Die Verwandlung* (written 1912, published 1915) codes as Christian. Although this aspect of recapitulation theory is not the focus of this study, Kafka in all likelihood combines the two theories of human evolution, scientific and spiritual, in order to create an aesthetic of degeneration and redemption, or redemption through degeneration and atavism. He does this as a way of imagining not a pure work of art but a pure artist capable of generating works of art in no way beholden to human judgment.

This book, then, follows Kafka's evolving thought on an aesthetics of devolution and recapitulation in both its scientific senses. In the individual works addressed and as a whole, Kafka presents an aesthetic theory of recapitulation that seeks to demonstrate how an artist becomes an artist. To do so, the artist must devolve, recapitulate, go through the stages of human evolution in reverse order. The being-as-becoming-artist begins by revealing an innate degenerate quality, here always expressed as sexuality. It then is rendered in terms of blackness and negritude. This state succumbs to that of the animal, which in turn is uncreated entirely. It is in this state of nothingness, or pure blackness, that the work of art is created.

That being said, the method I employ in presenting this material is to a large extent determined by Kafka's exposition of these theories. Kafka did not fancy himself a writer and critic of scientific racism, psychoanalysis, cultural materialism, historicism, and so forth. He was a bricoleur. His borrowings from science, theology, and other domains do not amount to expertise or even detailed engagement (reflections on the law excepted). He is attracted to a general idea that he then uses to spectacular effect to create works that function in a truly singular way. Kafka's appropriation of scientific racism, ethnography, and racial-cultural phenomena is serviceable. That said, this book concentrates on and is fundamentally about moments of such usage in Kafka and their direct, cultural, historical, psychological, and biographical sources in light of how they shaped his aesthetic presentation. To that end, a cultural, historical, and biographical frame is given in each chapter that then informs individual close readings. Such information will be woven into the close reading and, as necessary, at times supplant it; but for the most part the historical, cultural, and biographical background provided at the beginning of a chapter or section acts as the interpretive frame and touchstone for what follows. One exception is the discussion of Prague cabaret in chapter 3, in which a discussion of music is made to wait until other elements of *Die Verwandlung* are first discussed.

But in general, I frame each chapter or section with an account of how blackness determines, either directly or obliquely, the given major text at issue or relates to Kafka's life as he wrote that text, and then reinforce this frame where and when appropriate. The close readings would make no sense without the historical-cultural background; but this background would be nothing more than anecdotal without the close readings. The close reading that constitutes the bulk of each chapter is devoted to how that text fits literary-historically in Kafka's overall aesthetic devolutionary scheme. Each instance of close reading is fully determined by its frame and the critical narrative that has preceded it. Only chapter 2 deviates from this pattern, in that *Der Verschollene* has a critical apparatus attached to ideas of blackness, which I address in the way this body of work demands. In order to avoid the redundancy of terms like "Negro," "black," and "blackness," as well as the proliferation of already numerous scare quotes, I ask of readers that when I write of sexual deviancy, devolution, laziness, noise, and so on, they bear in mind that all these terms have here always already been demystified.

Kafka's mode of aesthetic fashioning did not come into the world fully formed; it is a process of which all the elements were present in the early writings and that developed, became more sophisticated, and became problematic over time. Because of this, blackness is more present at the apex of this trajectory than at its nadirs. This is not to say that blackness is not present throughout, say, "Das Urteil," but that it haunts that text, is its shadow without ever stepping outside itself, in order to allow the text to develop other, intimately related theses. Blackness, of course, conditions the story, but it does not show its face as directly as it does in *Der Verschollene*. This does not mean that when I discuss "Das Urteil" I am not treating blackness directly but that blackness is part of a system in Kafka, of which each element is related, but, in a literary-historical progression, not every element can take center stage.

The manner in which I present cultural-historical and biographical evidence, undertake close readings, and have methodologically constructed this book is deeply influenced by my training as a comparatist in German and

African American literature. And while I consider this book to be primarily an intervention in Kafka studies, it reflects my work in African American literature in the sense that many of the themes and historical moments referenced by and shaping this study fall outside the traditional boundaries of Kafka criticism. Aside from referencing works and theories that are commonplace in African American studies but that may not be known in Kafka studies—such as "black noise"; the slave's narrative and New World slavery more generally; racist ethnographical theories of black sexuality, criminality, and laziness—the book takes for granted that the rhetorical devices employed here, such as the persistent use of the word "Negro" and frank discussions of topics such as black noise, and the perceived inherent deviancy of black sexuality, will not be perceived by the reader as in themselves racist. Very often I am writing from within a racist argument and quite obviously not along with it. In this sense, and in the African American literary themes and theories referenced, this is how I have brought my thought as a black comparatist to this project.

Part 1 is divided into three chapters, each tracing a critical stage of development in Kafka's aesthetics of recapitulation. Chapter 1, "Becoming Negro," connects Kafka's conception of writing to his presentation of the biblical justification for New World slavery, the curse of Ham, and to his notion of deviant black sexuality. Kafka bases "Das Urteil" on the drunkenness of Noah and its concomitant curse in order to represent Noahic patriarchal power and the inception of the "black race." In "Das Urteil," Noahic patriarchal power depends on sexual propriety guaranteed by the presence of a chaste wife. At the outset of the story, a disequilibrium in the family has been created by the death of the mother, allowing for an illegitimate power alignment of son over father. However, Georg's inability to find a suitable, sexually chaste woman undoes his bid to consolidate his power once and for all over and above the father through a suitable marriage. This point is wedded biographically to a series of letters Kafka writes to Felice in which she claims, much to his delight, that she has a *Negergesicht* (Negroid facial features). This letter exchange is then set in relation to another letter, in which Kafka describes to Felice a night out with Max Brod in a cabaret, during which Kafka's only enjoyment is the extreme sensation of excitement he receives from a black woman singer. The chapter discerns in these letters a sexual preference on Kafka's part for the idea of sexually transgressive blackness that is named in the presentation in "Das Urteil" of deviant sexuality in the context of Hamic negritude and premarital sex. Because Georg has made an inappropriate match, or, said differently, a union with a sexually loose woman, he is able to be undermined by father and reinscribed within Noahic patriarchal power as Ham, the perpetual black slave. Ultimately, Georg's "death" is a flight from slavery into an exile of black sexual perversion and/as writing.

The next chapter, "Being Negro," first reminds us that, like Georg Bendemann, Karl Roßmann goes into exile because of premarital sexual impropriety. It then reads *Der Verschollene* through one of the major influences on the creation of that text, Holitscher's *Amerika, Heute und Morgen*. The chapter then connects Holitscher's discussions of black life, including black music, in America with Kafka's use of the word "Negro" and two photographs of lynched black men. It then links these passages to the name and physical appearance of "Der Heizer" by way of the Czech translation of the word *Heizer*, the German rhyme *Neger, Neger Schornsteinfeger*, and Holitscher's use of the word *Scholle*. The chapter next moves to an account of the critical work that has been done on Kafka's use of the word "Negro" in the unfinished novel, followed by a grammatical analysis that shows that Karl had been using this name for a much longer period and so did not spontaneously name himself as such. Finally, the role of music in the Nature Theater of Oklahama [*sic*] is associated with Kafka's understanding of black music, and the name "Oklahama" is set in the context in which Kafka found it—as the caption under one of the pictures of a lynched black man in Holitscher's study. Conflating the freedom of the theater with the event of lynching, Karl becomes "Negro" in terms of aesthetic production conditioned by blackness and racism.

Chapter 3, "Beyond Negro," begins with an etymological-linguistic tracing of Gregor Samsa's entomological condition, showing the relation between the words *Käfer* and *Kaffer*. The chapter then reads the well-known link between *Die Verwandlung* and Leopold von Sacher-Masoch's *Venus im Pelz* (1870), providing the connection between Gregor's work status, indentured servitude, and slavery. The chapter next discusses the importance of musicality for *Die Verwandlung* and the ways in which the story's understanding of dinner music is implicated in blackness via Prague cabaret culture, brought out in the chapter's presentation of cabaret music and dance current in Prague during the time *Die Verwandlung* was written. Demonstrating that ragtime was all the rage, as were animal dances in which the participants "recapitulated" into beasts to the rhythm of black music, this chapter concludes that Gregor, already conditioned as black through his status as a *Käfer*, devolves to the point of disappearance as he transcends to a realm of pure art understood as black musicality.

Part 2 shows a fully formed aesthetics of recapitulation that Kafka begins to interrogate and deconstruct. Each story considered delineates in essence what the processes of becoming black and black becoming have produced. Chapter 4, "Negro's Machine," begins by showing that the ultimate appearance of the tattooing performed by the execution machine in "In der Strafkolonie" duplicates the designs of the Old Commandant—which are so dense as to be all but black. Establishing that the machine's "writing" transforms skin color to black, the chapter proceeds to a description of the importance of clothes and bodily ornamentation for the story. It then presents the critical debate on deportation surrounding "In der Strafkolonie" and its relation to postcolonial readings of the story's setting. Insisting that any reading of the victims of the machine as exclusively native flies in the face of the deportation debate Kafka is writing into, the chapter posits that the white soldiers and prisoners subjected to the machine undergo a complete change in skin color and are both literally and figuratively made black. This argument is supported by the colonial context of the story; the identification of Kafka's use of the common binary of savage and civilized instigated in the story by cannibalism; and the tropes of recapitulation and devolution. The chapter concludes that the machine is the representative of the black artist and that its art is made up of punished black bodies.

Chapter 5, "Negro's Manumisson," asserts that Rotpeter of "Ein Bericht für eine Akademie," (written and published 1917) can be read as an African slave and that the story itself functions like a slave narrative. The slaver in this case is Carl Hagenbeck and the work performed is not only in his zoos as an animal attraction but in his *Völkerschauen* as well. A connection is then made between Rotpeter and *dressierte Affen* (dressed-up apes) and scientific racist notions of *Menschenaffen* (man-apes). After having established these ties between the story, perceptions of Africans in the context of variety shows and zoos, and slave narratives, the chapter examines themes and narrative progressions shared by slave narratives and "Ein Bericht." The chapter finds that Rotpeter is determined by the same inherent sense of mimicry thought common to simians and blacks, and that through black mimicry he becomes more than human. For Rotpeter believes that humans merely mimic being human, whereas he has learned to mimic such mimicry, in essence laying the essence of human being bare. This *Ausweg* (way out) enables him to escape the very definition of the human that enslaved him in the first place.

The book's final chapter, "Negro's Martyrdom," sees "Ein Hungerkünstler" (written and published 1922) as Kafka's summation of his reflection on racial blackness. The chapter begins with Kafka's interest in twenty-two black Ugandan martyrs and then considers two fragments from Kafka's diaries in which he imagines in one an *Austellungsneger* returning to Africa only to go insane for *Heimweh* (homesickness) and in the other an African ritual. The history of the Ugandan martyrs as Kafka understood it and these two fragments are synthesized with Kafka's thought on cannibalism and linked to the story of the hunger artist, who exemplifies, down to the choice of his attire of an all-black, skintight bodysuit, a repetition of the recapitulative Negro on display and the black body in pain. By returning us to the scene of lynching first presented in *Der Verschollene* and hinted at throughout, Kafka offers in the hunger artist his most complete picture of the black(ened) artist (the *Ausstellungsneger*) as ex-slave at once prepared for martyrdom to his cause and subject to barbarous lynching.

The book ends with a wider consideration of the stakes, intellectual and institutional, involved in presenting a "black" Kafka.

Part I

Chapter 1

✦

Becoming Negro

I. *Mein Vater ist noch immer ein Riese*

Kafka himself asserted that "Das Urteil" marked the *Durchbruch* in his art. As Stanley Corngold has shown, Kafka's breakthrough story is also at the same time a sexual maturation, in that writing for Kafka is a form of sex, and it is with "Das Urteil" that he learned to do it right (Corngold 2000, 136).[1] "Das Urteil" also marks the moment in which the erotics and exotics of writing clearly trump those of normative sexual partnership. As Jahraus notes,

> Wenn man zusätzlich bedenkt, dass Kafka Felice Bauer nicht nur das Manuskript des Urteils geschickt, sondern ihr diese Erzählung auch gewidmet hat, dann wird klar, dass die Erotik des Schreibens gegen die Erotik der Partnerschaft ausgespielt wird, ja mehr noch, dass die Partnerschaft nur dazu dient, dass Kafka aus ihr jene erotischen Momente abzuziehen und auf das eigene Schreiben übertragen kann, so als ob es darum ginge, im Schreiben Erfüllung zu finden und Anforderungen zu genügen, was Kafka in einer Ehe für unmöglich hält. (Jahraus 2002, 410)

> Moreover, if one considers the fact that Kafka not only sent Felice Bauer the manuscript of "The Judgment," but also dedicated the story to her, then it becomes clear that the erotics of writing are being played over and against the erotics of partnership and, furthermore, that this partnership only serves one purpose: so that Kafka can pull out of it its every erotic moment and use it for his writing, as if the point of the relationship were for Kafka to find the excitement and fulfillment in writing that he believed was impossible to find in marriage.

It is through the lack of marital fulfillment that writing becomes fulfilling.[2] The type of writing that rejects domestic alliance in favor of its own favors and, indeed, feeds off of illegitimate, exotic sexual relations, is itself exotic and illegitimate.

Thus proper and improper, endogamous and exogamous forms of sexual conduct are linked to legitimate and illegitimate forms of writing.[3] Ultimately, control over the body (and so over an unmediated language of pure signification) that inhabits the legitimating space of patriarchal power is determined by sexual possession.[4] This is why the father in "Das Urteil" intimates that he could easily have Fräulein Brandenfeld, his son Georg's fiancée: the woman's character makes her unsuitable to the structural needs of patriarchal power.[5] This *Machtapparat* (power apparatus), as Jahraus calls it,

> lässt sich . . . durch drei Merkmale definieren: Erstens: Ein Machtapparat setzt voraus, dass die sozialen, erotischen und ökonomischen Strukturen als Bestimmungsmomente der bürgerlichen Existenz des Subjekts untrennbar miteinander verzahnt sind. Zweitens: Diese Verzahnung wiederum beruht auf einem Element der Verbindung—und das ist Macht. Nicht nur alle Relationen, in denen Figuren stehen, sondern die Konstitution des Subjekts selbst beruht ausschließlich auf Macht. Heiraten beispielsweise ist eine zentrale Frage der Macht. Und drittens organisiert sich die Macht nach dem Prinzip der Machtökonomie, was Machtakkumulation—vergleichbar der Kapitalakkumulation—bedeuten kann, aber letzten Endes in jedem Fall so etwas wie Übergang oder Aufteilung bedeutet (Jahraus 2006, 418).[6]

> can be defined . . . by three characteristics. First, a mechanism of power assumes that social, erotic and economic structures serve as touchstones for the existence of the bourgeois subject, and are indivisible from it. Second, the binding force of these characteristics with bourgeois existence is power. Not only the relations between characteristics, but the constitution of the subject itself is fully determined by power. For instance, marriage is a central question of power. And third, power is organized by the principles of its economy, that which accumulation—comparable to the accumulation of capital—can ultimately mean in terms of expansion or partition.

As the central question of the *Machtapparat*, marriage is a thing of the past for the father and no longer possible in the future for the son. In the vacuum left behind by the death of the mother, a power struggle ensues that is as much about sexual potency as it is about traditional bourgeois values. Attempting to usurp the father's position as head of the family and sovereign in charge of the *Machtapparat*, Georg indirectly calls the father's sexual potency into question. This is in part brought out in the story by biblical allusion and is key to the story's rumination on racial blackness.[7]

Of course, "Das Urteil" contains interpretive references to the Bible, all potential hermeneutic tools for readings of the story and meditations on Kafka's relation to Judaism.[8] However, Kafka's use of religious tropes are idiosyncratic to such an extent that even in cases where there is a clear rethinking of a story from Genesis, the appropriation itself obviously need not be limited to a meditation on Jewish themes.[9] As Robertson writes,

> Kafka is a highly individual and challenging religious thinker. His thought does not proceed within the framework of any one religion, but defines itself against a number of theologies and philosophies. . . . For one simplifies Kafka and denies his originality and his eclecticism if one locates his thought within any religious system. Rewarding though it has been to see Kafka through lenses provided by Judaism, we need to see it only as one of the sources on which he drew for his highly personal intellectual and spiritual exploration. (Robertson 1985, 120)

One such moment of "eclecticism" in "Das Urteil" pushes such readings in a different direction. When Georg sees his father undressed, or "naked" (he wears only an open robe, a pair of filthy underwear, and socks), "Das Urteil" makes use of the Genesis story of the curse of Ham, a biblical allusion Kafka had already explicitly made in "Beschreibung eines Kampfes" (written between 1903 and 1907), referring to "Noah in his cups" (*C* 13).[10] In the biblical passage, Noah, Ham's father, has drunk himself into a stupor and fallen, naked, unconscious, only to wake to find that his son, Ham, has seen him in his natural state. As punishment for this "crime," Noah curses Ham's descendants, who are described as swarthy in skin color, to perpetual servitude. The tribe of Ham is now identified as that of Africa, constituting the biblical story as the origin of the "black race" and the scriptural authorization for New World slavery.[11] Indeed, the argument was avidly and popularly taken up by proponents of slavery looking to justify biblically the African slave trade and black enslavement. Historically speaking, this use of the story is its most well known and politically remarkable, and Kafka's appropriation of the drunkenness of Noah, this chapter contends, contains the thread of blackness and the African slave trade within it. Ultimately, this chapter finds that Georg Bendemann is one of Kafka's artist figures condemned to his vocation in and as Hamic exile and, in this way as well as by being associated with "deviant" sexuality, is implicated in slavery and blackness.

The story begins with Georg contemplating how to break the news of his recent engagement to Frieda Brandenfeld to a failing friend set up in Russia, and to his father.[12] Where the friend in Russia has habitually failed, Georg has succeeded.[13] In his father's stead as head of the family business, the concern has flourished. And with his coming nuptials, Georg is poised to take over the role of paterfamilias in every sense, thus covering up his father for good. Not only is the family business under Georg's control earning more money than ever before but also Georg intends to bring a woman into the family to replace his mother. Through marriage, Georg will consolidate his power. Following what might seem like the natural course of events, the son will supplant the father in every conceivable way.

When Georg enters his father's room to inform him of the good news, Georg's father stands and literally reveals himself to his son:

> Der Vater saß beim Fenster in einer Ecke, die mit verschiedenen Andenken an die selige Mutter ausgeschmückt war, und las die Zeitung, die er seitlich vor die Augen hielt, wodurch er irgendeine Augenschwäche auszugleichen suchte. Auf dem Tisch standen die Reste des Frühstücks, von dem nicht viel verzehrt zu sein schien.
>
> "Ah, Georg!" sagte der Vater und ging ihm gleich entgegen. Sein schwerer Schlafrock öffnete sich im Gehen, die Enden umflatterten ihn—"mein Vater ist noch immer ein Riese," sagte sich Georg. (*D* 50)

> His father was sitting by the window in a corner hung with various mementoes of Georg's dead mother, reading a newspaper which he held to one side before his eyes in an attempt to overcome a defect of vision. On the table stood the remains of his breakfast, not much of which seemed to have been eaten.
>
> "Ah, Georg," said his father, rising at once to meet him. His heavy dressing gown swung open as he walked and the skirts of it fluttered around him.—"My father is still a giant of a man," said Georg to himself (*C* 53).

In this primal Noahic (and noetic) scene, the father's dressing gown opens, prompting Georg to comment on his father's enormous stature, or simply on the father's enormity. The body of the father asserts itself against Georg through its sheer physicality (Jahraus 2008, 414). The logic of the father's body, the absolute coherence and clarity of its language, is juxtaposed with the seemingly disjointed, fragmentary, indeed drunken nature of his verbal locutions. And despite his linguistic dexterity later in the story, the content articulated by the father could be tantamount to nonsense and seems to be authoritative only because of Georg's argumentative ineptitude. As Berman writes of Georg, "Language gets the better of him, or remains beyond his grasp, sometimes erratic, sometimes recalcitrant, but never fully under his control. Without an effective command of language, he is hardly in a position to argue his own case. Evidently, the logic of argumentative judgment cannot count on the linguistic capacity that it would require to be successful" (Berman 2002, 95). Berman's point is valid; and yet the same could be said of the father, who seems fully in control of his linguistic utterances. He speaks well, but what he says makes sense only insofar as there is no credible opposition to it. Thus "the logic of argumentative judgment" is inadequate.

An example of this logic's nonsensical, drunken character issues directly from, and is figured as, the father's mouth. Where the father's mouth lengthens to reveal a black, toothless maw, the words that issue from the infernal chasm are hieratic, ending with the question, "Hast du wirklich diesen Freund in Petersburg?" (*D* 52) ("Do you really have this friend in St. Petersburg?" [C 56]). No amount of friends, society, or brotherhood can replace the father in Georg's inner life. The father occupies the central place in Georg's existence, and, upon rising and Noahically revealing his phallic power while at the same time opening his black hole of a mouth—one that sucks in the sense of words while sparing their sound—the father destabilizes Georg's petit bourgeois life.

The ensuing struggle between father and son, the verbal confrontation that ends with the son's Hamic exile qua suicide, is won and lost before the first word is spoken. The body of the father curses Georg the moment it rises. If there was a doubt or hesitation on Georg's part to conclude that his father was still "ein Riese," the sight of the father as he stands, as his robe opens to reveal the enormity of his body, and presumably his penis, is enough to silence all concerns. The father's body speaks louder and is far more articulate than anything he actually has to say. Indeed, it is the father's physical condition that provides the grounds for cursing the son: "Beim Anblick der nicht besonders reinen Wäsche machte er sich Vorwürfe, den Vater vernachlässigt zu haben. Es wäre sicherlich auch seine Pflicht gewesen, über den Wäschewechsel seines Vaters zu wachen" (*D* 54) (The not particularly clean appearance of his underwear made him reproach himself for having been neglectful. It should have certainly been his duty to see that his father had clean changes of underwear [C 84]).

At no other time in the story does Georg admit to having been neglectful or in the wrong. His Hamic "suicide" and its attendant apology, because of their disjointed, chaotic character, nullify any coherent sense of remorse Georg seems to show. More than regret, Georg displays a growing feeling of Hamic horror, which is awakened by the father's feverish movements: "Auf seinen Armen trug er den Vater ins Bett. Ein schreckliches Gefühl hatte er, als er während der paar Schritte zum Bett hin merkte, daß an seiner Brust der Vater mit seiner Uhrkette spiele. Er konnte ihn nicht gleich ins Bett legen, so fest hielt er sich an dieser Uhrkette" (*D* 55) (He carried his father to bed in his arms. It gave him a dreadful feeling to notice that while he took the few steps toward the bed the old man on his breast was playing with his watch chain [C 84]).

Seeing the father play with the watch chain provokes an indescribable fear. The reason for Georg's disgust and ominous sense of terror is not narrated because it cannot be narrated. To speak Hamic dread would be to diffuse its disruptive potential. The only way for Georg to relate his inner state without falsifying it is to allow his body to articulate the emotion, to let his body speak for itself, to pronounce it without voice and in so doing avoid the dissonance inherent in translation. Indeed, where the body is concerned, there is here no need of translation. Here body language is prior to the spoken; it is the language of Babel open to all and without need of mediation and interpretation. The body speaks and is language unto itself. In this way, when the father's body becomes pronounced, it is irrelevant what drunken words come out of his mouth. The body speaks the curse because it is the scene of the crime. What the father actually says only becomes intelligible and meaningful as the story progresses, as he "sobers up."

Thus, the Noahic body of the father pronounces its damning sentence simply by the fact of its movements. This is why Georg, horror-struck, seeks to cover up his father's body:

> "Bin ich jetzt gut zugedeckt?" fragte der Vater, als könne er nicht nachschauen, ob die Füße genug bedeckt seien.
>
> "Es gefällt dir also schon im Bett," sagte Georg und legte das Deckzeug besser um ihn.
>
> "Bin ich gut zugedeckt?" fragte der Vater noch einmal und schien auf die Antwort besonders aufzupassen.
>
> "Sei nur ruhig, du bist gut zugedeckt."
>
> "Nein!" rief der Vater, daß die Antwort an die Frage stieß, warf die Decke zurück mit einer Kraft, daß sie einen Augenblick im Fluge sich ganz entfaltete, und stand aufrecht im Bett. Nur eine Hand hielt er leicht an den Plafond. (*D* 55–56)

> "Am I well covered up now?" asked his father, as if he were not able to see whether his feet were properly tucked in or not.
>
> "So you find it snug in bed already," said Georg, and tucked the blankets more closely around him.
>
> "Am I well covered up?" asked the father once more, seeming to be strangely intent upon the answer.
>
> "Don't worry, you're well covered up."
>
> "No!" cried the father, cutting short the answer, threw the blankets off with a strength that sent them all flying in a moment and sprang erect in bed. Only one hand lightly touched the ceiling to steady him. (C 84)

The father "schien auf die Antwort besonders aufzupassen" to his question, "Bin ich gut zugedeckt?" because to cover the body is in this situation to destroy the person as a communicative being and so to stifle his judgment and power to curse. By covering up the father's Noahic body the way Noah's other sons did after Ham's "treachery" had been exposed, Georg seeks to demolish the father's word, his power, his malediction. The struggle between father and son is dramatized by the physical-linguistic battle being played out between the sheets. That Georg's father has enough strength to throw back the covers literally validates and proves his assertion that he still has enough power left to rebuke the son's attempt to usurp his patriarchal sovereignty, and that Ham's transgression cannot be forgiven. Control of the body, then, is control over linguistic utterance here understood as body language and the power to curse; as such, it delimits total control. The body and the language it speaks portray the ebb and flow of Noahic power between father and son, such that their biblical confrontation is indeed as much physical as it is verbal. This is crucial, for this "physical" confrontation does nothing less than create human racial difference through an act of sexual impropriety.

Let us recall that this is a physical confrontation between father and son premised upon inappropriately seeing the naked body of the father. The sexual connotations here, however unseemly, are palpable and obvious. The extreme physical and sexual nature of the conflict between Georg and his father repeats that between Noah and Ham. In challenging his father's phallic potency by seeing his naked, drunken, and unconscious body, Ham unwittingly gives birth to racial blackness and the understanding of blacks as natural-born slaves in relation to deviant sexuality. The story does not posit a purely biological determination of blackness; it insists that race is a spiritual disposition handed down by God and exercised through Noah that is marked by swarthiness, servitude, and sexual impropriety. Because he emasculated his father by seeing him naked, Ham's descendants are spiritually and bodily cursed to blackness and servitude to a series of white "fathers" attempting to remove perverse and degenerate sexual elements from familial society. From the viewpoint of "Das Urteil," *deviant sexuality is racial blackness*. Furthermore, Noahic power here means the authority and ability to exile or segregate racial blackness as deviant sexuality from the family and patriarchal society.

This originary act of racial creation and differentiation based on perceived abnormal sexual behavior is played out in part by Georg Bendemann when he sees his father in a compromised position and, in so doing, attempts consciously or otherwise to surfeit his sovereign, Noahic power. But whereas Noah has objective authority over all men, the power of Georg's father is purely subjective; it is "a partly arbitrary ('subjective') law with the validity and power of a wholly objective law. . . . Or, finally: [Kafka] shows us the working of an oxymoron called 'subjective law' " (Stern 1972, 123). The father's power, then, does not have the force of God behind it but nevertheless functions as if it did.[14] Reminiscent of Kafka's perception of his own father's power, Herr Bendemann has the authority unto himself to determine the sexual crime and racial character of Georg's punishment and to insist that to be black is to be tainted with an original sex crime, a procedural assumption that recapitulates the "scientific" terms of turn-of-the-century ethnography, criminology, and recapitulation theory.[15] Georg's quandary and question become, how can a man live in a world governed by his father's Word, *which is his curse*?

II. *Das Negergesicht*

In answering this question for Georg, his father will condemn the son to drowning as disinheritance through racial recapitulation, as transformation into the biblical subaltern, into the sexually recapitulative African. Lacking divine sanction, the father has the authority to do this through the semantic force of his enormous body. In essence, his body is the evidentiary proof of Georg's transgression not first and foremost against the father but against the legacy and law of Noah. Without Georg's initial Hamic transgression, the father would not have the power to condemn Georg to drowning. The curse of Ham creates for Georg as his ontological ground a congenital black servant, thus forcing him to obey the father's command.

By virtue of seeing his father in a dirty state of undress, Georg has committed an untoward, indeed sexually perverse act, or an act of recapitulative sex. In light of the consequences of the curse of Ham and those of its secular variations, ethnographic-scientifically inherent black criminality and deviant sexuality, Georg is racially perverse. His Hamic transgression begins a racial regression as it makes him beholden to Noahic law. Georg is thus unfit for proper married life as master of his domain. He is a perpetual servant, a Negro, not the head of a major concern. Following a chronological pattern of a race-based aesthetic-structural development, the story privileges the first moment of the cycle of recapitulation and transformation that passes through the Negro on the way to becoming, for Kafka, a being outside the chain of being: the artist. Conditioned by the Negro in nuce, "Das Urteil" primarily represents the first phase in the future artist's recapitulation—namely, the degenerate or sexual deviant. Unable thus to be productive either at work or in marriage, Georg is doomed to wasting time, to another common ethnographic assumption of the day, constitutional black laziness, an idée fixe established about Africans as early as Carl (Carolus) Linnaeus's *Systema Naturae* (1767). He is congenitally guilty in part of that which Kafka's mother understood her son's writing to be: *Zeitvertrieb* (*BF* 100).

Zeitvertrieb or not, "Das Urteil" was by his own admission Kafka's breakthrough in his development as an artist. Describing the process of writing the story, Kafka, in a journal entry of September 23, 1912, the day he finished "Das Urteil," now famously writes,

> Diese Geschichte "Das Urteil" habe ich in der Nacht vom 22. bis 23. von zehn Uhr abends bis sechs Uhr früh in einem Zug geschrieben. Die vom Sitzen steif gewordenen Beine konnte ich kaum unter dem Schreibtisch hervorziehn. Die fürchterliche Anstrengung und Freude, wie sich die Geschichte vor mir entwickelte, wie ich in einem Gewässer vorwärtskam. Mehrmals in dieser Nacht trug ich mein Gewicht auf dem Rücken. Wie alles gesagt werden kann, wie für alle, die fremdesten Einfälle ein großes Feuer bereitet ist, in dem sie vergehn und

> auferstehn. Wie es vor dem Fenster blau wurde. Ein Wagen fuhr. Zwei Männer über die Brücke gingen. Um zwei Uhr schaute ich zum letzten Male auf die Uhr. Wie das Dienstmädchen zum ersten Male durchs Vorzimmer ging, schrieb ich den letzten Satz nieder. Auslöschen der Lampe und Tageshelle. Die leichten Herzschmerzen. Die in der Mitte der Nacht vergehende Müdigkeit. Das zitternde Eintreten ins Zimmer der Schwestern. Vorlesung. Vorher das Sichstrecken vor dem Dienstmädchen und Sagen: "Ich habe bis jetzt geschrieben." Das Aussehn des unberührten Bettes, als sei es jetzt hereingetragen worden. Die bestätigte Überzeugung, dass ich mich mit meinem Romanschreiben in schändlichen Niederungen des Schreibens befinde. Nur so kann geschrieben werden, nur in einem solchen Zusammenhang, mit solcher vollständigen Öffnung des Leibes und der Seele. Vormittag im Bett. Die immer klaren Augen. (*T* 460–61)

> The story, "The Judgment," I wrote at one sitting during the night of the 22nd–23rd, from ten o'clock at night to six o'clock in the morning. I was hardly able to pull my legs from out under the desk, they had got so stiff from sitting. The fearful strain and joy, how the story developed before me, as if I were advancing over water. Several times during this night I heaved my own weight on my back. How everything can be said, how for everything, for the strangest fancies, there waits a great fire in which they perish and rise up again. How it turned blue outside the window. A wagon rolled by. Two men walked across the bridge. At two I looked at the clock for the last time. As the maid walked through the ante-room for the first time I wrote the last sentence. Turning out the light and the light of day. The slight pains around my heart. The weariness that disappeared in the middle of the night. The trembling entrance into my sister's room. Reading aloud. Before that, stretching in the presence of the maid and saying, "I've been writing until now." The appearance of the undisturbed bed, as though it had just been brought in. The conviction verified that with my novel-writing I am in the shameful lowlands of writing. Only in this way can writing be done, only with such coherence, with such a complete opening out of the body and the soul. Morning in bed. The always clear eyes. (*J* 212–13)

Kafka feels exhilarated. The writing process has lasted all night and proceeded in a state of giddiness, or ecstasy. The narration of aesthetic experience is highly eroticized (which here also means exoticized), including a trip to his sister's bedroom and ending with an encounter with the maid, with whom the writer shares his secret by perversely indicating the bed in which he has not slept and in effect saying, "I was out all night having sex"; or, worse, "I was in all night having sex in another bed." For, given the sexualization of the scene of writing, the suggestion of incest (the tribal, recapitulative deviant sex act par excellence) between brother and sister is strong and is also recapitulated in *Die Verwandlung*.

The sensation of writing well is one that Kafka would, in letters to Felice, liken to sexual release and giving birth. In a letter to his fiancée of December 16, 1912, Kafka relates that,

> Es ist ½ 4 nachts, mich zu lange und doch zu kurz bei meinem Roman aufgehalten und habe überdies fast Bedenken, jetzt zu Dir zurückzukehren, denn ich habe förmlich die Finger noch schmutzig von einer widerlichen, mit besonderer (für die Gestaltung leider übergroßen) Natürlichkeit aus mir fließenden Szene. (*BF* 186)
>
> It is 3:30 A.M. I have spent too much and yet too little time on my novel; and now I am almost reluctant to return to you, for my fingers are still downright dirty from a repulsive scene that came pouring out of me with exceptional ease (excessive, alas, for the description of the scene). (*LF* 108)

Kafka would like to be with Felice in the moment after writing but has soiled himself through this unseemly act as if he had just finished masturbating. His finger is dirty from something that has flowed out of him.

Kafka views the "sex act" of writing as an unwholesome, filthy experience, something unworthy of his future bride—a qualification similar to the one ascribed to Georg's "sex act," or, rather, acts. For Georg is guilty not merely of seeing his father compromised in a state of undress but also of premarital sex. The transgression against the person of the father names race and its critical sexual disposition. It is not that Georg wasn't sexually deviant before his physical confrontation with his father but that his father did not have the authority or hermeneutic frame to condemn Georg as such until the son saw the father in a state of undress. Georg's misuse of his fiancée is one more "proof," after the fact, of Georg's deviant black sexuality.

Oddly enough, Felice Bauer, the person to whom Kafka dedicated the story and the model for Frieda Brandenfeld, once described her own face to Kafka in a letter as a *Negergesicht* (Negro face).[16] Although Kafka destroyed Felice's side of the correspondence, it is clear from his responses that Felice, in 1912, sent him a photo of herself and indicated that she had another but that she hesitated to mail it to him because in it she looks as if she had black facial features. Showing gratitude for the photo he received and trying to coax her into sending the Negro picture, Kafka's first response ends, "Einen langen Kuß auf den wehmütigen Mund des Mädchens auf der letzten Photographie und Zuspitzen des Mundes für das kommende Negermädchen" (*BF* 173) (A lingering kiss for the melancholy lips of the girl in the last photograph, and a pursing of the lips for the Negro girl soon to come [*LF* 98]). After having read this, Felice did send the picture, to which Kafka responds, "Nun ist also endlich das ganze liebe Mädchen da! Und durchaus nicht negerhaft, sondern so wie man sie im Kopf und Herzen hat" (*BF* 174) (Now at last the whole of the dear girl has arrived! And not in the least like a Negro, but just as she is in one's mind and heart [*LF* 99]). Kafka assures Felice that she does not look black (*negerhaft*) at all but instead as he pictures her in his head and heart. This may have been read as cold comfort; for while it denies that she looks "Negroid" per se, Negroid is qualified by Kafka in the second half of the sentence as an emotional disposition in relation to an ideal image. It insists that, even if she does *objectively* appear to have Negroid facial features, he sees her only as he loves her, or *subjectively*.

But here love and sexual desire do not amount to the same thing. Kafka seems eager to see and kiss Felice's *Negergesicht* picture. Furthermore, in the very same letter, he writes, "Deine Bemerkung über das Negergesicht bringt mich auf den Gedanken, daß noch eine zweite Photographie existiert. Ist es so, unvorsichtige Liebste?" (*BF* 174) (Your remark about you looking like a Negro girl makes me think there must be another photograph. Am I right, dear careless one? [*LF* 99]). The black face picture reminds Kafka that Felice has another, potentially more risqué picture to send him. Felice, in association with black women, is a reckless love, and the connection Kafka makes through her is between blackness and sexual daring.

It can even be said that Kafka may have found Felice more attractive because of her *Negergesicht*, since such features held the promise of exotic sexual encounter. On July 6, 1913, Kafka writes to Felice a particularly racy account of a night out, admitting a sexual attraction to a black woman:

> Wir, Max, seine Frau, sein Schwager, Felix und ich, waren in einem Chantant, in das meine Frau nicht hingehen dürfte. Ich habe im allgemeinen sehr viel Sinn für solche Sachen, glaube sie von Grund aus, von einem unabsehbaren Grund aus zu erfassen und genieße sie mit Herzklopfen, gestern aber versagte ich außer gegenüber einer tanzenden und singenden Negerin fast gänzlich. (*BF* 422)

> We—Max, his wife, his brother-in-law, Felix, and I—went to a cabaret to which my wife would not be allowed to go. Generally speaking, I appreciate this kind of thing, I believe I have a deep, an immensely deep understanding for it and enjoy it with my pulse racing, but yesterday, except for the dancing and singing of one Negro girl, it meant nothing to me. (*LF* 285)

Kafka spent time in such places where black music could be heard and took enough interest in its "authentic" practitioners as to fantasize sexually about them. Indeed, on this particular night out only the dancing, singing "Negress" affords Kafka any pleasure at all.

Kafka also tells Felice that although he usually very much enjoys such cabarets, they are no place where he would want his wife to enter, even though Max Brod allows his own wife to be in attendance on such evenings. However, Kafka has no difficulty describing such pleasures to Felice, but she may not be included in them as anything other than as their ideal reader. Sexually risqué behavior is inappropriate for an engaged or married couple and can take place only outside the bounds of common marital decency. Thus we see a division in how Kafka views sex. Sex between husband and wife is normatively "clean." Outside marital propriety, sex is obscene, savage, and is thus enjoyed with (or because of) a sense of guilt engendered and exploited by the black atavistic transgression exoticism provides.

As Kafka is at pains to explain to Felice, there are places to which wives and fiancées ought not be subjected. As in "Das Urteil," the status of the fiancée, if she is to become a wife within the Noahic scheme of power, is defined by sexual propriety. Likewise, the legitimacy of a man's claim to Noahic power is determined by his domestic union with a woman. If a man is married to a sexually loose woman, then he has no right to patriarchal authority. Given Georg's father's lowly condition as a widower at the outset of the story, he must derive his authority at least in part from an outside source—the curse of Ham as Noahic legacy. He is not simply powerful in himself; he requires this supplemental authority even before he can rally the friend in Russia to his side. The reason for this is simple. The father himself has degenerated, or recapitulated, in the wake of his wife's death. The mother, or a proper sexual bond, consolidates Noahic power. And while the mother does not come back from the grave to reinvest her husband with this authority, he is able to revivify, at least temporarily, his failing strength through his wife's memory.

III. *Wer sich mit Hunden zu Bett legt, steht mit Wanzen auf*

For, it is during the mother's lifetime that Georg Bendemann's father reaches the height of his power:

> Vielleicht hatte ihn der Vater bei Lebzeiten der Mutter dadurch, daß er im Geschäft nur seine Ansicht gelten lassen wollte, an einer wirklichen eigenen Tätigkeit gehindert, vielleicht war der Vater seit dem Tode der Mutter, trotzdem er noch immer im Geschäfte arbeitete, zurückhaltender geworden, vielleicht spielten—was sogar sehr wahrscheinlich war—glückliche Zufälle eine weit wichtigere Rolle, jedenfalls aber hatte sich das Geschäft in diesen zwei Jahren ganz unerwartet entwickelt, das Personal hatte man verdoppeln müssen, der Umsatz hatte sich verfünffacht, ein weiterer Fortschritt stand zweifellos bevor. (*D* 46)

> Perhaps during his mother's lifetime his father's insistence on having everything his own way in the business had hindered him from developing any real activity of his own, perhaps since her death his father had become less aggressive, although he was still active in the business, perhaps it was mostly due to an accidental run of good fortune—which was very probable indeed—but at any rate during those two years the business had developed in a most unexpected way, the stall had had to be doubled, the turnover was five times as great; no doubt about it, further progress lay just ahead. (*C* 78–9)

The father's vast influence is in part generated by the successful family business. This family enterprise allows the father the patriarchal capital to determine the development of his son's life. Georg has lived by the father's economic support. The father has invested in the life of his son and, in having done so, has the right to determine the limits of its development; the father has a vested and controlling interest in Georg's life.

However, this control or share in Georg's existence is not measured by a purely economical index. The father's overdetermined familial power is also linked to marital status. Once the mother is dead, the father is not able to continue to perform his patriarchal duties. For it is not enough for a man to be successful in business if he is to be invested with absolute Noahic authority; he must have also formed a strong, proper, active domestic alliance. The role of wife and mother, if performed well, legitimates Noahic power and delegitimates all other modes of transcendent self-assertion. Likewise, if the wrong type of woman is found for this role, she a priori undermines the power of the man to whom she is wed in every aspect of his being. As Kafka's father firmly believed, "Wer sich mit Hunden zu Bett legt, steht mit Wanzen auf" (*T* 223) ("Whoever lies down with dogs gets up with fleas" [*J* 103]). Indeed, as Niehaus writes, "Kafkas kleine Geschichte [inszeniert] einen Prozeß der 'Delegitimation'. Es ist unmittelbar klar, dass Georg Bendemann der Daseingrund entzogen wird—seine Auseinandersetzung mit dem Vater ist gleichsam eine Szene der Entgründung" (Kafka's short story represents a process of "delegitimization." It is absolutely clear that Georg Bendemann is torn from the very fabric of his being—his struggle with his father is at the same time a scene of dissolution) (Niehaus 2002, 345). The trial that Georg undergoes will end in his recapitulative *Entgründung* because of his inability to make a suitable marriage. For, in her willingness to engage in premarital sex, Frieda, after the fact, will be construed as having shown her black face. She has a *Negergesicht* because, after Georg has been cursed, that is how sexual impropriety will be seen.

Thus, for the father's assault on Georg to be fully successful, he must also destroy Georg's hope of marriage—the very thing with which the story begins. In order to undermine Georg's relationship with his fiancée, and so disrupt Georg's structural claims to Noahic sovereignty, the father reveals yet another ace in his hand. The father reconsolidates his power by uncannily revealing not only his own undergarments, or that which should have remained hidden, but also by exposing Georg's fiancée's undergarments. A woman who "lifted up her skirts" prematurely, who, according to the father, engaged in deviant premarital sex with Georg, has de facto invalidated her coming marriage. Through the fiancée, Kafka is also making reference to Hippolytus's (d. 235) account of Noah's family, in which Noah is about to kill Ham's wife for divulging the truth too soon of the coming of the deluge, only to have his hand stayed at the last moment by God (Roberts and Donaldson 1886, 197). Indeed, the fiancée introduces Georg into the Noahic order of the curse; she taints Georg with the sin of the original, aboriginal deviant sex act, priming him for racial malediction and exile. Unlike the venerated and presumably sexually proper mother, Fräulein Brandenfeld has given herself away too early, thus opening herself to the patriarchal Noahic judgment that finds her to be sexually inappropriate.[17] A woman the likes of Fräulein Brandenfeld could never take the place of Georg's mother, and therefore the domestic marital bond essential for Georg to usurp his father's Noahic power completely is now impossible. By discrediting Georg's potential domestic partner, the father affirms his return to power and is able literally to stand on his own two feet. "Und er stand vollkommen frei und warf die Beine. Er strahlte vor Einsicht" (*D* 57) (And he stood up quite unsupported and kicked his legs out. His insight made him radiant [*C* 85]). At this moment of absolute triumph, Georg's father stands "unsupported" and "radiant."

By reinstating the memory of the mother in its proper place, one defined by sexual propriety, the father regains his strength physically, linguistically, and structurally. Understanding the structure of Noahic power as triadic (Noah-mother [wife]-Ham), the place of the mother is being held by proxy. Befitting the biblical uncertainty as to who Noah's wife actually was, the body of the mother is absent, but the idea of her remains.[18] She was a woman of unquestioned sexual propriety. The reason why this is of the utmost importance is that chastity and obeisance before the laws forbidding premarital sex ensure that a woman does not give birth to illegitimate, recapitulative children. The fact that Georg's mother has given birth to a child of recapitulation does not impugn her reputation. The father's Noahic authority condemns Georg to blackness as it creates it. Blackness is engendered because of sex but not through it.

Establishing a link between writing, creation, and sexual misconduct, Kafka perceived writing as generative of filthy bastards. Describing in a journal entry of February 11, 1913, his preparation of "Das Urteil" for publication, Kafka writes,

> Anläßlich der Korrektur des 'Urteils' schreibe ich alle Beziehungen auf, die mir in der Geschichte klar geworden sind, soweit ich sie gegenwärtig habe. Es ist dies notwendig, denn die Geschichte ist wie

> eine regelrechte Geburt mit Schmutz und Schleim bedeckt aus mir herausgekommen. (*T* 296)

> While reading the proofs of "The Judgment," I'll write down all the relationships which have become clear to me in the story as far as I now remember them. This is necessary because the story came out of me like a real birth, covered with filth and slime. (*J* 214)

A filthy, indeed quasi-demonic act leads to an unsanitary consequence akin to how Kafka perceived what giving birth would be like.[19] In a letter to Robert Klopstock sent in March 1923, Kafka would also compare the relation between himself and writing "wie einer Frau ihre Schwangerschaft" (*B* 431) (as a woman her pregnancy). "Das Urteil" as love child takes first breath covered in dirt and slime, indicative of its status as a bastard produced by the illegitimate union of writer and work of art. Fittingly, this text as the product of an illicit sexual union contains within it the recapitulative seed of blackness. The story in its materiality is as much an inheritor of Noah's curse as its protagonist is.

The story itself, when associated in its inception with a deviant sex act, seems to offer no benediction to alleviate Noah's curse. Yet Kafka adds figurative power to Georg's plight as the accursed by imagining him as always already enslaved, or a slave via a congenital malediction naming a racial disposition exogamous to the family and bourgeois society. In doing so, Kafka gives Georg a way out (*Ausweg*); for once the boundaries of one's enslaved existence are made visible—which is precisely what the judgment does—flight from slavery becomes possible.

When Georg finally takes flight by leaping into the water,

> Noch hielt er sich mit schwächer werdenden Händen fest, erspähte zwischen den Geländerstangen einen Autoomnibus, der mit Leichtigkeit seinen Fall übertönen würde, rief leise: "Liebe Eltern, ich habe euch doch immer geliebt," und ließ sich hinfallen.
>
> In diesem Augenblick ging über die Brücke ein geradezu unendlicher Verkehr. (*D* 61)

> Already he was grasping at the railings as a starving man clutches food. He swung himself over, like the distinguished gymnast he had once been in his youth, to his parents' pride. With weakening grip he was still holding on when he spied between the railings a motor-bus coming which would easily cover the noise of his fall, called in a low voice: "Dear parents, I have always loved you, all the same," and let himself drop.
>
> At this moment an unending stream of traffic was just going over the bridge. (*C* 88)

His body is at once strong and absent. It is under the sway of, or enthralled by, that of the father. Georg swings himself like a gymnast in one moment and is gone in the next. The only way to disengage himself from the power of the father's body, the physical force that gives meaning to the father's command, is to remove his body from the scene of Noahic malediction. Georg loses himself as a body in *Verkehr*, meaning "traffic," "intercourse," and also "sex." He becomes one with the recapitulative sex act, with blackness. He becomes "Negro."

By so doing, he also becomes the act of writing, or writing as a racially coded, deviant sex act. For it is in the double sense of *Verkehr* as human intercourse and sex that Kafka describes the experience of writing in a letter to Felice of January 14–15, 1913: "Schreiben heißt ja sich öffnen bis zum Übermaß; die äußerste Offenherzigkeit und Hingabe, in der sich ein Mensch im menschlichen Verkehr schon zu verlieren glaubt" (*BF* 250) (For writing means revealing oneself to excess; that utmost of self-revelation and surrender, in which a human being, when involved with others, would feel he was losing himself [*LF* 156]). Also lost "im menschlichen Verkehr," Georg has opened himself to the *Übermaß* (also "orgy") of writing—the same one Kafka felt upon writing "Das Urteil." Even though his "freedom," or way out, is imposed on him by his father, by embracing blackness, by becoming "Negro," Georg is able to discover completely the openness required of the writer outside bourgeois constraints.

Indeed, the verb *erspähen* expresses the effort of searching for something, but also the effort of "finding out completely" (Ruhleder 1963, 17). It is this discovery that makes of the father's judgment not a death sentence but manumission by revealing the boundaries of Georg's enslavement and so allowing him to transgress and go beyond them.[20] Given that the frame of the story is that of the drunkenness of Noah, Georg finds transcendence through Hamic exile, or freedom through blackness.[21] For Georg's end need not be read as death. Localizing ourselves in Prague in the apartment Kafka lived in when he wrote the story (Pařížská 36, where he lived from 1907 to 1913), we are led not to the Charles Bridge but to the Czech Bridge (Čechův Most), at the time newly built and just beyond Kafka's doorstep and from whose meager height it is unlikely an athletic young man would die in the mild current at this juncture of the Moldau. Furthermore, the Civilian Swimming School was located directly on the bank of Prague's Kleinseite where the Czech Bridge lets out and was visible from Kafka's windows. We know that Kafka went there with his father, as he writes on May 19, 1924, from his deathbed to his parents, "In the past, as I often remember during the heat spells, we used to have beer together quite often, in that far-off time when Father would take me along to the Civilian Swimming School" (*L* 414). Georg would have jumped in the river at a very busy time right in front of the swim academy—the same one Kafka went to regularly with his father. Finally, at the level of the word, Kafka himself makes clear in a letter to Felice of June 2, 1913, "Das letzte Wort des vorletzten Satzes soll 'hinabfallen,' nicht 'hinfallen' sein" (*BF* 392) (The final word of the penultimate sentence should read "drop," not "fall" [*LF* 265–66]). *Hinabfallen* signifies a host of concepts beyond *hinfallen*, or "to fall in." It can mean also to drop off, secede, or *to apostatize*. In other words, Kafka's other word carries a religious sense of separation and even exile. Georg has seceded from the theosophical state governed by Noahic patriarchal power and in so doing has become apostate.

The sheer dynamism of the text's movement as well as the flood of light and water into which Georg disappears marks this passage into freedom through the loss of a stable body to be enslaved. As Nerad observes, "So hat Kafkas Schreibweise, indem sie sich vermeinten evidenten Lesarten entzieht, am Ende wenigstens die Möglichkeit gerettet, dass Georg sich nicht in den Tod, sondern ins Leben hat fallen lassen" (In this way Kafka's aesthetic, insofar as it opens itself to certain reading practices, in the end saves the possibility that Georg does not die but in the end comes to life) (Nerad 2003, 81). Kafka's "Schreibweise" is also one of dynamism. As Speirs points out, "The dynamism experienced by Kafka during the process of writing 'The Judgment' is reflected in the story itself, imbuing it with such inner coherence that Kafka even dared speak of the 'music' that had emerged along with the fear (*Angst*) he felt while composing it" (Speirs 2011, 222). Speirs goes on to write that, "As he disappears in the river below, one might say that Georg is being returned by the act of narration to the element from which the story as a whole emerged, the restless energy that formed the opening paragraph" (227). The energy of the story is, ultimately, that of dynamic recapitulative sexuality, one that frees a body from the Noahic order of power authorized by and premised upon the body. Georg's and the story's recapitulative sexuality is ethnographically bound to his otherwise biblical status as black. The dynamism of the river, the rush and seemingly sudden flow of the traffic (*Verkehr*), are savagely ejaculatory—which was Kafka's own sense of writing the story. Georg performs the vulgar phrase for having sex, "in den Teich springen." Not only is Georg free to become an artist but also art is bound to recapitulative, perceived black sexual perversion, to the "Negroid" sexually impermissible within the marital-familial bond.

Sexually becoming one with the narrative act, the body biblically coded black identifies with the scene of writing in order to escape Noahic judgment and means of social control. To attain this goal, however, one must first pass through the crucible of blackness, in this case to Noahic law, the precondition of which is becoming he who is naturally born a slave, Negro. By being inherently unsuitable to the position of Noahic sovereign, the here metaphorical yet ontologically prior black body is the "proper" entity to be doubled by he who is the eternal slave: the eternal son. But also by being of a race theologico-categorically different from that of the father, the black body is paradoxically excluded from the order of consanguineous patriarchal power. The Noahic patriarch must have a son, both as successor and as subaltern.

Having no legal rights, the black body is both before and beyond the law as bare life. For Georg, this is the key to freedom from bondage. The black body is no-body. It is free from the linguistic regime of the body, the body as writing, and writing as deviant black sex. In sending its protagonist into exile for deviant sexuality and becoming "Negro," "Das Urteil" follows a similar structural development to, and ends in the same way as, *Der Verschollene*.

Chapter 2

✦

Being Negro

I. *Eine amerikanische Musik gibt es nicht*

Karl Roßmann comes to America because he has had premarital sex that led to the family maid's pregnancy. He, too, is guilty of a sex crime and is sent into exile. Considering that Kafka started work on *Der Verschollene* shortly after writing "Das Urteil," one could view Karl's journey as the continuation of Georg's story. Be that as it may, America as exile is an interesting choice for Kafka to have made given that he had never been there. To fill the gap in his knowledge, Kafka read and used as a main source for his unfinished novel Holitscher's book *Amerika, Heute und Morgen*. Holitscher spends much time on the problem of the color line in America, devoting a long chapter to "Der Neger" in which, among other things, he highlights his acquaintanceship with W. E. B. Du Bois. Indeed, Holitscher was so deeply impressed with Du Bois that he provides the reader with a biographical sketch of the African American genius and translates passages from "A Litany of Atlanta" (1906), Du Bois's poetic meditation on Atlanta's 1906 race riots (Holitscher 1919, 360–74).

Another powerful narrative of racial violence in America appears in Holitscher's book, a photograph of a lynched African American, with the title "Idyll aus Oklahama" (sic). We know that the photo gave Kafka pause, as he used the name "Oklahama," misspelling and all, as the name of the *Naturtheater Der Verschollene*'s protagonist, Karl Roßmann, joins near the end of the novel.[1] *Amerika, Heute und Morgen*, also discusses Booker T. Washington and Tuskegee, Jim Crowism, and the overall social history and political life of African Americans. Holitscher displays a strange pride in his various interviews and interactions with African Americans and sums up the black experience in a report with which African American writers such as Richard Wright and James Baldwin surely would have found affinity: "Der Neger lernt die weiße Kirche verachten, in der von den gleichgeborenen Söhnen Gottes gefaselt wird, und gibt in seiner eigenen schwarzen Kirche hörbar seiner Zustimmung Ausdruck, wenn von der Kanzel herab das Wort fällt: 'Die Hölle, mit der das Gericht droht, erlebe der Schwarze ja schon diesseits'"

Figure 1. *Idyll aus Oklahama.*

(The Negro learns to feel contempt for the white church in which one babbles about the equality of the races, and he expresses with loud unanimity in the black church, when given the word from the pulpit: "We already live in the hell God's law threatens us with.") (Holitscher 1919, 368).

According to Holitscher's representation of his sources, the white church lies about race relations in America, whereas the black church provides a space and modicum of freedom in that it tells the truth, both of scripture and of American society. The "Jubilee songs," composed while working on slavery's plantations and sung in the postbellum era in part in the black church, name another source of Kafka's conception of black music and blacks as inherently musical. As Holitscher writes,

> Wenn der Amerikaner sentimental wird, fängt er an, schöne alte Negerlieder zu singen, die Plantagenlieder, "Jubilee-Songs." Das musikalische Genie des Negervolkes hat viel zu dem spezifischen Rhythmus des modernen Amerikas beigetragen. Ein schwerer Schatz von Melodien und Rhythmen eigenster Art liegt in diesen alten naiven Choralen und Rundgesängen aufbewahrt. Mit ihren rauhen afrikanischen Kehlen haben die "darkies" wirkliche Tonwerte für

> die englischen Worte gefunden, die ihnen ganz neu waren, und die sie lernen mußten, um die Befehle des Aufsehers zu verstehen und ausführen zu können. (Holitscher 1919, 371)

> Whenever an American becomes sentimental, he starts to sing beautiful old Negro songs, the plantation songs, Jubilee Songs. The musical genius of the Negro folk has added quite a bit to the specific rhythms of the modern America. One finds a treasure trove of melodies and rhythms of the most unique kind in these old, naive chorals and songs in the round. With their rudimentary African throats, the "darkies" have found the appropriate tonality for English words—words which were, for them, totally new and which they had to learn in order to understand and complete the orders of their overseers.

Holitscher's praise of the music is based on what he perceived to be its unwieldy, non-Western quality. The Negro's musical success is in part his ability to adapt African music from its unique melodies and rhythms to the English language and American tastes. The difference between the black noise of *Völkerschau* music and the fine melodies of African Americans is the standard racist trope of Western black fashioning. Having been around white culture for a much longer period, African Americans were, according to this logic, able to appropriate musical structure to their otherwise raw instinct for music. However, Kafka is not concerned with the details and qualitative judgments of cultural racism; from the two sources of black music he derives the general idea of an inherent, congenital black musicality. Holitscher, however, esteems the music of the "darkies" to such an extent that he can make the following comparison: "Man läuft durch die Straßen der Stadt, plötzlich, was hört man da: vier kleine zerlumpte Negerknäblein, 'coons,' stehen beisammen und singen Quartett mit einer Reinheit und Vollendung, derengleichen man sich in der Metropolitan Opera für zehn Dollar nicht er kaufen kann" (Holitscher 1919, 372). Why pay to hear great music when any "coon" on the street can provide you with higher-quality entertainment? The suggestion here is that, as opposed to the European artists flooding America's opera houses at this time, the Negro needs no formal training; he is inherently musical. Indeed, his primitive vocalizations surpass the warbling of the most sophisticated virtuoso.

Holitscher's lack of sensitivity is of course a product of its time; but for all his epithets, he is remarkably sympathetic to the African American cause. Using music as evidence of African American equality, Holitscher goes so far as to posit the following:

> Eine amerikanische Musik gibt es nicht. Die alten Weisen stammen, soweit es keine englischen Psalmen sind, aus Afrika, sind Eigentum der Neger (so wie die 'ungarische Musik' Eigentum der ebenfalls aus

> Afrika stammenden Zigeuner ist), und was gegenwärtig das Ohr des Americanos entzückt, das 'zerfetzte Tempo,' rag-time, eine Nachahmung der Negertanzrhythmen, ist von findigen russischen Juden fabriziert, allerdings mitunter mit fabelhafter Geschicklichkeit und musikalischem Können. (Holitscher 1919, 417)

> There is no American music. The old songs, insofar as they are not English Psalms, come out of Africa and belong to the Negro (just like "Hungarian music" belongs to gypsies—who also come from Africa—in Hungary). What today so attracts the ear of the Americanos, the frenetic tempo, ragtime, an imitation of Negro rhythms, is an invention of creatively clever Russian Jews, occasionally made with amazing skill and musical knowledge.

The statement is crucial, for it reveals another important prejudice of the book that so influenced Kafka. Not only is any "American" music always already African but also the music thought to be African American in origin, ragtime, is actually the product of Russian Jews living in New York attempting to imitate African Americans. In effect, for Holitscher, ragtime is nothing other than blackface music performed by Jews. It is not a question here of whether or not ragtime was inspired by African Americans; the issue is whether or not it is fully and exclusively an African American product. Holitscher does not believe so. This skepticism provides Kafka with an aesthetic-cultural link between blacks and Jews.

Although Holitscher's conflation of Jew and black, ironic and otherwise, may not come as a surprise, the credence Kafka gave to Holitscher's connection between music, Negroes, and Jews may still be shocking unless we consider the following. Kafka's best friend and literary executor, Max Brod, was, among other things, an accomplished composer and music critic. Brod had a great interest in Czech music, even translating Leoš Janáček's libretto for the opera *Jenůfa* into German. But the Czech composer for whom Brod had the highest regard was Antonín Dvořák, who spent significant time in the United States and enjoyed there celebrity status as he composed his Ninth Symphony (*From the New World*, 1893) and taught. His prized pupil was the gifted African American composer Harry T. Burleigh, who would later become famous for reconciling African American folk music with the classical tradition, for his transcriptions of African American spirituals, many of which were made at Dvořák's insistence, and for being the inspiration for James Weldon Johnson's *The Autobiography of an Ex-Coloured Man*. Speaking of his pupil in an interview of May 28, 1893, with the *Boston Herald*, Dvořák stated,

> Among my pupils in the National Conservatory of Music I have discovered strong talents. There is one young man upon whom I

> am building strong expectations. His compositions are based upon negro melodies, and I have encouraged him in this direction. The other members of the composition class seem to think that it is not in good taste to get ideas from the old plantation songs, but they are wrong, and I have tried to impress upon their minds the fact that the greatest composers have not considered it beneath their dignity to go to the humble folk songs for motifs. I did not come to America to interpret Beethoven or Wagner for the public. That is not my work, and I would not waste any time on it. I came to discover what young Americans had in them and to help them to express it. When the negro minstrels are here again I intend to take my young composers with me and have them comment on the melodies.

The interviewer describes what happened next, writing in the same article, "And saying so, Dvořák sat down at his piano and ran his fingers lightly over the keys. It was his favorite pupil's adaptation of a southern melody." Dvořák thus maintains that he came to America to discover exactly this music, the Negro spiritual, which he now knows from minstrels. He plays a minstrel tune, transcribed by Burleigh, as the prime example of what he had searched for in America.

Indeed, Dvořák was so deeply impressed with African American music that, in this article, he made the bold prediction,

> I am now satisfied that the future music of this country must be founded upon what are called the negro melodies. This must be the real foundation of any serious and original school of composition to be developed in the United States. When I first came here last year I was impressed with this idea, and it has developed into a settled conviction. These beautiful and varied themes are the product of the soil. They are American. I would like to trace out the individual authorship of the negro melodies, for it would throw a great deal of light upon the question I am most deeply interested in at present. These are the folk songs of America, and your composers must turn to them.

Thus, Dvořák made good on his stated goal in the United States: "I intend to do all in my power to call attention to this splendid treasure of melody [the Negro spiritual] which you have" (*Boston Herald* 1893, 23). Vowing to use his every resource to bring Negro music to light in a Western canonical context, Dvořák speculates that such music is the future of American cultural expression. The Negro is the avant-garde that is only now coming into popular consciousness—in part aided by Dvořák, whose Ninth Symphony quotes the spiritual "Swing Low, Sweet Chariot" to great effect. Indeed, Dvořák's provocative views on African American music coupled with his easily identifiable quote of the famous spiritual led his American critics to dub the Ninth

Symphony his "Negro Symphony."[2] It would be hard to imagine that Brod and Kafka never discussed Dvořák and his views on "Amerika" given that Kafka was writing a novel in Prague about the country in which the main character would give his name as "Negro" to the Nature Theater of Oklahama [sic].[3] This "deterritorialized" version of Prague, Kafka's America, is deterritorialized as such by Kafka's intellectual and cultural encounter with blacks in Holitscher and elsewhere.

II. *Neger, Neger, Schornsteinfeger*

Indeed, nowhere in Kafka's oeuvre are the deterritorializing effects of his writing more on display than in his suspiciously Prague-like America. *Amerika* presents Kafka with a landscape in which his Karl Roßmann can become an artist, not simply through America's "sameness" and "otherness" in comparison with Europe, but also through America's "others."[4] Said differently, Kafka exploits an image of blackness as one to be invaded and inhabited by *Der Verschollene*'s Karl Roßmann as a means of taking an artist position otherwise unavailable to him.[5]

This is already indicated at the beginning of the novel when Karl Roßmann meets the stoker (in German, *der Heizer*, which is also the title of a short story Kafka wrote in 1913 and which became the title of the first chapter of *Der Verschollene*) in the bowels of the ocean liner on which he travels to America. The German word *Heizer* dispels one of the more unfortunate myths about Kafka—namely, that he spoke only German. In fact, like his father, Kafka spoke and wrote in highly proficient Czech, probably taught to him by a nanny and servants in his household and evidenced by his ability to write letters in Czech and work, after 1918, in a Czech-speaking environment. Other instances of Kafka's Czech proficiency are some of his selections for character names, the most glaring example being that of *Das Schloß*'s enigmatic Klamm, a name associated with the Czech word for "illusion" or "aberration." Another example is *Heizer* itself, which translates into Czech as *topič*. Topič was also the name of the most prominent Czech literary publishing house and bookstore of Kafka's day. The massive Topič publishing house was within sight of the Czech National Theater and bears (to this day) on its facade its name in huge block letters that could not have been missed. The building, a stone's throw from one of Kafka's favorite haunts, Café Louvre, housed a massive bookstore on its ground floor. Among other things, *Heizer* is an interlinguistic reference to literary publishing and the Prague literary scene.

And yet, seemingly paradoxically, Karl is attracted to the *Heizer* in large part because he is a fellow countrymen, not because he has something Czech or black about him. Karl's attraction to the *Heizer* considered as one based on a shared German identity extends beyond the general. However, the *Heizer* by trade loads coal into the ship's furnace. An effect of his profession, his skin is covered in soot and so appears as black, much like the chimney sweep of the German folk rhyme "Neger, Neger, Schornsteinfeger," which was well known in Kafka's day. To put it bluntly, men clothed in soot from head to toe were from childhood metaphorically identified as *Neger*. When coupled with the fact that Karl Roßmann identifies with the *Heizer*'s German identity and, later, as "Negro" at the novel's end, we find that the novel projects its racial teleology from the body of the *Heizer* outward. Given that ethnicity is not an essential property of being, is nationally, socially, and historically contingent, and is therefore inherently mutable, Karl's narrative path is one from German to Negro, whereas the *Heizer*'s is not.[6] The *Heizer*'s blackness is akin to blackface and emblematic, metaphorically speaking, of the journey Karl takes from German to Negro. And when linked with the fact that for *Die Verwandlung*—the story Kafka broke off working on *Der Verschollene* to write—we know that Kafka wrote the beginning and the end of the story first, it becomes clear that the connection between the novel's opening, "Der Heizer," and ending, "Negro," is perhaps stronger than previously thought.[7] Like the *Schornsteinfeger* (chimney sweep), the *Heizer* connects a body blackened by coal and, again metaphorically, the literary scene of the Topič publishing house, with Roßmann as Negro and aspiring artist. Thus, Karl's interest in the *Heizer*'s German identity acts as a marker in the novel to show just how far he will move away from this ethnic identity by the novel's end toward becoming a black artist. He identifies with all the *Heizer*'s qualities, German and superficially Negro, setting up the novel as the story of Karl's transformation from an overtly German subjective posture to that of Negro. Finally, given that the novel ends with Karl officially assuming the name "Negro" when he registers for employment with the Nature Theater of Oklahama, there are echoes of Karl's Atlantic passage and encounter with the *Heizer* not only in the Middle Passage but also with the journey blacks and animals underwent in being transported to *Völkerschauen* in North America. Karl is on his way to becoming an (un)musical *Ausstellungsneger*.

Indeed, Kafka felt that "Der Heizer" as material text was essentially musical. The work was first published as a short story in 1913 and translated as such into Czech for the first time in 1920 by Milena. In fact, Kafka came to know the love of his second great letter correspondence after she wrote to him asking permission to translate the story. In a letter of August 28, 1920, Kafka comments on Milena's work:

> Die Übersetzung des Schlußsatzes ist sehr gut. In jener Geschichte hängt jeder Satz, jedes Wort, jede—wenn's erlaubt ist—Musik mit der "Angst" zusammen, damals brach die Wunde zum erstenmal auf in einer langen Nacht und diesen Zusammenhang trifft die Übersetzung für mein Gefühl genau, mit jener zauberhaften Hand, die eben Deine ist. (*BM* 235)

> The translation of the final sentence is very good. Every sentence, every word, every—if I may say so—music in that story is connected with the "fear." It was then, during one long night, that the wound broke open for the first time, and in my opinion the translation catches this association exactly, with that magic hand which is yours. (*LM* 173–74)

The description Kafka gives of his writing begins with the word and ends in music. The meaning and materiality of Kafka's writing are composition in the musical sense. Writing is music; it is the substance of every word of "Der Heizer." The meaning of "Der Heizer" as character and image is thus bound to that of the text's aesthetic. The music of the *Ausstellungsneger* returns in the figure of *der Heizer* (Topič) and as the text's "black" aesthetic strategy. In this sense, "Der Heizer" is an emblematic allegorical figure for the role of blackness in aesthetic practice and the discordant music (writing) that this practice produces

III. *Ja*, Negro

Perhaps not surprisingly, then, the allegorical figure par excellence in *Der Verschollene* is not a character, or literature alone, but music. Kafka's great American hero, Karl Roßmann, does not write but instead plays the piano. "What interests Kafka," Deleuze and Guattari explain, writing in relation to Karl Roßmann's talent as a pianist, "is a pure and intense sonorous material that is always connected to its own abolition—a deterritorialized musical sound, a cry that escapes signification, composition, song, words—a sonority that ruptures in order to break away from a chain that is still all too signifying. . . . In short, sound doesn't show up here as a form of expression, but rather as an unformed material of expression" (Deleuze and Guattari 1975, 6). At the very moment that the "sonorous material" asserts itself in a structure of musicological semantics and signification, it self-destructs or devolves, performing self-involutions until unrecognizable as anything but "musical sound," or sound that should be music.

What this deterritorialized sound provides are circuits through which flows the force of desire. For Deleuze and Guattari, "Desire evidently passes through these positions and states or, rather, through all these lines. Desire is not a form, but a procedure, a process" (Deleuze and Guattari 1975, 8). If this is true, if formless music in Kafka's texts and in *Der Verschollene* specifically provide a medium for the unhindered and disordered movement of want, then America is a deterritorialized site of becoming, or transformation based on aesthetic desire. Perhaps this is why Max Brod was able to record in his diary, "September 9 [1912]: 'Kafka is in ecstasy, writes whole nights through. A novel set in America.' October 1: 'Kafka in unbelievable ecstasy' " (Brod 1937, 128).

Walter Benjamin believed that Kafka was plagued by a "great sadness" and that Kafka's ecstasy over *Amerika* fed off of, as it annihilated, this deep sorrow.[8] "The ardent 'wish to become a Red Indian,'" Benjamin surmises, referring to Kafka's short piece *Wunsch, Indianer zu werden*, "may have consumed [his] great sadness at some point. . . . A great deal is contained in this wish. Its fulfillment, which he finds in America, yields up its secret" (Benjamin 1969, 119).[9] Ignoring the fact that "Red Indian" "music" was being played in Prague cabarets (see chapter 3), Benjamin nevertheless draws attention to the idea that becoming racially other not only provided Kafka with the means to escape the self and the material conditions that invoke great sadness in the suffering subject but also gave Kafka an aesthetic solution to the problem of representing the ineffable process of racial transformation. For Benjamin, Kafka's racial-musical charade creates an emotion denuded of intellectuality. "No matter how one may convey it intellectually," Benjamin asserts, "this purity of feeling may be a particularly sensitive measurement of gestic behavior; the Nature Theater of Oklahama in any case harkens back to the Chinese theater, which is a gestic theater" (Benjamin 1969, 120). At one moment American Indian, at another a member of a Chinese theater company, America offered Kafka a landscape in which to people his racial others, positioning them at various checkpoints of deterritorialization and desire.

It is because of this aesthetic of racial transformation and becoming that Kafka's American Negro must also be counted among the various causes of his racialized ecstasy. In the critical work that has treated Karl Roßmann's self-proclaimed negritude, this identification with African American blackness as he applies for a job at the great Nature Theater of Oklahama has been seen in various ways. "Enrolling himself as 'Negro,'" Anne Fuchs laments, "he now aligns himself with the most stigmatized and oppressed group in American history. . . . Karl's grotesque categorization as 'Negro, technical worker' underlines once more the loss of his social status, true history, name, and voice" (Fuchs 2002, 38). Although the label is unfortunate, it is not grotesque. Fuchs labors under the assumption that to be a Negro is a bad thing, that it is totally undesirable, and that it entails solely stigmatization and oppression. Two deeply erroneous assumptions condition Fuchs's argument: that the black experience in America (and *Amerika*) outlines a purely negative position and that Kafka limited himself to such a rigorously undialectical attitude.

Rolf J. Goebel's brilliant analysis posits that "Negro" is "a deeply emblematic signifier for [Karl's] hybrid position between cultures." But it is not the case that through his Negro status, "Karl comes to shed the pretenses of theatrical artistry for the stereotypical affiliation of minority status with menial labor" (Goebel 2002, 196). For Goebel's excellent understanding of the type of labor Karl will perform as part of the Nature Theater of Oklahama—namely, "technical worker"—forgets what the theater designates itself as, an organ for the production of artists *and nothing else*. In the context of this highly fanciful theater that claims to produce only artists, "technical worker" is perhaps not so easily defined, either in what Karl's duties will be or in what they will become.

Amerika, Heute und Morgen gives further clues to a fuller understanding of (the) Negro's role as technical worker in the theater and in *Der Verschollene* for at least one reason. First, in the opening pages of *Amerika, Heute und Morgen*, Holitscher describes his arrival, by ship, in New York Harbor—a scene *Der Verschollene* would re-create. Of the poor who had to travel in squalid conditions deep in the bowels of the ship, Holitscher writes,

> Diese Armen da unten, die Leute "aus der Tiefe," heut noch fünf Tage lang dürfen sie sich Menschen nennen. Sie sind nicht von ihrer Scholle losgerissen, denn wer unter ihnen hat denn heut noch seine Scholle? Was heißt denn das heute: Scholle? (Holitscher 1919, 16)

> These poor people below deck, the people "out of the depths," for the last five days they were still able to call themselves human. They are not torn from their homes, for who among them has a home today? What does that mean today: home?

This rhetorical bombast found in *Amerika, Heute und Morgen*'s introductory pages articulates the main question that Holitscher's and Kafka's books seek to answer. The German noun *die Scholle* is the root of *Der Verschollene*, the title Kafka gives to his unfinished novel.[10] *Der Verschollene* means, literally, "the lost one" or "the one who went missing" and is translated as the title of Kafka's novel as *The Man Who Disappeared*. The word *Scholle* is of particular importance aboard ships because it also indicates those who have gone overboard and are considered lost at sea. *Scholle* also commonly refers to a flatfish or clump of earth or a clod. The related English word, important for the nautical context we find ourselves in, is "shoal." Holitscher uses *Scholle* as a way, within his nautical context of fish, rocks, and shoals, to question the advanced and at the same time barbaric state of economic exploitation aboard his ship of passage. Indeed, the image of the ship and *Scholle* is so strong in Holitscher's work that the last page of his book is simply a picture of an ocean liner much like the one aboard which Karl would have traveled to America. Deep below decks of the liner, "aus der Tiefe," Holitscher hears the cry of the poor and wonders how they can bear their state of homelessness and, one could say, negritude. They are homeless because, Holitscher tacitly assumes, most who would travel in this manner and endure such hardship are attempting to escape an even greater hardship, to immigrate to America, to the land of opportunity. Relying on the many traces to be followed in the word *Scholle*, Holitscher silently equates the poor with fish in a barrel (fish that come *aus der Tiefe* and must remind themselves that they are human). The immigrants below have no shoal of their own, no oasis from the sea of poverty on which they live. America promises *eine Scholle* as much for Karl Roßmann as for Holitscher's poor. Fleeing not poverty but certain shameful circumstances, Karl immigrates. While aboard ship, in between lives and decks, homeless, Karl lives among the lowly deep in the belly of the boat as he takes his own middle passage in an attempt to reach the shallows and, ultimately, the *Scholle* of the theater. It is here below decks that Karl meets the *Heizer*, who is himself a type of engineer and technical worker while being an emblem of art and blackness.

One thing is certain: Kafka's Negro does not, as one critic would have it, allude to *Schwarzarbeit*, the type of work Karl undertakes both before joining and at the great Nature Theater of Oklahama (Politzer 1966, 159, 161). The term was not in use as such at the time Kafka was writing. Another interpretation sees Negro as foreshadowing Karl's dealings with gangsters, even though there is no suggestion of gangsterism in *Amerika*. Furthermore, African Americans were not involved in organized crime at the turn of the century and were thus not to be easily and readily identifiable as gangsters at this time (Binder, *Kommentar*, 1976, 148). Finally, the suggestion that African Americans are coeval with crime at this or any time is offensive.

Following a dialogue in the diaries and offering a more credible reading of "Negro," Wolfgang Jahn invests in the fact that "Negro" was changed from "Leo," a name that would have vaguely invoked, via *Löwe*, Kafka's mother's maiden name, Löwy, and so Kafka himself (Jahn 1965, 100).This possibility leads Ralf R. Nicolai to suggest,

> Was Kafka dazu bewog, den Namen 'Leo' zu 'Negro' zu ändern, wird dunkel bleiben, doch unbedingt der Wechsel der Richtung, die der Handlungsverlauf zu nehmen hat. Der Name 'Leo' läßt auf die Entwicklung zum höchsten Bewußtsein und dem von Brod erwähnten versöhnlichen Ausgang schließen; Negro drückt das Gegenteil aus und führt in die Stagnierung. (Nicolai 1981, 240)
>
> What possessed Kafka to change the name from "Leo" to "Negro," and the vast difference this change made to the possible way in which the novel could have unfolded, will remain forever unknown. Whereas "Leo" would have allowed for a teleological reading leading to the highest form of self-awareness and, as Max Brod believed, reconciliation, "Negro" has the exact opposite effect, one of stagnation.

Again, Kafka's association with the word "Negro" is seen as overwhelmingly negative in the sense of self-imposed stagnation, as if to be a Negro in America can only lead to no good. The case is more akin to Gerhard Loose's assumption, "Ein völlig neues Leben will er beginnen und wechselt daher den Namen. Negro bezeichnet die Schicht, um deren Entrechtung und gesetzlose Behandlung auch Kafka wußte" (Karl wishes to begin a completely new life and starts by changing his name. Negro describes a group within society defined by white abuse and lawlessness of which Kafka also knew) (Loose 1968, 69). While it is the case that Kafka sees an analogy between the unjust, unlawful ways in which blacks were treated and the treatment of Jews, it should go without saying that he did not know "die Entrechtung und gesetzlose Behandlung" by whites African Americans experienced on a daily basis. Neither he nor Karl were persecuted in the same way that African Americans were. What he did know was Holitscher's description of it and the reproduction of a photograph of a lynched African American male. Nothing accompanied the photo aside from its caption, not even a brief explanation under the photo or in the text. Oklahoma was misspelled (Oklahama), a mistake Kafka retains—intentionally or otherwise, it doesn't really matter—throughout the text of *Der Verschollene* (Loose 1968, 239). But the caption, or label, of "Idyll" is just as important as the misspelling of "Oklahama." Defining, however ironically or cruelly, a scene of lynching as an idyll transforms the act into romantic, pastoral poetry. In other words, abject suffering becomes cause for poetic inspiration and execution; it becomes an aesthetic. Robbing the gruesome image of its historical content leads to its transformation into exotic mythopoeia.

And whereas Anderson and Zilcosky agree that "Negro" signifies a moment of already overdetermined exoticism in the text, Zilcosky adds to this reading when he suggests that Karl as Negro is off to be lynched in Oklahoma (Anderson 1992, 98–122; Zilcosky 2003, 21, 66–70). Citing the connection between the appellation "Negro" and the photo of a lynched African American male reproduced in Holitscher and linking it to the novel's last sentence, in which Karl feels the cold of the mountains and shudders, Zilcosky believes Kafka wrote a more chilling ending for his protagonist. Zilcosky then reminds us of the bloody Tulsa race riot (or, for many, war) of 1921. Of course, Zilcosky doesn't mean that Kafka was clairvoyant but that race relations were particularly tense in Oklahoma, enough so to spark one of the bloodiest race riots in American history. There is enough that is ambiguous and picaresque in *Der Verschollene* to see this particular fate of Karl Roßmann as out of harmony with the novel as it exists in its fragmentary state. Despite Kafka's Negro sources, such an ending would demand a different novel. But Zilcosky's point is well taken and is, in fact, the telos of this current study. For while Kafka harbors at this moment in his aesthetic process contradictory "idyllic" notions of blackness as suffering and artistic freedom, by the time he writes "Ein Hüngerkünstler," it is clear to him that some form of lynching is how all such stories end.

For most of *Amerika*'s critics, then, Karl's endless process of transformation (and not becoming) reaches the apex of abjection, if one can speak of such a thing, when he calls himself "Negro," which Kafka wrote in English. The word Kafka uses is neither *Neger* nor *Schwarzer* (the latter of which wasn't in use as such at the time, anyway) but the English "Negro." The strong current of disbelief that runs through the theater's registrar cannot go unnoticed and surpasses mere doubt as to the veracity of Karl's name in terms of its legal validity. At issue for the registrar is precisely the applicability of the racial designation Karl gives as he submits his name. In order to determine if Karl has misrepresented himself racially, the registrar does not ask him questions but instead looks at him, as if to suggest that the truth of Karl's status as a "Negro" is written on his face. Karl takes the name itself from the "title" given either to him or to workers at one of the many menial jobs he has performed which are not mentioned Kafka's text. The relevant passage is translated by Michael Hofmann as "nothing else came to mind just then, he gave what had been *his* nickname on his last jobs" (*AH* 210, emphasis added). In Kafka's German it is, more precisely, grammatically unclear if the nickname "Negro" belongs entirely to Karl. Kafka writes *den*, not *seinen*. Although *den* in this context generally means *seinen*, or "his," the substitution allows for slippage, if in no other sense than the purely grammatical.

Amerika's early translators, Willa and Edwin Muir, sought to solve the "Negro" problem by eliminating the plurality of jobs to which Kafka refers: "[Karl] gave the nickname he had had in his last post" (*AM* 286). Even though the idea that Karl was named "Negro" at only one job makes for a smoother, more logical narrative progression, this is absolutely grammatically false. Kafka writes "aus seinen letzten Stellungen." The plurality of jobs is clear. Nowhere does Kafka indicate that Karl has ever called himself by this name before. Indeed, the novel is scrupulous on this point: asked several times throughout the narrative what his full name is, each time Karl emphatically gives his name as simply "Karl." If, then, he was spontaneously called Negro at several jobs, then the disbelief of the theater workers makes no sense, as there would be something *self-evident in coloring or demeanor* about the appropriateness of this designation vis-à-vis Karl's appearance. Instead, we must maintain the indeterminacy produced by Kafka's intentional lack of grammatical clarity and understand that the nickname was in use at several of Karl's menial jobs and, furthermore, that it indicates the otherwise phantom presence of Negro coworkers, and African Americans in general, in *Amerika* with whom Karl was lumped. Karl gives his name as "Negro" because he worked with Negroes and now identifies with them.

Karl's self-selection as Negro, however, does not go totally unchallenged in the text:

> "Sie haben doch nicht Negro aufgeschrieben," fuhr ihn der Leiter an. "Ja, Negro," sagte der Schreiber ruhig und machte eine Handbewegung, als habe nun der Leiter das Weitere zuveranlassen. . . . Der Leiter bezwang sich auch, stand auf und sagte: "Sie sind für das Theater von Oklahama." Aber weiter kam er nicht, er konnte nichts gegen sein Gewissen tun, setzte sich und sagte: "Er heißt nicht Negro." . . . Er [Der Herr des Theaters] stellte an Karl zunächst gar keine Fragen,

> sondern sagte zu einem Herrn, der mit gekreuzten Beinen, die Hand am Kinn neben ihm lehnte: "Negro, ein europaeischer Mittelschüler." (*V* 307–8)

> "You didn't write down Negro, did you," the boss shouted at him. "Yes, Negro," said the secretary placidly, and gestured to the boss to conclude the formalities. . . . The boss restrained himself, stood up and said: "I hereby proclaim that the Theater of Oklahama—" But he got no further, he could not violate his conscience, sat down, and said: "His name is not Negro." . . . He [the head of the theater] asked Karl no questions to begin with, but merely observed to another gentleman who was leaning next to him, with feet crossed, and his chin cupped in his hand: "Negro, a secondary schoolboy from Europe." (*AH* 210–11)

Despite being certain that Karl's name is not "Negro" and so that Karl is not a Negro, the registrar and the theater group's leader accept Karl as Negro. But Karl's new identity as Negro does not come without qualification. He is Negro, the European intermediary school student. As if to set him partially within his "proper" national and racial milieu, the registrar situates Karl's origins somewhere between Africa, African America, and Europe but also still within the process of becoming. As a student, Karl is not yet formed. Of mixed race, Karl, like *Amerika* itself, can never truly be formed as anything other than hybrid, a crossbreed, a figure of which Kafka was quite fond.

But unlike the crossbreed in Kafka's very short story "Eine Kreuzung," Karl is not doomed to the butcher's block (*KA*, *Beim Bau der chinesischen Mauer*, 92–93). With a new name and a new job title, Karl is off to Oklahoma:

> Während Karl hinunterstieg wurde zur Seite der Treppe auf der Anzeigetafel die Aufschrift hochgezogen: "Negro, technischer Arbeiter." Da alles hier seinen ordentlichen Gang nahm, hätte es Karl nicht mehr so sehr bedauert, wenn auf der Tafel sein wirklicher Name zu lesen gewesen ware. (*V* 312)

> As Karl climbed down the stairs, next to him the scoreboard was pulled up, and on it the words: 'Negro, Technical Worker'. As everything had gone so well, Karl wouldn't have minded too much if it had been his real name up on the board. (*AH* 213–14)

Karl's professional moniker is "technical worker," which here, once again, could mean anything. Like Negro, the tag of "technical worker" distorts the representation of Karl's identity in order to forge it anew as that which it always was. Where the name "Karl" obeys a strange racial morphology in order to become Negro, *Künstler* transforms into *technischer Arbeiter*. Karl becomes artist by first becoming a Negro technical worker. And it is right after—and because of—this metamorphosis that Karl can and does get on the bus, this time to Oklahoma, where they accept everyone, even a Negro European middle school student, so long as he or she desires to become a Negro, which is to say an artist.

IV. *Künstlerwerden wollte niemand*

Karl finds his new show business career by answering an advertisement that reads, "Jeder ist willkommen! Wer Künstler werden will, melde sich!" (*V* 295) (All welcome! Anyone who wants to be an artist, step forward! [*AH* 202]). The advertisement for the great Nature Theater of Oklahama is deceptively clear. Mentioning nothing of wages, activities, working conditions, and so on, the theater promises training. The troupe's self-representation on the surface frustrates the very expectation one should have met in a job listing—namely, the nature of the job. By insisting that the theater seeks workers to fill various unnamed positions, the poster Karl sees in fact promotes not so much an occupation as a transformation. The usual prerequisites—experience, education, and training—mean, or at least seem to mean, nothing here. The work at hand will be a process of becoming, of metamorphosis, into Artist. There is in fact only one requirement for employment at the theater: the desire to be an artist. One must *desire* to become an artist to be taken on as a hired hand at the Nature Theater of Oklahama. Therefore, if Karl is to be accepted into the theater's ranks, which he will be, he must tacitly or unconsciously already possess the desire to be an artist.

And yet Karl Roßmann seems the last person to want to become an artist. After reading the Nature Theater of Oklahama's advertisement for work, Karl affirms that "Künstlerwerden wollte niemand, wohl aber wollte jeder für seine Arbeit bezahlt werden" (*V* 295) (No one wanted to be an artist, but everyone wanted to be paid for his work [*AH* 202]). To be an artist and to be paid for one's work are here at odds. The tacit assumption operative in Karl's proclamation on the viability of the artist's life is that art does not pay. Karl also assumes that the production of art is, categorically, a form of technical work. Although no one wants to become an artist, and everyone wants to get paid for her work, the two statements are not mutually antagonistic to each other in this context; nor do they have a relation to each other beyond the purely grammatical. It could very well be that one is an artist despite having lacked the desire to become one *precisely* because one gets well paid for one's art. It could be, in other words, that no one wants to become an artist but that one does so anyway because, in a given situation, it pays well. The list of permutations, or eradications, of the seemingly easy logic of Karl's assertion is quite long and in fact ends only at the limits of imagination. What we find on the border of implied sense and the aporia opened up by the deception of the apparent grammatical ordering of meaning in Kafka's text is ambivalence. Where Karl appears to deny absolutely the insurmountable precondition of becoming an artist—namely, desire—he negatively affirms the probability of the artist instinct within him. Lack of desire cannot position itself between Karl and his becoming artist. Instead, it is Karl's inability to concede that he possesses such a desire in the first place that leads to the tension and ambiguity that holds *Amerika* together as it breaks it apart.

Throughout his journey across *Amerika*, Karl deploys various strategies of denial that do not subvert so much as distort and defer the teleological end of this novel without end. Karl's desire to admit to his desire to become an artist is palpable in his piano playing. But he cannot do so without first performing a series of evasions, misrecognitions, and misrepresentations that cause him to disappear at the moment he seeks to affirm his identity. In fact, Karl must disappear in order to circumvent his own desire and present himself to himself as artist. The Nature Theater of Oklahama offers Karl the ability not merely to train as an artist (assuming he has the desire to do so) but also to fulfill a logical requirement of becoming other. The annihilation of the self in terms of a past that would hinder his metamorphosis into an artist must occur before the positive transformation can take place. If it is the case the theater welcomes anyone and everyone, then "Alles was er bisher getan hatte, war vergessen, niemand wollte daraus einen Vorwurf machen" (*V* 295) (Everything he had done up until now would be forgotten, no one would hold it against him [*AH* 202]).

Working with a clean slate, Karl believes that he can no longer be held responsible for his past sins. In becoming artist, Karl must first become innocent. "Innocence" here does not mean free of sin but free from reproach. Having forgotten past lascivious behavior, those who will stand in judgment of Karl, should they pick up the trace of crime of deviant sexuality, will not want to admonish him for his indiscretions and transgressions. Therefore, becoming an artist necessitates both the desire to be an artist and a support structure that allows for this becoming by providing a space in which the various transformations mandated by this trial of becoming artist take place. This space does not create a value-free environment but one determined only by the strictures of art itself. In other words, the seemingly endless, and endlessly permutable, Nature Theater of Oklahama provides a stage upon which only the laws of art apply. Against this backdrop of endless referentiality, the theater stages no referent. In the absence of a referent, everything would be forgotten, would disappear without a trace, and almost unbelievably so. This is why "Karl las das Plakat nicht zum zweitenmale, suchte aber noch einmal den Satz: 'Jeder ist willkommen' hervor" (*V* 296) (Karl didn't read the poster through again, he just looked out the sentence 'All welcome' once more [*AH* 203]). "All welcome" means here that anyone can disappear, dissolve into someone or something else, even and perhaps especially a sexual deviant.

Given that the only artistic talent Karl shows in the novel is musical in nature, it is not surprising that his first impression of the theater comes from the music of trumpets: “Als er in Clayton ausstieg, hörte er den Lärm vieler Trompeten. Es war ein wirrer Lärm, die Trompeten waren nicht gegeneinander abgestimmt, es wurde rücksichtlos geblasen” (*V* 296) (When he got out in Clayton, the sound of many trumpets greeted his ears. It was a confused noise, the trumpets weren’t playing in tune, there was just wild playing [*AH* 203]). Like the atonal music generated in “Forschungen eines Hundes” and “Josefine,” the blast of sound that greets Karl lacks form and contour, this quality of lack signaling all the more in Kafka’s work the presence of the work of art. The music of the trumpets evades its audience as it imposes itself upon it; it transforms itself instantaneously and constantly, as to deny access to a central axis point and point of reference. Karl is greeted by symphonic cacophony, by the noise of the Negro, which is the music of the angels. Indeed, the trumpets are played by “hunderte Frauen als Engel gekleidet” (*V* 297) (hundreds of women dressed as angels [*AH* 203; translation modified]).

By dressing his musicians as angels, Kafka displaces the scene of the theater, or at least distorts it to such an extent that the music being played is not entirely sublunary. Never forgetting that this angelic music is played by women dressed as angels, the illusion of a celestial orchestra is made all the more complete by the fact that “die Gestalten der Frauen riesenhaft aus[sahen]” (*V* 297) (the forms of the women looked gigantic [*AH* 203; translation modified]). Seen here are the *forms* of the women, the angels, not the women themselves. Kafka removes from the women any attribute beyond a formal one, creating in the process a vision of the angelic as pure form. Forms without the possibility of knowable contents, or without legible contents, name not merely the celestial but also the negative aesthetic. The music being blown out by the heavenly trumpet players is, like the many forms of the angels, fragmented and without content. No demonstrable sense can be made of the noise Karl hears except to say that it announces itself within the realm of the aesthetic, and that it is self-referential, or reflexive, insofar as it speaks of nothing except its own self-referential system or reflexivity.

Perhaps it is because of this reflexivity that Kafka employs his musical Negroes in his diaries as similes for his art. As Adorno asserts, “It is not for nothing that Kafka, like no writer before him, should have assigned a place of honour to music in a number of memorable texts. He treated the meanings of spoken, intentional language as if they were those of music, parables broken off in mid-phrase” (Adorno 3). The meaning and the materiality of Kafka’s writing is composition in the musical sense. This is why, when asked by the Nature Theater of Oklahama for his name, Karl Roßmann “antwortete nicht gleich, er hatte eine Scheu, seinen wirklichen Namen zu nennen und aufschreiben zu lassen” (*V* 306) (didn’t reply right away, he was reluctant to give his real name and have that entered [*AH* 210]). Afraid to reveal his true identity and as if attempting to test, negatively, the theater's policy of accepting everyone, even a no one, or a false name, Karl

> nannte daher, da ihm im Augenblick kein anderer Name einfiel, nur den Rufnamen aus seinen letzten Stellungen: "Negro." "Negro?" fragte der Leiter, drehte den Kopf und machte eine Grimasse, als hätte Karl jetzt den Höhepunkt der Unglaubwürdigkeit erreicht. Auch der Schreiber sah Karl eine Weile prüfend an, dann aber wiederholte er, Negro, und schrieb den Namen ein. (*V* 306–7)

> Therefore, as nothing else came to mind just then, he gave what had been his nickname on his last jobs: 'Negro.' 'Negro?' asked the boss, turning his head and pulling a face, as though Karl had now reached the height of preposterousness. The secretary too looked at Karl a while, but then repeated 'Negro' and wrote it down. (*AH* 210)

Kafka wrote it down as well. *Der Verschollene* presents a landscape in which the protagonist, Karl Roßmann, can become an artist by acts of racial appropriation and mimesis via the misprision of African American "blackness" construed through black noise. The novel conflates an aesthetics of becoming with black identity as a way for Karl Roßmann to take a subject position as artist. In effect, becoming black is the only way to become an artist.

Chapter 3

Beyond Negro

I. *Käfer*, *Kaffer*, Kafka

As mentioned above, Kafka broke off writing *Der Verschollene* in order to begin work on *Die Verwandlung*. When it appeared in print in 1915, Kafka insisted that the cover of *Die Verwandlung* not show Gregor Samsa.[1] Much like Karl Roßmann's Negro, the "creature" that Gregor had become was to remain visually enigmatic. Complicit with this wish, the ways in which the novella describe him leave much distorted or incomplete, denying easy classification by presenting and then undoing identifiable but irresolvable oppositions, thus promoting allegorical readings. Indeed, the understanding of Gregor as an allegorical figure is the predominant critical position taken in interpreting the text. The question then becomes that of the type of allegorical structure to which Gregor Samsa adheres.

Offering Medieval allegory as the determinative model of Samsa's indeterminate being, Gavriel Ben-Ephraim writes,

> Demonstrating his ability to combine oppositions without resolving them, Kafka simultaneously builds and dismantles an allegorical ladder ascending the four levels of traditional interpretation. We recall that Medieval commentators like Bede, Aquinas, and Dante divided allegory into the literal (presented), allegorical (hidden), tropological (moral), and anagogical (metaphysical) levels of meaning. These may be reformulated as sign, symbol, significance, and spirit in figural narrative. The scheme makes the anagogia the very goal of allegory as it identifies figurative meaning with spiritual reality. Kafka's *Metamorphosis* finds its true context in an equation it threatens to destroy. (Ben-Ephraim 1994, 451)

Die Verwandlung is ambiguous enough to allow and disqualify this interpretation. Crucially, however, the supposition of medieval allegory highlights the fraught yet decisive role of metaphor in the text. Kafka presents the reader with anagogic metaphors in order to show their destructive, recapitulative possibilities as necessary to aesthetic production. "Die Metaphern," he writes in a journal entry of December 6, 1921, taken from a letter,

> sind eines in dem Vielen, was mich am Schreiben verzweifeln läßt. Unselbstständigkeit des Schreibens, die Abhängigkeit von dem Dienstmädchen, das einheizt, von der Katze, die sich am Ofen wärmt, selbst vom armen alten Menschen, der sich wärmt. Alles dies sind selbständige, eigengesetzliche Verrichtungen, nur das Schreiben ist hilflos, wohnt nicht in sich selbst, ist Spaß und Verzweiflung. (*T* 875)

> are one among many things which make me despair of writing. Writing's lack of independence of the world, its dependence on the maid who tends the fire, on the cat warming itself by the stove; it is even dependent on the poor old human being warming himself by the stove. All these are independent activities ruled by their own laws; only writing is helpless, cannot live in itself, is a joke and a despair. (*J* 398)

Writing is helpless because it cannot stand alone in its essence; it is dependent on its conventions, in particular on metaphors. Metaphors are the great enablers that both weaken and make writing possible, that transform writing into despair and mere "fun" or pastime (*Zeitvertrieb*), as Kafka's mother referred to his occupation as a writer. As Simon Ryan puts it, "The narrative is also about the destructive power of abusive metaphors and their relationship to cultural and ethnic identity at risk" (Simon Ryan, 1). Gregor as insectival being is, then, an anagogic allegorical figure that undoes its own spiritual signification in favor of a cultural reading of ethnicity and exoticism (Zilcosky 2003, 76–78). He is in this sense *unidentifiable* as what the text purposively suggests he is—namely, an allegory of the human condition, an *opaque* sign (Corngold 1973, 12).

Only one character in the novella dares identify Gregor in terms of his species and genus, potentially disrupting an anagogic reading of Gregor's body. The cleaning woman refers to him as a *Mistkäfer*, commonly translated as a "dung beetle." It is of little importance whether or not the woman is correct in her entomological assessment.

As Sean Ireton insists, "Es geht aber letzten Endes nicht darum, ob Gregor Samsa als entfremdeter Mensch oder verwandeltes Tier zu interpretieren ist. Wichtig bleibt vielmehr die Erzählstrategie, der sich Kafka bedient, um die Identität des arbeitssichtigen (man möchte fast sagen des 'Arbeitstiers') Gregor Samsa zu problematisieren und künstlerisch zu gestalten" (Ultimately, it is not a question of whether or not Gregor Samsa is to be interpreted as alienated man or transformed animal. More important is the narrative strategy Kafka employs in order to problematize the work-oriented [one would almost like to say beast of burden] identity of Gregor Samsa and re-imagine it as aesthetic in nature) (Ireton 1998, 35).

In order to understand Gregor as beast of burden, the text deploys not an entomological but an etymological strategy directly opposed to its manifest entomological process. Crucial is not what Gregor is *but that the text deploys the word* Mistkäfer *at all.*

For although Gregor's mystique is here preserved with regard to species—the cleaning woman may have easily misidentified him—the use of the word *Käfer* tells us much about what Gregor represents. In a story in which Kafka acknowledges that he is using his own name as a referent (Samsa = Kafka), *Käfer* is as close to Kafka as is Samsa, if not closer. Gregor Samsa's designation as a type of *Käfer* is, as will be shown below, a complex play on the German (and Afrikaans) word *Kaffer*, a common fin-de-siècle derogatory term for blacks akin to "nigger."

The *Etymologisches Wörterbuch* of *Das Digitale Wörterbuch der deutschen Sprache* defines *Kaffer* in these terms:

> Kaffer m. 'blöder Kerl'. Möglicherweise Übernahme (18. Jh.) von jidd. *kafer* 'Bauer,' gelegentlich auch 'Mann,' in die Gauner- und Studentensprache, wo es sich zum Schimpfwort entwickelt. Zweifelhaft ist die Herleitung des jidd. Ausdrucks aus hebr. *kāfār* 'Dorf'. Oft wird *Kaffer* wohl im Sinne von 'Dörfler' als gaunersprachliche Ableitung von Kaff (s. d.) angesehen. Anderer Herkunft hingegen ist *Kaffer* als südafrikanische Stammesbezeichnung. Es handelt sich um eine Entlehnung (19. Jh.) von nl., vornehmlich afrikaans *kaffer* im Sinne von 'Eingeborener, Schwarzer, Ungebildeter, Barbar,' das seinerseits (nach Etym. Wb. Nl. 2,603 über vermittelndes port. *cafre*) auf arab. *kāfir* 'Ungläubiger' (in der Sprache früherer arabischer Sklavenhändler) beruht. Im Dt. fallen beide lautgleichen Ausdrücke auch inhaltlich als Schmäh- und Schimpfwort zusammen und werden als dasselbe Wort empfunden.

Deviations from *Kaffer* also name in German parts of colonial Africa, for example *Britisch-kaffraria*, and Namibia was referred to as the *Kaffenküste*. One philological regression of *Kaffer* finds that the word comes from the Arabic *kāfir*, meaning in Islamic doctrinal practice "unbeliever" and used primarily in the Arab slave trade, and picking up the sense in which Kafka uses the word *Ungeziefer* to describe Gregor Samsa—a word that commonly means "vermin" but in a ritual context signifies an unclean animal unfit for sacrifice. Such an "unbeliever" would not have the sense God gave him, or would be stupid. And indeed *Kaffer*, the racial epithet, although most likely derived from *kāfir*, has its homologue in Yiddish. Stemming from *Kapher*, *Kaffer* is in Yiddish a word for "farmer" or "clumsy dolt" (Kluge 2002, 417; Pfeiffer 1996, 200). And in Vienna, stupidity was attached to *Kaffer* (or *Khaffa*) as an insult in any racial context (Hornung and Grüner 2002, 526).

Just as in the case of *Ungeziefer*, *Kaffer* contains the double meaning of vermin and unbeliever. In fin-de-siècle Silesia, Lausitz, and Posen, where geographical, cultural, and sociopolitical proximity must have led to a strong resemblance between iterations of Bohemian German, *Kaffer* (also spelled here *Käffer*) meant a small hole, or more commonly an attic window (*Kafferloch*) (Bernd 1820, 109). This type of window was named as such because of the sense that it should have remained closed, reflected in the old regional saying "Der Kaffer sei offen und der Vogel werde ausfliegen" (Bernd 1820, 109). It is clear that the window is meant to keep something out as well as in. Given the association with birds, one has to assume that *Kaffer* or *Käffer* means regionally *Käfer* in the more general sense of "vermin." In other words, one wished to avoid having a vermin infestation facilitated by an open *Kafferloch* ("vermin hole"). More important, the chain of *Kaffer* as *Käffer* as *Käfer* as "vermin" aligns perfectly with the text's two senses of *Ungeziefer*, the only name by which the narrator designates Gregor Samsa's new physical state.

Furthermore, aside from forming the beginning Kafka's own name, *Kaf* means "skin," with *Kafiller* designating the skin or skinned fur of an animal. We recall that all that will be physically left of Gregor is his skin. Also related to *Käfer* are *Käfig*, a word commonly used in Kafka's oeuvre and meaning "cage"; *Käfter*, synonymous with "prisoner"; and *Käfterchen*, signifying a small prison cell or room, much like the one in which Gregor lives. Consider, then, this sentence, making the appropriate substitutions: Kafka's dung beetle lives like a prisoner in his small room. Thus in one word, *Käfer*, Kafka is able to encompass significations for vermin; his name; Negroes; sacrilege; stupidity; skin or pelt; prisons; and prisoners.

Hence the word *Mistkäfer* is not in the text to give us the identity of the genus of insect Kafka otherwise so stridently fought against identifying; it is a tropological device to be used in conjunction with *Ungeziefer* to name the anagogic allegorical work that Gregor as insectival being performs in and for the text.[2] This chapter shows that, for as much as Gregor Samsa is in the process of transforming into a bug, he is also becoming a Negro, a prisoner, a pile of skin, and ultimately that which can contain and represent all these conditions at one time without contradiction, a work of art written by "Kafka." Gregor's transformation is not completed prior to or at the beginning of the story; it is the story, which is, metaphorically speaking, as much about racial transformation and the societal alienation of the artist as it is about a man becoming an insect.

Indeed, *Die Verwandlung* narrates as it embodies *the process* of transforming. The title of *Die Verwandlung* is usually considered to mean a completed act that has transpired before the story's opening. But it is also possible to understand the story's title as a description of events to follow. In this view, a metamorphosis has only begun to take place by the time Gregor awakens in bed. What has happened to Gregor Samsa during his night of "unruhigen

Träumen" is only the onset of his transformation. In fact, the situation is ambiguous enough to lead at least one critic to hypothesize, "When Gregor Samsa awakes . . . one naturally supposes that he has indeed become a gigantic insect. I think that there is significant internal evidence to the contrary. Gregor . . . has a human body at the outset, a human body trapped inside of an insect" (Hartman 1985, 32). Although I do not go this far, it is the case that, like any insectival metamorphosis, Gregor's transformation takes place in stages, making of him a recapitulative human-insect hybrid throughout most of the story. This hybridity is in turn thematized in every aspect of the text's unfolding. "Moreover," as Melissa De Bruyker writes, "Kafka's imaginary worlds have an argumentative function: they help the reader to understand the social crisis of the protagonists by 'contextualizing' the image of the hybrid. . . . Hybridity thus also signals a contested boundary between social norms and the individual" (De Bruyker 2010, 191–92). It is ultimately the social aspect of Gregor's transformation as subjective event that is at issue in the story. Each permutation of the hybrid marks another recapitulative stage in social devolution in accordance with degenerate subjective being.

However, the issues of hybridization, foreignness, and exoticism are not to be understood originally as social-psychological problems. As Benno Wagner points out,

> Fremdheit und Entfremdung stellen für den Schriftsteller Kafka . . . kein ursprüngliches *Problem* dar, keinen anthropologischen oder sozialen Mangel. Vielmehr dienen sie ihm zum einen als diskursives *Medium*, aus dem seine vielfältigen Problemprotokolle als Formen emergieren, zum anderen bilden sie die Grundlage für sein ästhetisches *Verfahren*. (Wagner 2006, 197, emphasis in original)

> Foreignness and alienation do not mean for Kafka the writer an original problem or anthropological or social conundrum. They serve first as a discursive medium from which emerge his multifaceted problemata as forms; second, they serve as the basis for his aesthetic process.

This is not to say that hybridity and its concomitant senses of foreignness and exoticism are not social-psychological problems but that they are here first and foremost unalloyed aesthetic concerns. The multiple stages of Gregor's transformation are an "ästhetisches *Verfahren*." That being said, this aesthetic process at its inception is premised upon said hybridity, foreignness, and exoticism.

Only at the end of the story can we say for certain that the transformation has come to a conclusion. This is to say that *Die Verwandlung* as material text and Gregor's transformation are contingent upon each other and describe each other's attributes. Furthermore, although the title specifies only one transformation, Gregor's metamorphosis, metanarratological process, takes place not as the single event but in protracted movements, or chapters in a story; the narrative describes multiple permutations of a single anagogic metamorphosis. As Margot Norris shows, a "strategy in Kafka's stories is to transform rationality into a site of perversity that allows the fictional animal to speak itself through. . . . In other words, Kafka has his animal figures thinking or speaking through an untenable rationality that gestures toward animal being by acting out the erasure of the signs and markers that attend human being" (Norris 2010, 19). This "acting out" has its inverted reflection in subsidiary characters that move from a lowly state to higher human being. Gregor is thus not the only character in the novella undergoing a transformation. Running parallel to Gregor's metamorphosis is that of his family, who go from passive-dependent to self-sufficient subjective agents. Just as Gregor recapitulates—literally moving from man to animal and metaphorically exhibiting the traces of his passage through "Negro"—his family recovers from a degenerate state; they evolve. That is to say, in contradistinction to the Samsa family's developmental trajectory, Gregor's movement from human to insect to oblivion, or disappearance, is that of a racial-teleological shift, in this order: salesman/insect-Negro-prisoner/pile of skin/artist (lack of being). Race is not intended in this chapter to denote a supposed biological separation between Jew and gentile—an aspect of the term that has already been dealt with many times, as has the story's use of Christian themes (Holland 2009, 178). What I am suggesting is the mise-en-scène of an anagogic allegorical transformation, through the metaphorical recapitulative Africanization, of Gregor Samsa. In addition, this process is quietly augmented primarily by muted discourses of etymology/entomology, New World slavery, skin color, and sociocultural standing within the text.

This amalgamated discourse begins with the fact of Gregor Samsa's insectival body itself, understood outside the registers of pure fantasy or sociologically unalloyed magic realism. Of course, it is the case that Samsa awakens to find his body fantastically transformed into that of an insect, and that this transformation must be taken literally or figuratively. Indeed, in various critical readings, the insect body stands in for, say, existential reflection on the state of human being; a Marxist analysis of wage labor and the holy family; philosophical excursions in the fate of linguistic signification; or it signifies nothing other than a giant insect living among humans.[3] All these interpretations are valid. What I am suggesting, however, is that they do not exhaust the story's endless plenitude of meaning, and they in no way address the fact that Gregor's insect form becomes waste, or mere brown *Kaf*. For, as the action of the maid's sweeping away Gregor's papery dead body (*Kafiller*) from his room (*Käfterchen*) suggests, she associates him not only with a dung beetle but also with biological waste and, by extension, shit. Blacks (*Käfer*) were also often associated with excrement, a fact borne out by the vulgar slang phrase for defecation, *einen Neger abseilen* (to expel a nigger).

II. *Ins Gesicht springen*

The biological hierarchy of who can be considered to be human and what (a pile of skin, a bug, shit, a Negro) cannot has its limiting polarities. The inhuman is either the anthropomorphized deity or, at the bottom of the human scale of evolution, and sometimes off it, the Negro.[4] It is clear that Gregor's insect nature sets him firmly at the bottom of the scale of animal being, and in very specific human company. In other words, when we consider what it meant in 1912 to actually think the human in terms of vermin, of absolute, biologically determined inferiority, of radical racial and cultural alterity, we are left with the Jew *and* the Negro.[5] Thus, to remove race (understood here as either Jew, Negro, or both) as a component for reading *Die Verwandlung* seems to evade a crucial issue; and to read Gregor as an actual insect and nothing more, as Nabokov does, is fascinating and beside the point. As one critic notes, "What Nabokov fails to recognize is something fundamental about Kafka and his creations. Being or becoming an animal—or an insect—in Kafka's works is a highly specific affair and involves a process whereby a creature's humanity, for lack of a better word, tends to be augmented and accented" (Deladurantaye 2007, 327). And although, as one contrarian has noted, "critics should not ignore the fact that 'The Metamorphosis' is, on the most literal level, about a bug," critics should also never forget that Kafka forbade visualizations of Gregor in favor of abstraction (Swinford 2010, 215). It is Gregor's metaphorical status as recapitulative hybrid within an anagogic allegorical scheme that names the terms of the story's strategic investments. The matter at issue is not what type of insect Gregor has become but what type of human.

Another category of the human that nevertheless stands outside its own parameters is that of the slave. Indeed, the story's second paragraph supplies us with an allusion to the Leopold von Sacher-Masoch novel of contractual sexual slavery, *Venus im Pelz* (1870). Gregor

> hing das Bild, das er vor kurzem aus einer illustrierten Zeitschrift ausgeschnitten und in einem hübschen, vergoldeten Rahmen untergebracht hatte. Es stellte eine Dame dar, die mit einem Pelzhut und einer Pelzboa versehen, aufrecht dasaß und einen schweren Pelzmuff, in dem ihr ganzer Unterarm verschwunden war, dem Beschauer entgegenhob. (*D* 115–16)

> hung the picture which he had recently cut out of an illustrated magazine and put into a pretty gilt frame. It showed a lady, with a fur cap on and a fur stole, sitting upright and holding out to the spectator a huge fur muff into which the whole of her forearm had vanished! (*C* 89)

Along with his writing desk, this picture is Gregor's prized possession, and he will not give it up. The insect Gregor can identify with it, in that the lady's vanishing forearm suggests recapitulative transformation, or at least the start of an externalized embryonic transformation. Just as Gregor has only begun to change, the woman in the photograph is still recognizable as woman and not wholly animal. Whereas Gregor's body has become fully animal, his thoughts remain, like the greater part of the woman's body, wholly human, creating a dualist perspective with regard to Gregor's subjective disposition. "Although the reader initially accepts the dualist perspective," Sweeny observes, "Kafka gradually introduces an alternative to this original position, thereby raising doubts about whether the insect continues to be Gregor Samsa. As a result, the reader's attitude toward the underlying framework of the story begins to shift: while accepting the insect as Gregor, the reader comes to acknowledge evidence that undercuts this identity (Sweeney 1990, 26). Kafka himself was deeply disdainful of wearing furs. In a letter to Greta Bloch of May 21, 1914, Kafka describes first meeting her, when she was at this time wearing a coat like the one in Gregor's picture:

> Ich erwartete ein großes, starkes, älteres Mädchen zu treffen. Nicht stimmte nun, so hätte sich ja meine Phantasievorstellung mit der Wirklichkeit ausgleichen können. Darüber hinderte mich aber hauptsächlich, wie ich jetzt weiß, ihr Pelzwerk. Eine Boa war es nicht, ich glaube, man nennt dieses Kleidungsstück Stola oder ähnlich. Es paßte Ihnen nicht oder vielmehr ich merkte nicht, daß es Ihnen nicht paßte, es gefiel mir bloß nicht. . . . Auch habe ich seit jeher gegen dieser Art der Pelzbehandlung (Ausbreitung des Pelzes und untern Seidenfütterung) einen entschiedenen Widerwillen. Vielleicht spielt hierbei irgendein Gedanke daran mit, daß nomadenhafte Jäger die Felle so tragen dürfen, allerdings ohne sie mit Seide zu füttern. (*BF* 582)

> I imagined you all wrong; I was expecting to meet a big, strong, rather older girl. Nothing was right; nevertheless, my preconceived ideas could have adjusted themselves to reality. But it was mainly your furs, as I now know, that prevented this. It was not a boa; I believe this garment is known as a stole or something like that. It doesn't suit you, or rather I failed to notice that it didn't suit you, I just don't like it. And at first sight it struck me as so conspicuous there, at the entrance to the hotel. Moreover, I have always felt a definite distaste for furs treated in this manner (stretched skins with a silk lining underneath). Perhaps it has something to do with the notion that nomadic hunters may wear their skins in this way, though not lined with silk. (*LF* 410)

The sight of the woman wearing furs is disrupted by the image of an uncivilized, nomadic hunter, highlighting the disparity between the artificiality of fashion and the brute facticity of primitive necessity. Whereas the hunter's fur is both a symbol of his powerful "primitive" survival instincts and their maintenance, the fashionable woman's coat signifies alienation from vital being and destructive hypocrisy. That Gregor chooses to aestheticize a woman in furs indicates that the picture places more at stake for him than mere fashion and sexual attraction. Gregor's *Venus im Pelz* captures the romanticized ideal of the primitive, visceral spirit of the nomadic, antibourgeois struggle for survival. Furs clothe another, radically other form of human being, one that Gregor believes himself to represent, and from which he is at the same time radically estranged.

The schizoid split that takes place between Gregor Samsa the insect and this other being is in part enacted by the text's recourse to strong literary allusion. For the woman in the picture is also clearly recognizable as Sacher-Masoch's Wanda (Waldeck 1972, 147–52). In this sense, a purely literary transformation takes place alongside Gregor Samsa's bodily metamorphosis. *Die Verwandlung* cannibalizes *Venus im Pelz*, appropriates its themes, and redeploys its strength in a new configuration. One text frames and enframes the other in a type of gilded cage, or, in this case, a picture frame. Just as Gregor intended for himself, the reader is meant to look, decipher, contemplate, and appreciate both the picture as an autonomous aesthetic object and the manner in which the displaced, monadic nomad continues to represent the whole of a lost world.

The least we can say of *Die Verwandlung*'s appropriation of Sacher-Masoch is that it does not happen without reason; and much has been made of the place of Sacher-Masoch in the *Die Verwandlung*.[6] But in these readings one forgets the extent to which Sacher-Masoch meditated on New World slavery in forming a picture of his hero's desire. Sacher-Masoch imagined quite rightly that New World slavery was informed in part by the violent sexuality, or institutionalized rape, that flourished under plantation slavery. Aside from being a sexual slave, Sacher-Masoch's Gregor, the slave name of *Venus im Pelz*'s hero (otherwise known as Severin) as well as the namesake of Gregor Samsa, *works* for his mistress. He carries her bags, tends her garden, and is contractually bound to do whatever she demands, including but not exclusive to sex acts. Gregor (Samsa) is also contractually bound to his employer, finding himself in the position of indentured servant, forced to work to pay the debts of his father. In fact, what Gregor (Severin) practices seems more along the lines of indentured servitude. He binds himself contractually to Wanda. Severin's debt, or in other words, his true enslavement is psychological; he must work until his psyche is spent of its "unnatural" desire to be a slave, an event that transpires and is explained as such close to the novel's close.

Because Severin can never legally (and so truly) become Wanda's slave he, throughout *Venus im Pelz*, laments the abolition of slavery, the very thing that would turn his fantasy into reality. His contractual servitude fails because, as material debt, it can be, and is, overcome. To be an actual slave would mean servitude in perpetuity and at all costs—precisely what Severin desires with Wanda but is not, paradoxically, strong enough to attain. The end of slavery would be, and was, *death, disappearance, or a new life as a human being instead of a thing*. Here the two texts, *Die Verwandlung* and *Venus im Pelz*, diverge. While Severin does not die, disappear, or ever have his status as a human being called into question, Samsa's plight is one unto death, disappearance, and the loss of status as a human being. This means that Gregor Samsa's servitude goes beyond the indentured servitude described in the text as his legal predicament. There is every indication that his father's bills will never be paid, no matter how long or hard Gregor works. Where Severin called himself a slave, he was in fact an indentured servant; and where Samsa appears to be an indentured servant, he is in fact a slave.

Thus, in reaction to his condition as a means of production and his inability not only to set the value of his labor but also, as a slave, to have any value attached to it, Gregor experiences the fragmentation and distancing of the individual from the idea of a shared humanity in favor of a monadic (nomadic) yet self-alienating existence. As Walter Sokel describes it,

> Die Fragmentierung des modernen Menschen im bürokratischen Staat der Departments und Ressorts stellt für Schiller den Abfall und Verratenen die Entfremdung—des Individuums von der Idee der Menschheit, einem vielseitigen Ganzen, in ihm selbst dar. Dieser Abfall von der Menschheit im Individuum ist aber zugleich dessen Selbstentfremdung, da ja das "Individuum" nur als Unteilbares, als organische Ganzheit es selbst sein kann, was gerade seine hochspezialisierte, einseitige Ausbildung und Arbeitsweise verhindern müssen. Dieselbe Gleichsetzung von Selbstverlust mit Verlust des Menschseins wird uns sowohl bei Marx als auch bei Kafka begegnen. (Sokel 1981, 8)

> The fragmentation of modern man in the bureaucratic state of departments and resorts meant for Schiller the refusal, betrayal and alienation of individuality from the idea of humanity, a multifaceted totality. This refusal of humanity in individuality is at the same time self-alienation, which this "individuality" can only understand as incommunicable, as the organic unity of the self that the highly specialized, one-sided education and work habits necessarily hinder. As in Kafka, we see this same notion of the self-alienated subject combined with the loss of communal human-being in the work of Marx.

And yet, as accurate as this reading is, it remains unclear as to what Gregor becomes after losing himself.

But the story provides yet another snapshot of savagery, this time in the scene in which Gregor's mother and sister try to remove the framed woman in furs along with furniture from his room and he literally attaches himself to the image. Indeed, by appending himself to the picture, Gregor receives a creature comfort. The glass of the frame is cool to the touch, allowing him to soothe his "heißen Bauch," which is to say, providing him a way of cooling his loins. The transforming body experiences the explicit sexuality of the image as if that body itself belonged to a regime of images. Gregor can exact a measure of bodily release and pleasure from the picture and its frame as object. The image has become "real" insofar as Gregor has slipped into its literary-ideational realm, thus bringing about a physical conjoining of *Die Verwandlung* and *Venus im Pelz* in what can only be described as the copulation of two literary texts. A slave named Gregor again has sex with Wanda.

The pleasure the picture provides triumphs over the only other sensual connection the transformation gives Gregor. He would rather "Grete ins Gesicht springen" than release his hold on his *Venus im Pelz*. This can be read in a particularly vulgar way, in that *springen* can also mean *spritzen*, or "ejaculation." When read in this way, Gregor is indicating that his sex act with the picture is not yet finished and that he would literally rather ejaculate in Grete's face should she find herself in the wrong place at the wrong time than interrupt (or cover up) his unique form of coitus. But again, we must recall that the quality to which Gregor adheres in the picture is no longer the image of the sexually arousing, devolving woman but the physical sensation of cold on a hot belly (*C* 166). That is to say, Gregor clings to the picture because he is able to measure an erotic charge from it beyond that of the intellect. The picture frame as object allows Gregor to fuse material reality with the purely imaginative. He can do so only at the expense of, if not his humanity, then his human form. We must also recall that at the level of textual allusion, the picture connotes a sense of enslavement, otherness as the slave, and finally the exotic eroticism of slavery. In this sense, Gregor fuses himself to the symbolic order in which he had previously existed as unconscious observer, that of deviant black sexuality. Gregor no longer follows his desire or restrains it; he has become one with his desire in a transgressive sex act that includes incest only as one of its horrors.

Grete's reaction to this "perversion" is telling. For the first and last time during his transformation, Gregor's sister calls him by his name, in effect rehumanizing him in an attempt to dislodge him not just from the wall but also from the realm of pure fantasy with which he has direct sexual congress. Whether out of jealousy, shock over intuiting the perverse nature of Gregor's relationship with the image, or reflex, Grete imposes her will over Gregor by recalling him to his humanity at the very moment that he sinks below, or rises above, the human. This is also the only time in the text that Gregor's transformation is referred to as such. Thus we have a double act of naming, each pole of which moves irrevocably away from the very thing it names. As Grete reminds Gregor of his humanity, or whiteness, thus drawing him out of the closed circuit of unreality and blackness and bestiality, the narrator reinserts Gregor into his immaterial, proper place within it with all the more force. Underscoring his transformation, the narrator undercuts Grete's effort, decisively giving Gregor over to the foreignness of an unknown country in a text that shifts and transforms, that clings to its illusions and allusions as forcefully as Gregor clings to his, and with the same "perverse" pleasure.

Gregor is able to pry himself loose only at the sight of his fainted mother. Wishing to help his sister in finding a potion to revive the fallen woman, Gregor detaches himself from the picture, indeed forgets about it entirely and for the remainder of the story, and leaves his room. The mother's distress, coupled with Gregor's sudden appearance outside his prison cell, leads the father to believe that his insect son "sich irgendeine Gewalttat habe zuschulden kommen lassen" (*D* 168) (had been guilty of some violent act [*C* 107]), *which is in fact the truth*. The father erroneously concludes that Gregor *directly* attacked the mother and the sister, but his main interpretation of the scene, that Gregor has committed some violent act, is accurate.[7] If we see Gregor's communication with the picture as a sex act (which in Kafka is always identified with "primitive," "black," congenital sexual deviancy), then it is a form of sexual violence in at least two senses. The mode of Gregor's pleasure is quick and violent; he cools himself on an imaginary love imprisoned by him in a frame without, of course, recognizing the violence of his gesture. The picture is literally smothered in grotesque copulation that is both purely human, purely "Negro," and purely animal. On the one hand, what Gregor's mother and sister witness is unalloyed instinctual behavior designed for the singular purpose of physical release. On the other, certain aesthetic conditions must first be met before the animal can come off his chain. That is to say, Gregor's sexual violence is a highly intellectualized, aestheticized form of unreflective, ugly savagery.

The fact that this all-too-human inhuman act is done in the presence of his mother and sister is Gregor's second act of unspeakable violence. Subjected to the sight of the fulfillment of Gregor's bestial need—which is still perversely informed by the symbolic displacement and so recognition of Gregor's very human desire—the mother is overwhelmed by another act of incest. The savage act of symbolic reordering and reification is a revelation of the base and inhuman character of black "perversions." The giant insect clinging to, and taking physical comfort in, a fetishistic photo in *Venus im Pelz* serves to disrobe the emperor, to unveil the truth of Gregor the man and the primacy of primitive fetish in all sexual desire. In other words, this inhuman act stages the truth of the sex act as Gregor desired it, as a *Käfer* in the Bohemian sense of the word. More important, because Gregor as framer fabricates an object that is also a literary historical frame for *Die Verwandlung*, the act of making a literary allusion is perceived here in a perverse sexual way. Thus, writing in a literary manner, which always involves allusions to other literary texts, is itself understood here as sexually disgusting and racially perverse, as the grotesque copulation of two or more texts. Gregor's mother has indeed seen something unbearable, unmentionable. She has seen the concretization of a writer's literary-racial process and passion. And this is why the writing desk and the picture are coupled in the story; they are related in the way a certain type of work is associated with its specific, required tool.

It is precisely at this moment of expressive, essentially sexually deviant revelation that the father's power reasserts itself. Just as in "Das Urteil," Gregor's father steps in and brings Noahic order to the passions, to the savage sexual proclivities of an unruly son, by bringing him in line with a greater, but socially legitimate, form of savagery. As in the case for Georg Bendemann, the confrontation between father and son over sexual impropriety hinges on maternal sexual "innocence." Although Gregor will not ultimately survive his father's assault with the apple, as in "Das Urteil" this is not just an unhappy death. Gregor's transformation as death is a project of rebirth; the story itself is the hesitation before birth as recapitulation.[8]

III. *Und so leicht, so musikalisch*

Like Georg Bendemann's leap and Karl Roßmann's "disappearance," Gregor's impending "death" is also bound to music. Starving, unable to find appropriate nourishment despite the thoughtful, wide-ranging efforts of his sister, Gregor eventually loses his appetite for food. It is not that he does not want to eat what is presented to him or seen on the dining-room table; he requires this different type of nourishment: " 'Ich habe ja Appetit,' sagte sich Gregor sorgenvoll, 'aber nicht auf diese Dinge. Wie sich diese Zimmerherren nähren, und ich komme um!' " (*D* 183) ("I'm hungry enough," said Gregor sadly to himself, "but not for that kind of food. How these lodgers are stuffing themselves, and here am I dying of starvation!" [C 119]). It is only after his family has eaten dinner and the lodgers request that Gregor's sister play some music that Gregor awakens to that which he still cares about, finding the nourishment for which he has been longing and to which he belongs:

> Und doch spielte die Schwester so schön. Ihr Gesicht war zur Seite geneigt, prüfend und traurig folgten ihre Blicke den Notenzeilen. Gregor kroch noch ein Stück vorwärts und hielt den Kopf eng an den Boden, um möglicherweise ihren Blicken begegnen zu können. War er ein Tier, da ihn Musik so ergriff? Ihm war, als zeige sich ihm der Weg zu der ersehnten unbekannten Nahrung. Er war entschlossen, bis zur Schwester vorzudringen, sie am Rock zu zupfen und ihr dadurch anzudeuten, sie möge doch mit ihrer Violine in sein Zimmer kommen, denn niemand lohnte hier das Spiel so, wie er es lohnen wollte. (*D* 185–86)

> And yet Gregor's sister was playing so beautifully. Her face leaned sideways, intently and sadly her eyes followed the notes of music.

> Gregor crawled a little farther forward and lowered his head to the ground so that it might be possible for his eyes to meet hers. Was he an animal, that music had such an effect upon him? He felt as if the way were opening before him to the unknown nourishment he craved. He was determined to push forward till he reached his sister, to pull at her skirt and so let her know that she was to come into his room with her violin, for no one here appreciated her playing as he would appreciate it. (*C* 121)

Played by the sister for whom he was saving money to send eventually to a conservatory, music is the unknown nourishment.[9] The question then becomes, what type of music nourishes "vermin"? For, while the sister is in all likelihood performing a piece appropriate to a conservatory, the setting of the Samsa household—the father, still in uniform, the mother, three uncouth lodgers, and a giant insect—is more akin to a cabaret. Given the circumstances of the performance, it is no longer a matter of what is being performed but how setting and audience determine the reception and classification of a composition. What, in fact, does Gregor the insect and *Käfer*, and *Die Verwandlung*, understand under the label of "music"?

It is a curious choice on Kafka's part to make Gregor a potential patron of the musical arts, and to have him feed off music nearing the end of his transformation. For Kafka often complained of his "unmusicality." This does not mean, however, that he rejects any form of musicality with regard to his work but that his definition of musicality is idiosyncratic. Indeed, two different definitions of music are operative and in tension with each other in Kafka's musings on the subject. One is characterized by untroubled harmony. He extends this idea of music to mean anything that is in harmony with itself, including people. In a journal entry of March 9, 1922, he writes about "life in the jungle" as follows: "Eifersucht auf die glückliche, unerschöpfliche und doch sichtbar aus Not (nicht anders als ich) arbeitende, aber immer alle Forderungen des Gegners erfüllende Natur. Und so leicht, so musikalisch" (*T* 910) (Jealousy of the happiness and inexhaustibility of nature, whose impelling force (like mine) is yet distress, though always satisfying all the demands its antagonist lays upon it. And so effortlessly, so harmoniously [*J* 416]). The musical being is the indefatigable man fit for happiness and hard work, in harmony with nature's demands. The second, the unmusical, refers to all things existing in disharmony with themselves, which Kafka extends to his very being and his writing. For example, Kafka asks Milena, "Weißt du eigentlich, daß ich vollständig, in einer meiner Erfahrung nach überhaupt sonst nicht vorkommenden Vollständigkeit unmusikalisch bin?" (*BM* 65) (Do you know that I am completely unmusical, more than anyone I have ever known? [*LM* 48]) but also proclaims to her, "Ich verstehe nicht Musik aber diese Musik verstehe ich leider besser als alle Musikalischen" (*BM* 165) (I don't understand music but unfortunately I understand this music better than all musical people combined [*LM* 125]). There is a music outside music, comprehensible only to those thought to be unmusical in the prosaic sense. This "other" music is dialectically opposed to a light, happy, harmonious surface sound; it is a dark, nebulous, cluttered noise linked to creativity and sadness, "Jubilee song" and *Ausstellungsneger*, cabaret and cruelty. Kafka's reflections on the black music he heard in Prague's night haunts place it squarely within this conception of musicality. Negro music is to him melodious and sadly inharmonious at the same time. So, too, for Kafka is his own writing. This tension defines the Unmusical, or music that undoes itself as such. The Unmusical made tangible in Negro music is both the inherent value and the opacity of Kafka's work. In fact, Kafka's writing is so absorbed by its own unmusicality (its Africanicity) in the sense of creating seeming nonsense that it annihilates for him even the possibility of an interpretive philosophical contemplation of any "music":

> In mir kann ganz gut eine Konzentration auf das Schreiben hin erkannt werden. Als es in meinem Organismus klar geworden war, daß das Schreiben die ergiebigste Richtung meines Wesens sei, drängte sich alles hin und ließ alle Fähigkeiten leer stehn, die sich auf die Freuden des Geschlechtes, des Essens, der Trinkens, *des philosophischen Nachdenkens der Musik zuallererst* richteten. Ich magerte nach allen diesen Richtungen ab. (*T* 341, emphasis added)

> It is easy to recognize a concentration in me of all my forces on writing. When it became clear in my organism that writing was the most productive direction for my being to take, everything rushed in that direction and left empty all those abilities which were directed towards the joys of sex, eating, drinking, philosophical reflection, and above all music. I atrophied in all those directions. (*J* 163)

It is Kafka's unmusicality that comprehends his writing, which is not born of harmonious reflection and is not open to definition. It is a machinelike practice construed as the banging of the African gong; but it is also the voluptuous exoticism of Bizet.

For another source for the link between Africanicity and music in Kafka is Nietzsche, of whom Kafka was a great admirer and who, in an attack on Richard Wagner, backhandedly praised Bizet's music for its progressive "African" qualities, writing in *The Case of Wagner*,

> This music is cheerful, but not in a French or a German way. Its cheerfulness is African; fate hangs over it; its happiness is brief, sudden, without pardon. I envy Bizet for having had the courage for this sensibility which had hitherto had no language in the cultivated music of Europe—for this more southern, brown, burnt sensibility.—How

> the yellow afternoons of its happiness do us good! We look into the distance as we listen: did we ever find the sea smoother? And how soothingly the Moorish dance speaks to us! How even our instability for once gets to know satiety in this lascivious melancholy! (Nietzsche 1967, 159)[10]

One could just as well add Richard Strauss's infamous *Salome* (1905) to the list. In the cases of Dvořák, Nietzsche's Bizet, and Strauss's *Salome*, Nordau's predictions of the lascivious "degeneration" of European art were coming true. By 1912, primitivism and cubism in all the arts were having their "Moorish" heyday.[11] The idea that musical art was headed in the direction of Africa was already *en vogue* as Kafka sat down to write *Die Verwandlung*. Ragtime was an established pastime in Prague.[12] Performances of African American spirituals, either by white minstrels or by African Americans, had long since made their way back to the Old World.[13] And of course, like most of the fin-de-siècle Prague literati, Kafka would have been intimately familiar with Bizet's *Carmen*. But Kafka was familiar with another *Carmen*, one that made Nietzsche's understanding of the happy African melancholy of the opera all the more obvious, inadvertently or otherwise.

In 1908, in Prague, the lawyer Jiří Červený (George Red) founded Cabaret *Červená sedma* (The Red-Seven Cabaret), whose Večer Akademiků (The Night of Academics) set the standard for Prague cabaret culture.[14] A collection of seven student scholars of highly discerning taste (the Academy), the members of *Červená sedma* constituted Prague's cabaret elite, deciding what the most cutting-edge cultural trends were and presenting them to and as the city's nightlife. Performing mostly at Prague's then bilingual (Czech and German) cabaret and café Montmartre (owned by the impresario and writer Josef Waltner), *Červená sedma* were interested mostly in new developments in the avant-garde and popular culture and combining and staging them in highly intellectualized fashion. Their repertoire consisted of satire, parody, persiflage, travesty, various sketches, shadow play, and improvised soliloquies and dialogues—during which Kafka was present (Kotek 1998, 26). One of their productions was a burlesque of *Carmen* (they gave the same treatment to another "exotic" opera, Strauss's *Salome*), which included strong elements of the "new music" (Kazda 1981, 23). "American dances" were performed on the same evenings as *Carmen*, including animal dances such as The Bear (Langer 2003, 31), in which the dancers imitated the animal's namesake. Kafka and his friends all frequented not only Montmartre but also other night haunts that offered ragtime and Africanized, "protojazz" entertainments (Kotek 1975, 66).

Waltner did much to popularize ragtime and black music and dance in Prague. "Animal" and "Apache" dances became staples of Prague's young literati nightlife during the early decades of the twentieth century, following up on the Cakewalk, which, according to a firsthand account of black dance by the Czech writer and translator Otakar Theer, was introduced in Prague as early as 1903 (Kotek 1998, 19). The new music and dance influences were so strong that what started at Montmartre in 1911 as dancing only on Friday nights became, throughout 1913, dancing every night (Kotek 1975, 66). Waltner's 1913 book, *Kavárna Montmartre* (*Café Montmartre*), a complement to Theer's 1903 *Zlatá Praha* (*Golden Prague*), canonized Montmartre, as well as African dance (and thus music), for the Prague intelligentsia of the fin-de-siècle.

Červený himself never ceased to introduce black cultural forms into Cabaret *Červená sedma* until the group was disbanded in 1922. During their heyday, their performances often took the countenance of a combination of canonical classical music and opera such as *Carmen* with ragtime and African dance (Matzner, Poledňák, and Wasserberger 1983, 185). Or an approximation of African and Native American dance was performed, exaggerating the syncopated, percussive elements of the music to the point of turning it into mere "noise." An example of this is an instrument that was used in the Prague cabaret Konvikt Bar (Convict Bar), where, in 1920, the culmination of years of experimentation was brought out onto the stage and called a jazz instrument (Válek 1960, 17). As described by none other than Kafka's friend and "conversation" partner Gustav Janouch, the device

> was a huge, red-painted monster, surrounded with sixteen bell bars, four strings of bells and jingle bells, six cowbells, three cymbals, tam-tam, gong, and four small drums. Beside the usual set of pipes and cymbals, this "jazz" was equipped with a strange instrument consisting of six shotgun barrels, six pedals instead of triggers so that one could shoot six times during the performance—with a foot. That was, of course, an astonishing sensation, and the most popular piece of that time was therefore "Indianola," during which the drum player transformed into a dogged gunman. (Kotek 1975, 55)

The result could only have been cacophony. It is important to note that this "jazz" contraption was the product of a decade of cacophonous cabaret music thought to be based primarily on African American expressive culture. For "the operator [of the machine] had returned from the U.S. with his 'jazz,' and during the performance he sat in a cage. His name was Reimann" (Válek 1960, 16). In fact the owner of Konvikt Bar, Reimann produced black noise (Voskovec 1996, 26).

The dance and music forms thought to be of black origin leading up to the appearance of Reimann's infernal "jazz" machine in 1920 prepared the mavens of cabaret culture to such great extent for this pure black noise that no one was shocked by what she or he heard and saw. Indeed, the experience of the noise machine served to affirm the role of the cabaret avant-garde as the sole purveyors of the only living music. Accounting in 1927 for what these "jazz" precursors meant to Prague's popular cultural formation during the second decade of the twentieth century, E. F. Burian (the Czech poet, journalist, singer, actor, musician, composer, dramatic adviser, playwright, and director—as well as the author of the book *Černošské tance* [*Negro Dances*, 1929]) writes in his essay "Tanec v novém světle" ("Dance in a New Light"), "Dance was invented by jazz and was brought to us by jazz. . . . We invented dancing, we invented collective art. . . . Dance has proven its collective character. And dance has proven much more than that: we dance atonal dances of the most radical character. From the simple farmer to the American banker from Broadway [Wall Street], everybody will dance according to Schönberg" (Burian 1981, 31).

Despite syncopated rhythms, what was looked back upon in the 1920s as the Prague "jazz" and dance of the first two decades of the century was more akin to an improvised burlesque of Schönbergian atonality. Much in the way Bizet was "ragged," Schönberg was jazzed, or simply blackened. The result was wild noise given an exotic face and name. Whether through "Apache" dances or the Cakewalk, or through what was believed to be African drumming, or through "Bear Dancing," Prague's cabaret avant-garde presented their entertainments as what they were: ambiguous cultural hybrids intellectualized and then ironized to the point of becoming highly influential aesthetic practices. As the composer Jaroslav Ježek characterized the early influence of what is being referred to as jazz after the fact, "The power of jazz was not in just captivating sensitive musicians. Its merit was that it came across to nonmusicians and that they felt in it a manifestation of contemporary life. It seems that jazz meant another, deeper dimension for the contemporary musical and social life (Válek 1960, 15). Whereas concerto music was thought to be dead, the modern music of the cabaret was vibrant and young, despite or because of its cacophonous nature. "Bizet's blackness" was indeed deeply in tune with Kafka's contemporary world. And animal dances allowed for interspecies transformation as an art form.

This conception of music and dance, in which animal transformation is made possible by black aesthetic influence in the space of the cabaret (and the three lodgers certainly do not behave as if they were at the concert hall), is the ultimate goal of the transformation; its teleology is a complete fusion of the black musico-aesthetic realm with the body—something made possible solely by passage through blackness and slavery. First, Gregor's body transforms into a *Käfer*, or, synonymous in Prague German, a *Kaffer*. Then, Gregor satisfies a physical need for the aesthetic at one remove when he cools himself with a "reading" of Sacher-Masoch's enslaved Gregor of *Venus im Pelz*—a deviant black sex act worthy of Georg Bendemann that implicates him in a schematic and ahistorical meditation on New World slavery and the gateway experience to an engagement with erotics of exotic "black" popular culture. Through the sister's music, or rather the time, setting, and reception of her performance, Gregor finds a way out (*Ausweg*) in the context of Prague's cabaret scene and its rich appropriation of ragtime, "jazz," and American popular dance forms. Because music, here inflected with the black noise and spectacle of the unmusicality of Prague's cabarets, is the sense of his being, Gregor is able to escape the prison of one life, perhaps to begin another.[15]

Part II

Chapter 4

✦

Negro's Machine

I. *Es ist doch deutlich*

In Gregor's transformation into a being in flight, race plays a pivotal role. The trope of flight connects Kafka's *Söhne* trilogy ("Der Heizer," "Das Urteil," and *Die Verwandlung*) and the planned *Strafen* stories ("Das Urteil" and *Die Verwandlung*), which might also include *Der Verschollene* as represented by "Der Heizer"; for Kafka felt that the two stories shared an affinity to such an extent that "wenn die beiden Elemente—am ausgepragtesten im 'Heizer' und 'Strafkolonie'—nicht vereinigen, bin ich am Ende" (*T* 726) (If the two elements—most pronounced in "The Stoker" and "In the Penal Colony"—do not combine, I am finished [*J* 330]).[1] As Michael P. Ryan sees it, "escape, the means of an attempted literary escape, coupled with [an] emphasis on the family unit, might more fully account for the 'secret connection' among *Die Söhne*" (Ryan 2001, 74).

As shown in part 1 of this study, "escape" is here a racial transformation into "Negro," which then names slavery as the condition from which the protagonist must take flight. In "Das Urteil" and *Die Verwandlung*, blackness and slavery are indicated, respectively and among other ways, by biblical allusion and by the cryptological interjection of slavery in the text via Sacher-Masoch's *Venus im Pelz*. Indeed, the very idea of slavery in the nineteenth century carries within it a racial discourse, one of which Kafka was of course well aware. Gregor becomes Negro to show that he was always Negro, thus freeing him in and through his slavery to become an outsider, an artist. Gregor's hybrid blackness is literally written in part as his skin (*Kaf*), in the same way that the writing machine of "In der Strafkolonie" writes not only the judgment but also a racialized entity on and in the skin of the prisoner (*Käfter*). For it has been commonly assumed that the writing machine actually writes a definite script. However, we have only the officer's word for this. In point of fact, the description of the machine's final product is of a script that is so dense that it turns the skin a uniform black:

> Der Reisende hätte gerne etwas Anerkennendes gesagt, aber er sah nur labyrinthartige, einander vielfach kreuzende Linien, die so dicht das Papier bedeckten, daß man nur mit Mühe die weißen Zwischenräume erkannte. "Lesen Sie," sagte der Offizier. "Ich kann nicht," sagte der Reisende. "Es ist doch deutlich," sagte der Offizier. "Es ist sehr kunstvoll," sagte der Reisende ausweichend, "aber ich kann es nicht entziffern." "Ja," sagte der Offizier, lachte und steckte die Mappe wieder ein, "es ist keine Schönschrift für Schulkinder. Man muß lange darin lesen. Auch Sie würden es schließlich gewiß erkennen. Es darf natürlich keine einfache Schrift sein; sie soll ja nicht sofort töten, sondern durchschnittlich erst in einem Zeitraum von zwölf Stunden; für die sechste Stunde ist der Wendepunkt berechnet. Es müssen also viele, viele Zieraten die eigentliche Schrift umgeben; die wirkliche Schrift umzieht den Leib nur in einem schmalen Gürtel; der übrige Körper ist für Verzierungen bestimmt." (*D* 217–18)

> The explorer would have liked to say something appreciative, but all he could see was a labyrinth of lines crossing and re-crossing each other, which covered the paper so thickly that it was difficult to discern the blank spaces between them. "Read it," said the officer. "I can't," said the explorer. "Yet it's clear enough," said the officer. "It's very ingenious," said the explorer evasively, "but I can't make it out." "Yes," said the officer with a laugh, putting the paper away again, "it's no calligraphy for school children. It needs to be studied closely. I'm quite sure that in the end you would understand it too. Of course the script can't be a simple one; it's not supposed to kill a man straight off, but only after an interval of, on an average, twelve hours; the turning point is reckoned to come at the sixth hour. So there have to be lots and lots of flourishes around the actual script; the script itself runs around the body only in a narrow girdle; the rest of the body is reserved for the embellishments." (*C* 148–49)

There are two scripts represented in the story, one of the machine and another of the Old Commandant's designs. Whereas the script of the machine remains throughout the story hard to pin down in terms of its actual appearance, the Old Commandant's designs are clearly described as being so dense that one can hardly see the white of the page that would define its outlines. That is to say, the Old Commandant's script appears as an immutably black page. It is a writing that effaces its words as it writes them, leaving behind only punctuation as puncture.[2] This is why the explorer cannot read what is "written" there. The objection that the machine's writing is of a different representative order than the writing of the designs is invalid; for the officer conflates the appearance of the two scripts. In discussing the script of the designs with the explorer, the officer seamlessly slips into describing the script of the machine, in essence marking no difference between the appearance of what is written on the page and what is written on the body.

Furthermore, the fact that the officer knows his own judgment in advance of the machine's writing it into his body is unprecedented. Pointing in the book of designs, the officer announces his judgment to the explorer:

> Von jetzt ab kümmerte sich aber der Offizier kaum mehr um ihn. Er ging auf den Reisenden zu, zog wieder die kleine Ledermappe hervor, blätterte in ihr, fand schließlich das Blatt, das er suchte, und zeigte es dem Reisenden. "Lesen Sie," sagte er. "Ich kann nicht," sagte der Reisende, "ich sagte schon, ich kann diese Blätter nicht lesen." "Sehen Sie das Blatt doch genau an," sagte der Offizier und trat neben den Reisenden, um mit ihm zu lesen. Als auch das nichts half, fuhr er mit dem kleinen Finger in großer Höhe, als dürfe das Blatt auf keinen Fall berührt werden, über das Papier hin, um auf diese Weise dem Reisenden das Lesen zu erleichtern. Der Reisende gab sich auch Mühe, um wenigstens darin dem Offizier gefällig sein zu können, aber es war ihm unmöglich. Nun begann der Offizier die Aufschrift zu buchstabieren und dann las er sie noch einmal im Zusammenhang. "Sei gerecht!—heißt es," sagte er, "jetzt können Sie es doch lesen." Der Reisende beugte sich so tief über das Papier, daß der Offizier aus Angst vor einer Berührung es weiter entfernte; nun sagte der Reisende zwar nichts mehr, aber es war klar, daß er es noch immer nicht hatte lesen können. "'Sei gerecht!'—heißt es," sagte der Offizier nochmals. "Mag sein," sagte der Reisende, "ich glaube es, daß es dort steht." (*D* 238)

> From now on, however, the officer paid hardly any attention to him. He went up to the explorer, pulled out the small leather wallet again, turned over the papers in it, found the one he wanted, and showed it to the explorer. "Read it," he said. "I can't," said the explorer, "I told you before that I can't make out these scripts." "Try taking a close look at it," said the officer and came quite near to the explorer so that they might read it together. But when even that proved useless, he outlined the script with his little finer, holding it high above the paper as if the surface dared not be sullied by touch, in order to help the explorer to follow the script in that way. The explorer did make an effort, meaning to please the officer in this respect at least, but he was quite unable to follow. Now the officer began to spell it, letter by letter, and then read out the words. "'BE JUST!' is what is written there," he said, "surely you can read it now." The explorer bent so close to the paper that the officer feared he might touch it and drew it farther away; the explorer made no remark, yet it was clear that he

> still could not decipher it. "'BE JUST!' is what is written there," said the officer once more. "Maybe," said the explorer, "I am prepared to believe you." (*C* 161)

And yet the condemned becomes aware of his judgment only after the machine has begun doing its work. The officer is able to read his judgment in the designs of the Old Commandant only if the ability to know the judgment is the capacity to read the script that writes it. No one other than the officer can read this without first experiencing it on the body as a lesson in penal literacy. The problem here is of course that there is no script to read. The designs of the Old Commandant are in appearance the same as those of the machine on the body, virtual blackness, and judgments are literally prefigured in the designs. Through the transcendent quality of the designs and the working of the machine, the skin of the condemned man becomes uniformly ink-black, leaving no trace of a script, and metaphorically qualifying him by sheer outer appearance as a Negro.

This fact cannot be overlooked, as the ability to read outer appearances as accessories, tattoos, and uniforms is of paramount importance to meaning in the text. Uniforms in particular are an encumbrance that must be endured for the sake of cultural legibility. For when the explorer points out what seems to be the obvious, that the officer's heavy uniform is too hot for the tropics, the officer insists that one does not wish to forget the homeland. It is only after the body has been stripped of its uniform, its link to a legalized world of responsibility, that it goes beyond legible justice and into a realm of absolute blackness—a passage marked once again by death.

The uniform also serves as necessary reinforcement to, and panoptic reminder of, the status of the prisoner. A man of intellect and great reputation, the explorer knows this. His comment about uniforms is not meant to address the necessity and practicality of uniforms as such in the tropics. He questions the necessity for the use of the heavy material out of which the uniforms are made:

> "Diese Uniformen sind doch für die Tropen zu schwer," sagte der Reisende, statt sich, wie es der Offizier erwartet hatte, nach dem Apparat zu erkundigen. "Gewiß," sagte der Offizier und wusch sich die von Öl und Fett beschmutzten Hände in einem bereitstehenden Wasserkübel, "aber sie bedeuten die Heimat; wir wollen nicht die Heimat verlieren." (*D* 204)

> "These uniforms are too heavy for the tropics, surely," said the explorer, instead of making some inquiry about the apparatus, as the officer had expected. "Of course," said the officer, washing his oily and greasy hands in a bucket of water that stood ready, "but they mean home to us; we don't want to forget about home." (*C* 192)

The officer's answer seems cryptic and nonsensical. Certainly one could wear a uniform that is faithful to the homeland and appropriate to the heat of the tropics, *unless the two spaces are absolutely irreconcilable with each other*. The officer's designation of the uniform as emblem of the homeland serves, then, multiple purposes. It establishes the homeland as essentially, radically other than the penal colony. The adherence to the inappropriate, in fact torturous, uniforms in the tropical climate as well as the insistence on the uniforms as portable monuments to the homeland also indicate the extreme nature of the colony's dependence on second skins as indicators of an internal state. To shed the skin of the uniform is literally to become nothing, to die. What one views on the outside is what one is on the inside, even and perhaps especially among savages.

II. *Wirf die Peitsche weg, oder ich fresse dich*

There is no conclusive evidence as to the location of the penal colony, and therefore racial disposition of the indigenous population is unknown. Given the space and colonial disposition of the tropical island, it is probable that the island's native population is made up of "savages." But the story also suggests that such designations as "savage" and "civilized" are as artificial and inappropriate as the uniforms worn by the soldiers. "In der Strafkolonie" in fact obliterates the distinction between savage and civilized at the level of the apparatus itself, as well as at that of the occupying army's comportment, and at that of the guard's interchangeability with the condemned man. It is more a question here of the existence of savagery as a concept in the realm of nineteenth-century ethnology than it is of assigning savagery to one side or the other. The sides themselves are illusions. The only distinction between them is the uniform one wears.

What appears to be savagery in the penal colony is aligned with criminality, another common trope of nineteenth-century ethnology.[3] The condemned man's crime is insubordination. He fails to do his duty by falling asleep while guarding an officer's quarters. After being whipped across the face for his lapse, the man threatens, "Wirf die Peitsche weg, oder ich fresse dich" (*D* 213) ("Throw that whip away or I'll eat you alive" [C 146]).

It is not clear that insubordination or falling asleep at his post is in fact the man's crime. The infraction will be made known with the judgment, which is to be written on the body by the machine in an indecipherable script that amounts to pure blackness. Although this may be a simple case of insubordination, or failure to do one's duty, or both, the fact is that the condemned man threatened, presumably in all seriousness, to cannibalize his superior officer. Here is the seeming paradox of the officer's law: if the judgment cannot be known until after the machine has performed its grisly work, how can the crime ever truly be known before the judgment is revealed? But this is, in fact, not a problem. The machine turns the skin black, in effect transforming the condemned man into a Negro, a savage. If the crime committed displays an inherent, racialized savagery, then the judgment as de- and reracialization *will always be just*. The punishment for acting like a Negro (inherent criminality displayed by the threat of cannibalism) is to be transformed into a Negro (congenital criminal). To threaten to cannibalize anyone, much less a superior officer, is to act like a Negro because Negroes are savages and thus inherently criminal and subject to committing any and all crimes, including and perhaps most especially that of cannibalism. The machine does not tarry with individual crimes; it adduces the essence of criminality, which is always savagery and blackness. Thus, its writing reveals the condemned man's inherent savagery through racial identification. The judgment says nothing. "BE JUST" is not written anywhere in the designs or on the body. What signifies is uniform blackness (negritude) as the essence of crime.

This is the crux of the matter; it brings Negro savagery, in the form of cannibalism, to the fore. Thus cannibalism threatens to consume the entire system of penal justice, in that if the subaltern devours a superior, if he commits this true act of insubordination, then he in point of fact consumes the other and becomes him, distorting the rank and file upon which justice and judgment are predicated. Justice would become uncivilized, Africanized, and so no justice at all. It would become prey to the very feelings Kafka describes himself as experiencing in 1914 while writing this story, and which represent well the story's condemned man: "Ich bin zerrittet statt erholt. Ein leeres Gefäss, noch ganz und schon unter Scherben oder schon Scherbe und noch unter den Ganzen. Voll Luge, Hass und Neid. Voll Unfähigkeit, Dummheit, Begriffstützigkeit. Voll Faulheit, Schwache und Wehrlosigkeit" (*T* 545) (I am more broken down than recovered. An empty vessel, still intact yet already in the dust among the broken fragments; or already in fragments yet still ranged among those that are intact. Full of lies, hate, and envy. Full of incompetence, stupidity, thickheadedness. Full of laziness, weakness, and helplessness [*J* 301]).

Such feelings of being degenerate and borderline criminal, with regard to himself and his engagement, may have inspired Kafka to take a deep interest in current debates over deportation. Walter Müller-Seidl has meticulously insisted that Kafka wrote "Strafkolonie" with contemporary deportation debates in mind, potentially mitigating a reading of colonialism in the text. Yet despite Müller-Seidl's exhaustive work on the role that deportation plays in Kafka's story,

> Kafka's "penal" or "punishment colony," his *Strafkolonie*, is, upon closer examination, in fact quite unlike any penal colony ever known—including Devil's Island, with which, because of the historical background of the Dreyfus case, it has understandably been associated. It does, however, bear an astonishingly close resemblance to the actual historic practices of colonialism. And it is precisely in the

> confrontation with the literary, historical, and documentary record of colonialism itself that this *Korrespondenzverhältnis* may perhaps be brought most tellingly to light. (Peters 2001, 402)

Robert Lemon provides a riposte to those critics who would focus exclusively on the colonial context at the expense of Müller-Seidel's deportation reading, citing that "such an approach ignores the fact that the penal colony arose far more out of a concern with the punishment of European convicts than with the colonization of overseas populations. Indeed, the debate over the penal colonies in Germany and Austria centered on the health and welfare of the Volk, which, it was claimed, could only be preserved through the permanent removal of degenerate elements" (Lemon 2007, 280–81).

Lemon's critique is well heeded. While deportation and colonialism often went hand in hand, to eliminate the context of deportation simply because Kafka's fictional penal colony does not function like that of a historical penal colony would be to add an imperative to fiction and to literary criticism that does not pertain in either domain. Losing sight of the deportation context also leads to the mistake of reading the condemned man as a "native" and not an exported convict or soldier. The prisoner, and those subject to penal-military law, are certainly white Europeans and not indigenous peoples of (since one does not know the specific colonial context of the penal colony) different races and hues. Following a 1917 journal entry that reworks the story's ending, Kafka also wrote that, where the explorer, officer, and condemned man are concerned, "alle drei gehörten jetzt zusammen" (*T* 825) (all three now belonged together [*J* 381]).[4] In order to reach this point of triadic belonging, each character shares and is tainted by an initial context. The overriding contextual scheme is that of deportation. All three, including of course the condemned man, are displaced white Europeans.

Other sources in the deportation debate provided Kafka with material. These include, Thomas Weitin notes,

> die Schriften des Kriminologen Hans Groß, bei dem Kafka an der Prager Universität Vorlesungen zum Strafrecht hörte, und Robert Heindls 1912 erschienener Bericht *Meine Reise nach den Strafkolonien*. Beide stehen im Zusammenhang mit der Diskussion über Sinn und Zweck von Deportationsstrafen, die die junge Kolonialmacht Deutschland seit den letzten Jahren des 19. Jahrhunderts unter großer öffentlicher Anteilnahme führte. Groß machte sich vor allem dafür stark, "Degenerierte" zu deportieren, deren Gefährlichkeit mit den Mitteln des herkömmlichen Strafrechts nicht gebannt werden könne. (Weitin 2007, 255–56)

> the writings of criminologist Hans Gross, whom Kafka heard lecture on criminal law at Charles University in Prague, and Robert Heindl's

> 1912 report, "My Travels in Penal Colonies": both are related to the discussion about the reason and goal of deportation, which the new colonial power, Germany, practiced and publicly debated. Gross strongly supported deporting "degenerates," who posed a dangerous threat, he believed, which could not be contained by means of conventional penal codes.

Within this debate, those who would be and were deported are considered "degenerate" and as such too dangerous to be kept jailed at home. What is often missed in reflections on this debate in the context of Kafka's story is that the very notion of a degenerate type comes into being alongside ethnological praxis and scientific-racist discourse. "*In der Strafkolonie*," writes Harald Neumeyer, "verhandelt nicht allein dieses . . . heterogene und in sich widersprüchliche Ensemble von Funktionen der Deportationen. Des weiteren wendet sich die Erzählung den Rahmenbedingungen der Deportation zu: der Frage nach den Personengruppen, fuhr die Deportationen erwogen werden, und der Frage danach, wie das Strafsystem der Deportation vor Ort durchzuführen ist" ("In der Strafkolonie" debates not only this . . . heterogeneous and self-contradictory ensemble of functions of deportation. The story also investigates the framing discourses of deportation: questions of which groups of people are to be singled out for deportation, and the question of how the penal system of deportation is to be administrated onsite) (Neumeyer 2004, 296–97). One cannot so easily disentangle, then, the terms of engagement of deportation, colonialism, and racism. The very notion of deportation springs from and is made possible by colonial practices and hierarchical racial conceptions of human being that, at the end of the nineteenth century, had as much to do with race as with criminality.[5] Indeed, the reverse argument was made that if one is to avoid awakening recapitulative congenital Negro criminality and inherent black perversions, social conditions for the Negro must improve.[6] The degenerate deportee is a devolved European, a white Negro.

Along with elliptically engaging in the deportation debate, Kafka most certainly, as Tracey Dawe shows, "criticizes the belief that German rational colonialism is less savage than any other form of colonialism" (Dawe 2008, 135). For, having already stated that the division between civilized and savage is here subverted, "Strafkolonie" nevertheless affirms that savagery exists but that it is not clear if savagery is the norm that the illusion of military order both covers up and, dialectically, makes possible, or if military justice is simply savagery by another name. That is to say, the act for which the potential cannibal is condemned does not threaten the existence of the rank and file but demonstrates that the rank and file are as savage as the island's indigenous population, thus destroying the illusion that preserves the colony's penal system. The condemned man does not introduce savagery to the island; he articulates its veiled presence. As Zilcosky writes,

"Der Kolonialismus erzeugt in Kafkas Erzählung seinen eigenen Untergang") (Colonialism in Kafka's story brings about its own downfall) (Zilcosky 2004, 45). The "wild" colonial subject embodies "wild" European subjectivity, condemning the colony to its own inherent savagery.

Thus, the entire space of the penal colony, regardless of its location and its population's ethnological determination, exists in and as the space of savagery, which is here collusive with determinations of racial blackness. The condemned man's crime is, then, insubordination in the word's philological meaning; he literally undoes the given order of colonial ideology by shattering its reflective surface. As Hansjörg Bay observes, "lassen sich die in seinen späteren Texten entworfenen Begegnungs- und Beobachtungsszenarien . . . als Travestien der ethnographischen Situation beschreiben. Es sind Versuchsanordnungen, die den ethnographischen Blick zurückwenden auf den Beobachter und dessen eigene Kultur" (in his later texts, encounters and scenes of observation are presented as travesties of the ethnographic situation of description. The ethnographic gaze is returned to the observer as an examination of his own culture) (Bay 2009, 290). Ethnographic discourse reflects on itself, calling into question and fatally travestying its own presuppositions and findings. Here the subaltern does speak, and what he says is enough for the powers that be to silence him forever in a very public, ritualized demonstration.

III. *Du bist ein Fremder, sei still*

The explorer, too, feels the need to speak out, to denounce the apparatus as a, paradoxically, savage machine not fit for use in the modern, civilized world:

> Der Reisende überlegte: Es ist immer bedenklich, in fremde Verhältnisse entscheidend einzugreifen. Er war weder Bürger der Strafkolonie, noch Bürger des Staates, dem sie angehörte. Wenn er die Exekution verurteilen oder gar hintertreiben wollte, konnte man ihm sagen: Du bist ein Fremder, sei still. (*D* 222)
>
> The explorer thought to himself: It's always a ticklish matter to intervene decisively in other people's affairs. He was neither a member of the penal colony nor a citizen of the state to which it belonged. Were he to denounce this execution or actually try to stop it, they could say to him: You are a foreigner, mind your own business. (*C* 151)

For the moment, however, he silences himself, rationalizing that the powers that be will condemn him as a foreigner with no right to judge indigenous practices. The explorer's silence is also justified by the logic of the foreign operative in the text. Indeed, as Danilyn Rutherford writes, "The story suggests—even insists upon—the foreign character of power. Agents of justice are recognized as possessing qualities that place them at a remove from local politics, from the realm of comprehensible meanings, from conscious thought, from life itself" (Rutherford 2001, 304). The native and the foreign shall have nothing to do with each other and nothing to say about each other.[7] For to criticize one is to implicate the other in that which is being criticized.

Thus the officer makes a critical error when he appeals to the explorer for support in his quest to maintain the use of the machine and help to resurrect the apparatus's fading power. The officer makes it known to the explorer that, because he is world renowned, the explorer's opinions and reports of his time in the penal colony will be widely disseminated, respected, and heeded:

> Aber vielleicht wollen Sie das nicht, es entspricht nicht Ihrem Charakter, in Ihrer Heimat verhält man sich vielleicht in solchen Lagen anders, auch das ist richtig, auch das genügt vollkommen, stehen Sie gar nicht auf, sagen Sie nur ein paar Worte, flüstern Sie sie, daß sie gerade noch die Beamten unter Ihnen hören, es genügt, Sie müssen gar nicht selbst von der mangelnden Teilnahme an der Exekution, von dem kreischenden Rad, dem zerrissenen Riemen, dem widerlichen Filz reden, nein, alles Weitere übernehme ich, und, glauben Sie, wenn meine Rede ihn nicht aus dem Saale jagt, so wird sie ihn auf die Knie zwingen, daß er bekennen muß: Alter Kommandant, vor dir beuge ich mich.—Das ist mein Plan; wollen Sie mir zu seiner Ausführung helfen? (*D* 234)

> Yet perhaps you wouldn't care to do that, it's not in keeping with your character, in your country perhaps people do these things differently, well, that's all right too, that will be quite as effective, don't even stand up, just say a few words, even in a whisper, so that only the officials beneath you will hear them, that will be quite enough, you don't even need to mention the lack of public support for the execution, the creaking of the wheel, the broken strap, the filthy gag of felt, no, I'll take all that upon me, and, believe me, if my indictment doesn't drive him out of the conference hall, it will force him to his knees to make the acknowledgment: Old Commandant, I humble myself before you.—That is my plan; will you help me to carry it out? (*C* 159)

And yet there is no question of the explorer's foreignness as a hindrance to judgment on the penal colony's older juridical practices. In fact, the case is quite the opposite. Nevertheless, the officer persists in believing that, by the very fact that the explorer is an outsider, and so is an "objective" observer, he will be listened to.

In any event, the explorer takes no stock in what the officer believes; what concerns him is the morality of the officer's statements. But even for the explorer to pose the question of morality is disingenuous. The explorer is as reactionary as he is progressive; his moral stance is a necessary textual pose in order to bring the singular, extramoral quality of the machine more strongly in relief. In this sense, the explorer does make for an unwillingly objective observer, the ideal reader of the apparatus's text. His vision pierces two worlds, that of the Old Commandant and that of the new, implying a theory of reading, as Clayton Koelb suggests, "wherein the reader does not act upon the text, but rather the text takes the initiative and acts upon the reader. The reader submits, and this submission is the only thing he need do. The book then takes charge and both picks up the reader and forces its way inside him. The text writes upon the reader and even makes him into a kind of copy of itself" (Koelb 1982, 513). The apparatus and its concomitant system of "primitive" rituals define the almost atavistic, black realm of the Old Commandant in which, through a series of reading practices, the explorer is called upon to witness and to judge.

And yet writing in this world is hieroglyphic and takes place not merely on the body but also of the body, making the activity of reading into that of making sense of nonsense presented as grammatically placed bodies in space. As in "Das Urteil," writing is the opaque, seemingly divine judgment to which the body must submit completely as it calls it forth.[8] Structurally and with constant regard to the mechanisms and mandates of the reading and writing outside petit bourgeois moral constraints, "In der Strafkolonie" is no different from the major stories that come before it. All demand the actual transformation of the body into a black subject and then into writing itself. This transformation is effectuated by a biological degeneration or an atavistic return, which in turn stands in for the amoral, id-like primitive world of artistic creation. The chain of recapitulative transformation can be linked as such: the circus in *Der Verschollene* becomes the machine and world of the Old Commandant in "In der Strafkolonie." The story "transfers this theme from the immigrant's journey through First World capitalism to the ethnological construction of the colonial 'periphery' by European metropolitan consciousness" (Goebel 2002, 196). Just as Karl is trapped in the New World, so, too, is the officer.

It is clear in "In der Strafkolonie" that, despite the prophecy, the world of the Old Commandant will not return. Even if the Old Commandant were to rise again, he would in all likelihood be arrested for a crime similar to the one committed by the condemned man. The fact that the explorer leaves the island under the conditions he does so is both a testament to and testimony against the claims both worlds make on him. For in the new commandant's world order, without the presence of the officer the explorer is in danger. The New Order is every bit as savage, as black, as the old; it merely expresses its blackness differently. But because both orders are implicated in a fundamental savagery, the power relations between them become essentially meaningless, destabilizing the authoritarian structure separating the various characters. As Claudia Albert and Andreas Disselnkötter write, "Kafka spannt aber die Handlung nicht nur in die Opposition von altem und neuem Kommandanten ein—genaueres über dessen Strafsystem erfährt man ohnehin nicht—er verändert auch fast unmerklich das Machtverhältnis zwischen dem Verurteilten und dem Soldaten auf der einen, dem Reisenden und dem Offizier auf der anderen Seite" (Kafka creates tension not only between the opposition of old and new Commandants—in fact, one learns really nothing about this penal system—he also changes, almost imperceptibly, the relations of power between the condemned man and the soldier on one side, and the explorer and the officer on the other) (Albert and Disselnkötter 2002, 178). The text nevertheless does articulate a difference between the totalities of the two orders that is constitutive as opposed to contingent. The essential point of separation is the machine. The apparatus belongs to the age of the Old Commandant, a time in which justice was coterminous with spectacle. The officer relates the impact the public executions had on the penal colony, including the silent reverence of native inhabitants (*D* 225–26; *C* 154). The spectacle of the execution transcended cultural and linguistic barriers and the otherwise absolute separations of domestic and foreign, civilized and savage. The officer tells of a universal justice that, in the old order of the machine's effects, was in need of no translation practices; its seemingly illegible meaning could be understood without mediation.

The apparatus's effects on the body signified a universal, and so universally graspable, meaning. As Corngold writes, "The moment of ecstasy is not that of understanding the script(ure); it is a moment of recognizing that here there is script to be deciphered" (Corngold 2001, 289). This means that in the moment of recognition, in which the condemned man "reads" what is written into his body and transmits this knowledge in his deathly gaze, it is shared unmediated by all as a text decipherable only insofar as it has been written. Unable actually to read the judgment or translate its substance into words, the written text, *which is a virtual black body in a space of unmitigated blackness*, can be understood only as an expressive or aesthetic experience beyond or before words and so outside the domain of translation. As Andreas Gailus aptly concludes, "'In the Penal Colony' is Kafka's attempt to traverse the fantasy of revelation by unveiling the mechanical nature of its production" (Gailus 2001, 296).

The community thus shares and is united in virtual blackness, in savage Negro identity, which is here conceived as the pure, and at the same time mechanically produced, Aesthetic. The expressive black being of the community, realized in the ritual of judgment that is but one of Kafka's lynching variants already hinted at in *Der Verschollene*, transcends all binary distinctions (savage/civilized) and codes of morality. That which stands absolutely outside the community unites it. In other words, the spectacle of the apparatus, which is in essence aesthetic blackness, transcends all linguistic and cultural divisions, making all things, in this moment, in this space outside space, equal. As Malynne Sternstein writes, "If the project of those in power is to fix the language of the Law onto the body of its citizens, to make it legible, Kafka's is to force this eminent 'legibility' into 'overexposure,' which then 'blocks every essay of interpretation.' The struggle for signification—the officer's and the reader's—is laughable. What better language to defy paradigmatic signification than that of bodily praxis? This code of gesture, of bodily signs and postures, is Kafka's foremost language" (Sternstein 2001, 319).

The judgment speaks the same "language" with the same force to each spectator because bodily praxis, as in "Das Urteil," stands before language, is instinctive, and so can be understood by everyone. All who witness and partake in its force are black insofar as blackness, or Africanicity, is here understood as a mode of cultural-societal being that has no recourse to writing but only to bodily gesture and oral record. Blackness destroys the readability of writing, turning writing itself into a visual art defined by praxis and no longer beholden to standard reading practices. And just as blackness is the savage truth of the criminal and his crime, it is also the essence of the penal colony and the apparatus as lynching machine. In "In der Strafkolonie," Gregor's *Käfterchen* is extended to an entire island, and the forced labor of the penitentiary becomes equivalent with slavery. Thus, the essence of everyone in the penal colony, from officer to condemned man to native, is that of the African ex-slave as contemporary criminal. The machine performs the artist function sought after by Georg Bendemann, Karl Roßmann, and Gregor Samsa. Through its inscription, it engenders blackness. Furthermore, this very concept of blackness that Kafka viewed as positively productive of the literary text in *Die Söhne* trilogy is now understood as that which both creates and undoes the work of art in its legibility. In the penal colony, bodies are unreadable black works of art engendered by the machine as inhuman black artist. What I am suggesting is that the machine is in essence what Kafka's "sons" become.

The machine as black artist at work nullifies the hierarchical order upon which the penal colony as colonial institution depends for its survival and in so doing does not "free" its inhabitants from such determinations but enslaves them to artificial divisions, such as uniforms. Following Friedrich Kittler, who reads the machine not as one of Heindl's torture instruments but as a gramophone, the machine recapitulates Kafka's black musical theme (Kittler 1986). For while the machine's normal functioning is virtually silent, as it kills the officer it comes to resemble one of the popular jazz noise machines in Prague's cabarets, such as the Konvikt Bar. Black noise takes over precisely where the idea of transcendental judgment unravels.[9] Just as the condemned man revealed in his crime the illusory aspect of this hierarchical organization, the true threat the machine as (un)musical black artist (which for Kafka is coterminous with the writer) poses to the New Order is of the same untenable character as the notion of divine judgment and universal punishment. Each time the machine delivers its verdict, its work of art, it abrogates that verdict for all but the condemned man, who, in death, passes beyond judgment. In death, the condemned man becomes both less and more than a man; his body is parchment and palimpsest for an illegible message, which is the evidence of a communicative, communal process (Ryan 2002, 213–27). He becomes a ritual work of art.

The ritual nature of the work's communication transcends hierarchical order and the need of mediation. That which needs no mediation cannot be read, only bodily experienced; it is an illegible script that is nevertheless correctly interpreted by a precognitive facility of judgment or as a ritual black aesthetic experience. The dead body of the condemned is, then, literally a black work of art that, as such, stands outside the realm of intelligibility and in the space of not divine but primitive ritual signification. It is emblematic of "the status of nonsense—or rather, the limits of sense—both in the text and in the administration of justice as represented by the text" (Santner and Levin 2001, 279). The limit of sense is the purely sensual realm of ritual black aesthetic procedure.

Thus the dead black body as the product of black writing exists outside of the regime of uniforms and tattoos, all of which are still the emblems of secular, comprehensible authoritarian orders.[10] The salient feature of the machine's narrative, then, is not the story that it tells but the manner in which it tells it and the aesthetic quality of its purely ornamental descriptions. As Mark Anderson brilliantly shows, "Simply writing the judgment on the prisoner's body would kill him; it would not induce the 'transfiguration' which distinguishes this penal invention from other, all too familiar means of execution. The decorative margin to the judgment (which is also the time of 'Spiel,' understood as both spectacle and sado-masochistic play) is thus the decisive element in the process of a transfigured death" (Anderson 1988, 127). What matters, aesthetically speaking, is the experience of receiving a full-body tattoo so intricately ornate, so densely arabesque, that all that can be understood of it is its color. This art, then, is ultimately a sacrificial ritual practice that seeks to alter the body in radical, racialized ways. The artist-body, the body of work, is first a racial pantomime and then transformation that is a complete and total disappearance; a metamorphosis into an insect; a new skin color; death as flight and disappearance. The difference here between this story and those of *Die Söhne* trilogy is that, in the machine, we are shown the mechanism that drives on to become artist as it racially qualifies his or her candidacy.[11]

Once again, art and the artist merge to create the work that, in the act of creation, is not a thing but a painful bodily experience of racial transformation. In each case examined thus far, the work of art and the working artist are implicated in a regimen of racial significations of blackness and pain.[12] Race as a biological condition and a radical conditioning of the body is here experienced as an aesthetic phenomenon of and on the body. That is to say, race not only contributes to but also is the work of art in its material-cultural lifeworld. Kafka uses conceptions of "Negro" to communicate an aesthetic theory and the essence of the writer's life. The experience of the enslaved or imprisoned body in pain, the body forced to labor in a radicalized context, is the work of art as the final product of a process of physical transformation that ends in flight from bondage or, as in the penal colony, untransfigured death.

Thus, Kafka offers a phenomenology of aesthetic vision that is intimately bound with race and metamorphosis. With the "sons" we see a man transforming into the recapitulative artist; "Strafkolonie" and what follows present us with men becoming recapitulative art. Because the dead or dying black body as work of art emerges only within a system of racial coding, the racialized entity cannot be determined and fixed within an authoritarian conceptual order. This aesthetic elaboration of race annihilates the very notions of race that it depends on to make the category of blackness appear. In this sense, Kafka's racialized bodies are like the Old Commandant's designs. They are illegible in and for themselves yet existent and are responsible for the very mechanism they describe.

Racial character and being in Kafka are not, then, inherent qualities but variables that are determined by appearance. This means that racial identity, like ethnicity, is as stable as the clothes one wears, as uniforms and other modes of ornamentation. Race is a chimera that possesses the force of the real. The clothes make the man, the skin color the race. Yet skin color can be changed. Racialization in Kafka is always accompanied by a metamorphosis from one race to another. This is not because Kafka necessarily questions the authenticity of the racial determinations but because the transformation itself is understood as the supreme aesthetic act and so beyond any form of hierarchically construed determinative order. The black noise that accompanies the transformation is not produced by but rather is productive of the black body in pain.

Chapter 5

✦

Negro's Manumission

I. *Wie Affen in den Baumwipfeln*

Another journal entry, of January 7, 1912, locates the inscrutability of Negro noise as something close to home for Kafka:

> Als ich auf dem Kanapee lag und in beiden Zimmern mir zur Seite laut gesprochen wurde, links nur von Frauen, rechts mehr von Männern, hatte ich den Eindruck, daß es rohe, negerhafte, nicht zu besänftigende Wesen sind, die nicht wissen, was sie reden, und nur reden, um die Luft in Bewegung zu setzen, die beim Reden das Gesicht heben und den Worten, die sie aussprechen, nachsehn." (*T* 358)
>
> [When I lay on the sofa the loud talking in the room on either side of me, by the women on the left, by the men on the right, gave me the impression that they were coarse, savage beings who could not be appeased, who did not know what they were saying and spoke only in order to set the air in motion, who lifted their faces while speaking and followed the spoken words with their eyes. (*J* 172)

Cacophonous noise deletes easily accessible meaning and in so doing takes on the *negerhafte* quality of noise—here created by his father and his friends and his mother and sisters—made strictly for its own sake.

Perhaps it was this association of his family with blacks that led Kafka to believe that he was the family ape. For of all the animal figures Kafka represented in his work, it was the ape with which he most explicitly identified.[1] In a letter to Felice of November 28, 1912, he describes the situation: "Als Erstgeborener bin ich viel photographiert worden und es gibt also eine große Reihenfolge von Verwandlungen. Von jetzt an wird es in jedem Bild ärger, Du wirst es ja sehen. Gleich im nächsten Bild trete ich schon als Affe meiner Eltern auf (*BF* 138) (As the eldest, I was constantly being photographed and there exists a long succession of transformations. From now on it gets worse in every picture, but you'll see. In the very next one I appear as my parents' ape" [*LF* 172]). This is not the only time he will refer to himself as an ape to Felice. A few weeks later, on January 23–24, 1913, Kafka writes,

> Was bedeutet Dein Nichtschreiben? Etwas Schlimmes? . . . Abend konntest Du dann nicht, gut, Mittwoch am Tage konntest Du nicht, gut, aber dann schriebst Du, bitte, schriebst (ich bitte für die Vergangenheit) schriebst also am Mittwoch abend, und morgen früh mit der ersten Post habe ich Deinen Brief und lese, daß Du mich nicht verlassen willst, selbst wenn Du in mir statt einers Menschen, einen (wie man nach manchen Briefen glauben möchte) kranken, wild gewordenen Affen finden solltest (*BF* 267).

> What's the meaning of your not writing? Anything bad? You, whom I felt to be so close to me, have now gone your own way in Berlin for a whole day, and I know nothing about you. Which day was it? The last time you wrote was Tuesday lunchtime. Then in the evening you couldn't; all right; but then you wrote, pray wrote (I pray for the past tense), wrote on Wednesday evening; and tomorrow morning, first mail, I shall get your letter and read that you don't want to leave me, even if you were to find in me not a human being but (as one might well believe from some of my letters) a sick ape gone berserk. (*LF* 168–69)

Crucially, Kafka sees that the only way Felice would ever leave him is if he were to become an "ape." Once again, degeneracy, this time in the actual sense of a physical devolution, provides Kafka with a way out of marriage. Thus "being ape" excludes Kafka from family and exempts him from entering the marital cage.

Kafka returns to the ape theme with Felice a few months later, on July 8, 1913: "Du weißt nicht, Felice, was manche Literatur in manchen Köpfen ist. Das jagt beständig wie Affen in den Baumwipfeln statt auf den Boden zu gehen. Es ist verloren und kann nicht anders. Was soll man tun?" [*BF* 425]) (You have no idea, Felice, what havoc literature creates inside certain heads. It is like monkeys leaping about in the treetops, instead of staying firmly on the ground. It is being lost and not being able to help it. What can one do?" [*LF* 288]). Here, literature itself is transformed into a pack of apes. Kafka fuses himself with literature through this simian third term. This fusion or transformation creates a being ill-suited to marriage, family, and, presumably, the professional demands of bourgeois life. The ape that he is or would possibly become would be something like a *dressierter Menschenaffe*, a variety ape with human attributes dragged out into the spotlight at world's fairs and brought on Hagenbeck's zoo stages to amaze crowds. One such ape was the honorable Konsul Peter, whom Kafka probably saw perform in 1910 in Prague and may have been referred to in "Ein Bericht für eine Akademie" as the story's second Rotpeter. Another descendant of that primary primate was in all likelihood a *Menschenaffe* Kafka read about in the *Prager Tagblatt* in the year "Ein Bericht" was written.

But there is yet another type, human or otherwise, that conforms well to Rotpeter's description. This type has more to do with Ernst Haeckel's conception of *Menschenaffen* (man-apes), which Kafka studied at university, than Hagenbeck's, although Hagenbeck was clearly guided by Haeckel's theories of Africans as beings who exist somewhere between simians and humans on the evolutionary chain.[2] For transformation and transfiguration in "Ein Bericht" follow along the lines of capture, disfiguration, and enslavement. Rotpeter experiences a radical cultural, geographical, and psychological displacement. In this sense, Rotpeter is (re)born from a cage instead of a womb, taking his first breath between the decks of a nautical vessel. The details of the location of his (re)birth are not incidental. Slaves in chains were held as supercargo between the decks of slave ships, and sometimes in cages.[3] "Ein Bericht" narrates here the scene of the Middle Passage. Taken from the once slave-rich Gold Coast, stripped of his identity and his "manhood," Rotpeter is supercargo bound between decks aboard Hagenbeck's "slaver."

Furthermore, as the story unfurls during and after this makeshift middle passage, "Ein Bericht" follows closely both some of the physical brutality of the slave trade and the devastating psychological consequences of enslavement described in slave narratives.[4] James Olney's oft-quoted outline of the general characteristics of the slave narrative provide an interpretive model for Kafka's story:

> a first sentence beginning, "I was born . . . ," then specifying a place but not a date of birth;
> a sketchy account of parentage, often involving a white father;
> description of a cruel master, mistress, or overseer, details of first observed whipping and numerous subsequent whippings, with women very frequently the victims;
> an account of one extraordinarily strong, hardworking slave—often "pure African"—who, because there is no reason for it, refuses to be whipped;
> record of the barriers raised against slave literacy and the overwhelming difficulties encountered in learning to read and write;
> description of a "Christian" slaveholder (often of one such dying in terror) and the accompanying claim that "Christian" slaveholders are invariably worse than those professing no religion;
> description of the amounts and kinds of food and clothing given to slaves, the work required of them, the pattern of a day, a week, a year;
> account of a slave auction, of families being separated and destroyed, of distraught mothers clinging to their children as they are torn from them, of slave coffles being driven South;

descriptions of patrols, of failed attempt(s) to escape, of pursuit by men and dogs;
description of successful attempt(s) to escape, lying by during the day, travelling by night guided by the North Star, reception in a free state by Quakers who offer a lavish breakfast and much genial thee/thou conversation
taking of a new last name (frequently one suggested by a white abolitionist) to accord with new social identity as a free man, but retention of first name as a mark of continuity of individual identity;
reflections on slavery. (Olney 1985, 152–53)

Modifying Olney's list to sketch briefly the ways in which Rotpeter's narrative conforms *metaphorically* to that of the slave's, we find that

while the first sentence does not begin, "I was born . . . ," an account specifying a place but not a date of birth immediately follows. In addition, the first sentence's address to the *hohen Herren* corresponds to the list of subscribers, sympathetic abolitionist readers, and benefactors found at the beginning of, or implied at the beginning of, every slave narrative;
in Rotpeter's inability to speak with any certainty about his previous, ape existence, an implied sketchy account of parentage;
in Hagenbeck and in Rotpeter's wounds, a description of a cruel master, mistress, or overseer;
in Konsul Peter, an account of one extraordinarily strong, hardworking slave—often "pure African"—who, because there is no reason for it, refuses to be whipped;
in Rotpeter's struggles learning to speak and function in human society before he drinks the schnapps, a record of the barriers raised against slave literacy and the overwhelming difficulties encountered in learning to read and write;
in Rotpeter's representation of the ship's captain and the need to change positions in order to receive better treatment, a description of a "Christian" slaveholder (often of one such dying in terror) and the accompanying claim that "Christian" slaveholders are invariably worse than those professing no religion;
in Rotpeter's account of life as a zoo attraction, a description of the amounts and kinds of food and clothing given to slaves, the work required of them, the pattern of a day, a week, a year;
in Rotpeter's conceptualizations of human freedom and *Affenfreiheit*, an account of a slave auction, of families being separated and destroyed, of distraught mothers clinging to their children as they are torn from them, of slave coffles being driven South;

- in Rotpeter's discussions of his need to find an *Ausweg*, descriptions of patrols, of failed attempt(s) to escape, of pursuit by men and dogs;
- in the moment Rotpeter drinks the schnapps and comes to "human" consciousness, a description of successful attempt(s) to escape, lying by during the day, travelling by night guided by the North Star, reception in a free state by Quakers who offer a lavish breakfast and much genial thee/thou conversation;
- in Rotpeter's assertion of his new life as an artist, the taking of a new last name (frequently one suggested by a white abolitionist) to accord with new social identity as a free man, but retention of first name as a mark of continuity of individual identity;
- in Rotpeter's concluding comments, including the short discourse on his chimpanzee lover, reflections on slavery.

How could these parallels come about? Did Kafka read a slave narrative? Like most of his contemporaries, Kafka was probably familiar with Harriet Beecher Stowe's enduring international best seller, the novel of slavery, *Uncle Tom's Cabin* (1852; translated into German also in 1852). And Kafka was also fascinated by the movie *Die weiße Sklavin* (1911), a captivity narrative recounting a young woman's abduction and enslavement by exotic, oriental powers—the genre of literature out of which the slave narrative grew.[5] But whether or not Kafka consciously incorporated such potential influences into "Ein Bericht für eine Akademie," the story uncannily exhibits strong parallels with many of the general characteristics of the slave narrative listed above and to one slave narrative in particular, *The Interesting Narrative of the Life of Olaudah Equiano, or Gustavus Vassa, the African* (1789). And while I have found no direct evidence that Kafka read this narrative, it is worth noting that Equiano was the greatest missionary success story of the Moravian Church, a Czech-based Calvinist denomination with which Kafka, like any of his contemporaries, would have been familiar.

A slave of great intelligence, enterprise, and literary skill, Equiano writes of Europeans at a crucial juncture in his narrative of captivity and freedom: "I no longer looked upon them as spirits, but as men superior to us; and therefore I had the stronger desire to resemble them; to imbibe their spirit, and imitate their manners; I therefore embraced every occasion of improvement; and every new thing that I observed I treasured up in my memory. I had long wished to be able to read and write; and for this purpose I took every opportunity to gain instruction, but had made as yet very little progress. However, when I went to London with my master, I had soon an opportunity of improving myself, which I gladly embraced" (Andrews and Gates 2000, 95). Equiano's is an assimilation narrative that hinges on literacy and linguistic mastery as the key to freedom. Similar themes of cultural assimilation and racial freedom are echoed and, as we shall see, subverted in Rotpeter's self-presentation. Indeed, Kafka's text has often been read as a Jewish assimilation narrative. It was first published in *Der Jude* (*The Jew*) in 1917. But the journal's editor, the famous Jewish theologian and philosopher Martin Buber, himself didn't know what to make of the story, which was published together with another work by Kafka, "Schakale und Araber" ("Jackals and Arabs"). Buber suggested the stories be collectively called "Two Parables," but Kafka rejected this out of hand, saying that they were in no way parables and that they had no real classification but that if a collective title was required, "Zwei Tiergeschichten," or "Two Animal Stories," first suggested by Buber after "Two Parables," would do (Koch 2005, 175). And according to Max Brod, Buber related that he had them in the journal not because of their Jewish contents, if indeed for Buber there were any, but because he felt that they were important for the reader to know (Schulz-Behrend 1963, 3).

Given that even Buber had his doubts as to what this story was even casually about and that no text by Kafka can be reduced to a single thematic to the exclusion of all others, it is possible to diverge from the frame of Jewish assimilation narrative and investigate another possibility. For, all the above-listed attributes taken together with the place of the Negro in Kafka's thought traced thus far and the fact of a talking African ape from the Gold Coast—the most famous African point of departure for slavers loaded with supercargo—obsessed with freedom as the main character of "Ein Bericht" indicate that Kafka's story warrants serious consideration along the interpretive lines of New World slavery.

Indeed, Frances Smith Foster's description of the nineteenth-century slave narrative could just as well summarize Rotpeter's journey: "The action moves from the idyllic life of a garden of Eden into the wilderness, the struggle for survival, the providential help, and the arrival into the Promised Land. In addition, the plot of the slave narrative incorporates the parallel structure of birth into death and death into birth" (Foster 1979, 84). Foster discerns distinct phases through which the writer of the slave narrative passes. These phases aptly describe the life of Rotpeter as he presents it:

> In the slave narrative the mythological pattern is realized in four chronological phases. First comes the loss of innocence, which is objectified through the development of an awareness of what it means to be a slave. This can be compared to the descent from perfection or mortification. The mortification process includes purgation, for as the slave learns the meaning of slavery, he also tries to purge himself of those elements that would facilitate enslavement. Second is the realization of alternatives to bondage and the formulation of a resolve to be free. This decision begins the ascent to the ideal, or invigoration. The resolution to quit slavery is, in effect, a climax to a conversion experience. The third phase is the escape. (Foster 1979, 85)

Again, these connections are developed in the rest of this chapter. For now it suffices to say that Rotpeter is in no way merely an ape or simply a fanciful account of *dressierten Affen*. He is a complex allegory of aesthetic production represented as and through a grueling process of bodily transformation that combines the Hagenbeckian history of ape and African abduction with that of New World slavery.

Thus, while it is true, as one critic argues, that Rotpeter's experience follows that of actual apes captured at this time for use in Hagenbeck's zoos and shows, this in no way allows us to cease to go any further with the story and forget that Rotpeter is not an ordinary ape. Arguing for the "de-allegorization" of Kafka's animals, and in particular Rotpeter, Harel writes, "Although the story contains unrealistic elements, first and foremost Rotpeter's human speech, the story of Rotpeter—as an ape who lived in Africa, was shot and captured by Hagenbeck's hunting delegation, brought by boat to Hamburg, and there performed human gestures on stage, describes quite authentically an ape experience" (Harel 2010, 56–57). For as difficult as it is to say what an authentic "ape experience" might be, it is even more problematic to dismiss Rotpeter's "human speech" as a mere unrealistic narrative element not to be taken into serious consideration. Kafka's animals cannot so easily be "de-allegorized," especially not at the expense of the substance of his works. Furthermore, there is an easily identifiable historical practice virtually identical to Rotpeter's experiences involving humans who were by some literally perceived to be apes—namely, slavery. Finally and most important, Hagenbeck did not import only animals. His zoos did not merely feature caged beasts but also showcased, among others, Africans in their "native" habitats.[6] Even when we follow the Hagenbeckian thread, we find Africans in or in close proximity to kidnap and cages. Both Hagenbeck's and Kafka's works signify, albeit for different reasons, the colonial scenes that make them possible and through which "durchzieht sie Signifikantenketter Affe—dunkler Körper—Weiblichkeit—Sexualität—Wahnsinn" (traverses the chain of significations: ape, dark body; effeminacy; sexuality; and insanity) (Rösch 2007, 109).

II. *Nach Affenart*

As previously mentioned, Rotpeter comes originally from the slave-rich "Goldküste. Darüber, wie ich eingefangen wurde, bin ich auf fremde Berichte angewiesen" (*D* 301) (I belong to the Gold Coast. For the story of my capture I must depend on the evidence of others [*C* 251]). Unable to recount anything of his life that is not a matter of public record, the narrated events that come before Rotpeter's awakening to "human" consciousness are speculation. Although Rotpeter narrates the event of his capture and can say with certainty where he comes from, he does so based on secondary sources. In other words, he cannot falsify his memory; he must follow public record.

Rotpeter's relationship to his ape past coincides well with the slave's experience of absolute caesura of African past and European or New World present, even in the case of the most influential eighteenth-century slave narrative, *The Interesting Narrative of the Life of Olaudah Equiano*. The opening chapters of Equiano's narrative are devoted to a detailed account of his life in Africa until the age of eleven, when he was enslaved by Europeans.[7] This narrative pattern changes with a slave born a slave in the New World but still retains uncertainty as to origins. The standard example of the slave's representation of being born in bondage is that of Frederick Douglass, who writes,

> I was born in Tuckahoe, near Hillsborough, and about twelve miles from Easton, in Talbot county, Maryland. I have no accurate knowledge of my age, never having seen any authentic record containing it. By far the larger part of the slaves know as little of their ages as horses know of theirs, and it is the wish of most masters within my knowledge to keep their slaves thus ignorant. I do not remember to have ever met a slave who could tell of his birthday. They seldom come nearer to it than planting-time, harvest- time, cherry-time, spring-time, or fall-time. A want of information concerning my own was a source of unhappiness to me even during childhood. The white children could tell their ages. I could not tell why I ought to be deprived of the same privilege. I was not allowed to make any inquiries of my master concerning it. He deemed all such inquiries on the part of a slave improper and impertinent, and evidence of a restless spirit. The nearest estimate I can give makes me now between twenty-seven and twenty-eight years of age. I come to this, from hearing my master say, some time during 1835, I was about seventeen years old. (Andrews and Gates 2000, 1)

Douglass goes on to relate that he has virtually no memory of his mother and that his father's identity has been kept a secret from him. The slave's relationship to his past is one of darkness and conjecture, reliant upon public record where it exists and is to be procured.

According to public record, Rotpeter was wounded during capture:

> Einen in die Wange; der war leicht; hinterließ aber eine große ausrasierte rote Narbe, die mir den widerlichen, ganz und gar unzutreffenden, förmlich von einem Affen erfundenen Namen Rotpeter eingetragen hat, so als unterschiede ich mich von dem unlängst krepierten, hie und da bekannten, dressierten Affentier Peter nur durch den roten Fleck auf der Wange. Dies nebenbei.

> Der zweite Schuß traf mich unterhalb der Hüfte. Er war schwer, er hat es verschuldet, daß ich noch heute ein wenig hinke. Letzthin las ich in einem Aufsatz irgendeines der zehntausend Windhunde, die sich in den Zeitungen über mich auslassen: meine Affennatur sei noch nicht ganz unterdrückt; Beweis dessen sei, daß ich, wenn Besucher kommen, mit Vorliebe die Hosen ausziehe, um die Einlaufstelle jenes Schusses zu zeigen. Dem Kerl sollte jedes Fingerchen seiner schreibenden Hand einzeln weggeknallt werden. Ich, ich darf meine Hosen ausziehen, vor wem es mir beliebt; man wird dort nichts finden als einen wohlgepflegten Pelz und die Narbe nach einem—wählen wir hier zu einem bestimmten Zwecke ein bestimmtes Wort, das aber nicht mißverstanden werden wolle—die Narbe nach einem frevelhaften Schuß. (*D* 301–2)
>
> Once in the cheek; a slight wound; but it left a large, naked red scar which earned me the name of Red Peter, a horrible name, utterly inappropriate, which only some ape could have thought of, as if the only difference between me and the performing ape Peter, who died not so long ago and had some small local reputation, were the red mark on my cheek.
>
> The second shot hit me below the hip. It was a severe wound, it is the cause of my limping a little to this day. I read an article recently by one of the ten thousand windbags who vent themselves concerning me in the newspapers, saying: my ape nature is not yet under control; the proof being that when visitors come to see me, I have a predilection for taking down my trousers to show them where the shot went in. The hand which wrote that should have its fingers shot away one by one. As for me, I can take my trousers down before anyone if I like; you would find nothing but a well-groomed fur and the scar made—let me be particular in the choice of a word for this particular purpose, to avoid misunderstanding—the scar made by a wanton shot. (*C* 251–52)

Rotpeter is shot below the waist and, in effect, is castrated. At the scene of capture, the ape is stripped of his masculinity and sexual potency, a scene that easily corresponds to the breaking of slaves through various forms of physical torture, including genital mutilation as well as psychological emasculation. In this castration scene one also recognizes the logic of the narratological procedures of "Ein Bericht." The story offers the structure of a text that remains an open wound (Menninghaus 2002, 470–71, quoted in Shahar 2007, 461). Emasculated beyond repair, the story thematizes its wound, or its existence as eternal wound. As Shahar notes, "While Wagner's *Parsifal* ends with the closure of the King's wound, the cut on his side, and thus with a moment of theological and aesthetic catharsis, Kafka's story remains without a solution or a cure, as a fragment" (Shahar 2007, 461). For as emasculating and horrific as his fragmenting wound is, this loss gives Rotpeter the discretionary power to reveal himself to his audience. Castration becomes the basis of aesthetic presentation. For, although Rotpeter cannot reveal himself directly in terms of his narrative, which is first and foremost mediated, he can supplement the authenticity of his narrative by unveiling what he lacks. In what would have amounted to a burlesque or cabaret version of the scene of Noah's drunkenness (Rotpeter has already had his schnapps), to have seen the mark of castration would have been to verify an account that otherwise eludes all verification. Rotpeter attributes his willingness to perform what would otherwise be considered a lewd act to the prerogative of the great mind. Those who rise above the crowd need not obey the same moral codes of conduct that dominate the masses. However, Rotpeter knows that he cannot physically (not morally) perform the degenerate act he offers his public. And yet he proves himself capable of degeneracy beyond anything the academy would and could have expected. Castrated, there is nothing there to see. What Rotpeter would have "performed" in this instance of self-revealing would have been an aping of someone revealing himself. He would have mimicked someone flashing an audience.

A graphic example of this type of sexual mimicry comes at the end of the story. When he comes home at night, Rotpeter takes sexual comfort from a female chimpanzee, "nach Affenart" (*D* 313; or I might rewrite it as *eine Art nachaffen*). This chimpanzee is Rotpeter's constant, living reminder of his simian state and his "reflections on slavery." Rotpeter's companion gives testimony to enduring, perpetual slavery, embodying all those Rotpeter has irrevocably but only partially left behind.

The suggestion is that Rotpeter engages in bestial sensual delights that would insult the refinement of human intimacy. This is not true. Rotpeter cannot have sex; he has been castrated. Whatever he does with his chimpanzee girlfriend, if it involves sexual pleasure, it is not "bestial" in form but highly reflective, mediated, and intellectualized—making it all the more deviant. That is to say, Rotpeter's pleasures would have to be intellectual and aesthetic, the deliberate work of elaborate fantasy and mimicry. For we do have another clue as to what Rotpeter does with his girlfriend. To behave "nach Affenart" suggests that Rotpeter simulates sex, that the only comfort he can take now that he is "human" is in sex as simulation-stimulation, as unnatural, as perverse. Just as acrobats simulate the natural movements of apes, Rotpeter, the human, simulates human sex.

Perhaps this is why, before Elsa Brod gave a public reading of the story on December 20, 1917, Kafka insisted that, "should the text contain something dirty, don't leave it out" (*L* 168). Elsa's own experience of reading the text aloud before an audience was itself transformative, writing of it, "daß ich dabei buchstäblich affenmäßig fühle, ich rieche Affenschweiß und ströme ihn aus, natürlich nur während dieser Lektüre. Der Affe ist ein Meisterwerk"

(Koch 2005, 176) (that I in fact felt apelike while reading it, I smelled of ape sweat—of course only during this reading. The ape is a great work). Verified (or simulated-stimulated) by the dirty stench of ape sweat, Elsa confirms that the *Affe* is indeed a great work of art.

Verification of Rotpeter's narrative is possible only by seeing what is not there. Having bound his prerogative to disrobe in public to the liberties allowed great minds, Rotpeter displaces himself from the lofty heights he sought to reach. The lewd act he would perform, thus affirming his place among the clouds within the intellectual elite, cannot be lewd. Without the mastery of the phallus as proof of genius and its prerogatives, Rotpeter can never enjoy the fruits of human greatness; he can only suggest the possibility of the transcendence to human perfection. To concretize the audience's idea of his wound would be for Rotpeter to lose the ideality of the human he seeks to embody. Rotpeter's wounds, then, split him in two. With the loss of his manhood and the disfiguration of his face (representing, perhaps, ritual scarification), Rotpeter transforms, leaving himself behind in order to become his true self: "After these two shots I came to myself—and this is where my own memories gradually begin—between decks in the Hagenbeck steamer, inside a cage" (*C* 252).

III. *Affen denken mit dem Bauch*

Part of the slave narrative is, in fact, the slave's transformation from a white-perceived lower order of being into a man. Douglass's narrative famously asserts, "You have seen how a man was made a slave; you shall see how a slave was made a man," a sentiment echoed in Harriet Jacobs's *Incidents in the Life of a Slave Girl* (1861) and elsewhere. Equiano takes it a step further, becoming transfigured through a vision of Christ and thus gaining knowledge of his status as one of the elect of the Moravian Church (Andrews and Gates 2000, 199–203). It is exactly at the moment of Rotpeter's transfiguration between the decks of the slaver that we apparently see how a slave starts to become a man as he begins to speak for himself as a man: "Ich kann natürlich das damals affenmäßig Gefühlte heute nur mit Menschenworten nachzeichnen und verzeichne es infolgedessen, aber wenn ich auch die alte Affenwahrheit nicht mehr erreichen kann, wenigstens in der Richtung meiner Schilderung liegt sie, daran ist kein Zweifel (*D* 303) (Of course, what I felt then as an ape I can represent now only in human terms, and therefore I misrepresent it, but although I cannot reach back to the truth of the old ape life, there is no doubt that it lies somewhere in the direction I have indicated [*C* 253]).[8] Unable to articulate the truth of his ape existence, Rotpeter asserts the failure of language as its inability to translate the experience of the inhuman in human terms, in effect metaphorically representing the slave's preoccupation with the acquisition of European language(s), including a process of renaming the world among competing, constantly shifting linguistic traditions. The slave's linguistic predicament becomes one of living in translation where the target language has been fully effaced.

Rotpeter realizes that language can only blindly approximate or *mimic* his original state, the bestial, the primal. The unmediated experience of the inhuman is impossible to articulate. The "truth" in language exists—but cannot be located. That is to say, by extension, cultural and racial identity can be misrepresented, or altered, to suit the circumstances of a speech act. As a tool that cannot fix the truth of identity, language enables Rotpeter to shift and transform. And therein lies his freedom from bondage, as he well knows: "Aber Affen gehören bei Hagenbeck an die Kistenwand—nun, so hörte ich auf, Affe zu sein. Ein klarer, schöner Gedankengang, den ich irgendwie mit dem Bauch ausgeheckt haben muß, denn Affen denken mit dem Bauch" (*D* 304) (Yet as far as Hagenbeck was concerned, the place for apes was in front of a locker—well then, I had to stop being an ape. A fine, clear train of thought, which I must have constructed somehow with my belly, since apes think with their bellies [C 253]).

The movement between identities, the shifting from one place to another, is unreasonable. Position plays a role in the erasure and reconstruction of the human and inhuman and performs the role of the slave's coming to consciousness of literacy, figured in Equiano as a "talking book."[9] The talking book is in Equiano's narratives the slave's first experience of witnessing literacy in terms of its power to define the category of the human and potentially elevate the slave to this state of being. As Equiano elegantly puts it, "I had often seen my master and Dick employed in reading; and I had a great curiosity to talk to the books, as I thought they did; and so to learn how all things had a beginning: for that purpose I have often taken up a book, and have talked to it, and then put my ears to it, when alone, in hopes it would answer me; and I have been very much concerned when I found it remained silent" (Andrews and Gates 2000, 86). It is in part the memory of talking books that will drive Equiano's quest for literacy and human legitimacy. For the slave, literacy, discovered in a book that seems to talk to his master (and there are variations on this scene in other narratives, all signifying the same thing—namely, potential freedom from bondage through the attainment of "humanity" as literacy), is the fusion of body and language, the one having reciprocal effects on the other. The space of the book is that of freedom.[10]

For Rotpeter, it is a matter of standing; the actual space that Rotpeter occupies on the ship determines his subjective and objective positions. Thinking with his belly, Rotpeter determines to find a way out (*Ausweg*) of the prison in front of the locker. But this way out is found only in thought; bodily position or freedom of movement does not determine freedom in general. In this sense, both Rotpeter's apeness and his humanity are, as Rolf-Peter Janz writes, "nur vorgetäuscht. In Wahrheit führt er ein Doppelleben zwischen Mensch und Affe, er muß es führen, denn anders kann er nicht überleben.

Eine Rückkehr ins Leben als Affe ist ausgeschlossen" (Janz 2003, 113) (only faked. In reality he lives a double life between human and ape. He must do this, for it is the only way he can survive). Surmising that he thought with his belly, Rotpeter confirms that he can no longer think in the simian way if he is to be free.

Rotpeter thus does not elude the falsification of experience, the metaphorization of positional space and time through translation from the unspoken, aboriginal language of unmediated instinct into the intellectualized world of linguistic procedure. Indeed, he embraces and amplifies this primary cognitive function, doubling himself while losing all access to an original, unified being. From this point on, all of Rotpeter's actions and even his thoughts will be *vorgetäuscht*, creating, as Friedrich puts it, "eine Legitimationsaporie": "Weder bietet sie eine substantielle Vergegenwärtigung einer tierischen Vergangenheit, noch eine Wesenbestimmung des Menschen; die Erzählung verfängt sich von Anfang an in einer 'Legitimationsaporie,' die unhintergehbar ist" (Neither does it offer a substantial incorporation of a bestial past in the present, nor the possibility of becoming completely human; the story traps itself from the very beginning in an "aporia of legitimation," from which there is no escape) (Friedrich 2007, 208). From this untenable position of inauthenticity he seeks an *Ausweg*.

IV. *Der Ausweg*

As embodied unreflective nature, apes laugh instinctively at humans who train to do what comes naturally, unreflectively, to simians. Nature, then, is unreflective, unmediated thought as action. Word and deed are irrevocably intertwined in the animal kingdom. The body (belly) thinks, not the mind. There is no separation between mind and body. In effect, once Rotpeter loses his corporeal freedom and becomes conscious of and as his body in confined space, he also becomes aware of the unconscious, unreflective movement of "true" freedom.

Although as thinking animal Rotpeter is "free," he sees through human freedom:

> Nein, Freiheit wollte ich nicht. Nur einen Ausweg; rechts, links, wohin immer; ich stellte keine anderen Forderungen; sollte der Ausweg auch nur eine Täuschung sein; die Forderung war klein, die Täuschung würde nicht größer sein. Weiterkommen, weiterkommen! Nur nicht mit aufgehobenen Armen stillestehn, angedrückt an eine Kistenwand. (*D* 305)

> No, freedom was not what I wanted. Only a way out; right or left, or in any direction; I made no other demand; even should the way out

> prove to be an illusion; the demand was a small one, the disappointment could be no bigger. To get out somewhere, to get out! Only not to stay motionless with raised arms, crushed against a wooden wall. (*C* 253–54)

Human "freedom" is here the defining characteristic of the human and perceived to be hypocrisy. For this reason, Rotpeter not only rejects human "freedom" but also humanity as such. As Martin Buber intuited, his narrative is not one of assimilation or even resistance through assimilation as the whole of Equiano's can be understood; it is a withering critique, much in the way that sections of slave narratives would chastise their Christian masters for supporting a most un-Christian institution and routinely perpetrating un-Christian crimes.

Over and against the hypocrisy of human freedom, Rotpeter's only concern is to be in motion, to be able to navigate between one point and another. The quality of the freedom restless motion grants him is by this point beside the point. Any unconscious movement is better than unrelenting confinement within self-directed motion. And escape from freedom is not an option for Rotpeter:

> Die Ruhe, die ich mir im Kreise dieser Leute erwarb, hielt mich vor allem von jedem Fluchtversuch ab. Von heute aus gesehen scheint es mir, als hätte ich zumindest geahnt, daß ich einen Ausweg finden müsse, wenn ich leben wolle, daß dieser Ausweg aber nicht durch Flucht zu erreichen sei. Ich weiß nicht mehr, ob Flucht möglich war, aber ich glaube es; einem Affen sollte Flucht immer möglich sein. (*D* 306)

> The calmness I acquired among these people kept me above all from trying to escape. As I look back now, it seems to me I must have had at least an inkling that I had to find a way out or die, but that my way out could not be reached through flight. I cannot tell now whether escape was possible, but I believe it must have been; for an ape it must always be possible. (*C* 254)

Rotpeter's *Ausweg* is unattainable through flight; but for an ape, escape is always possible. The embrace of the way out as opposed to flight serves to strengthen the bonds of his chains while offering a purely negative mode of detachment and operational freedom. At this point, Rotpeter is no longer ape, in that he no longer possesses the essential simian quality of freedom of unconscious movement, understood here as the absolutely unreflective thought of the body in motion. The thought of flight does not occur to him because it cannot. Although Rotpeter is able to recall instinctually what the ape's instinct *may have* been, he can no longer experience unmediated thought, or the body as thinking organism in itself. He can only mimic experience, both human and ape. Thus, assimilation or, as Theisen puts it, "Anpassung wird bei Kafka zu einer komplexen Chiffre, in der eine so verstandene Zivilisation gerade durch eine Mimikry am von ihr geforderten, zum Überleben notwendigen Verhalten unterlaufen wird: sie wird zur Chiffre fuhr den 'Ausweg' " (Adaptation becomes in Kafka a complex code, through which a civilization—as it is understood in this way—demanding mimicry in order to survive will undermine its own fundamentals: this adaptation becomes the code for the way out) (Theisen 2004, 274). It is important to remember here that just as the primary simian behavioral characteristic was believed to be precisely this type of mimicry, it was also thought to be a "human" trait exhibited by Africans. Mimicry, or aping (*nachaffen*), was considered to be the reason why Africans of genius, defined here in purely Western terms, were able to produce, say, great poetry. As the case of the African-born New England slave poet Phillis Wheatley shows, talent, and in particular great artistic ability, was not believed to be innate in blacks but a product of their instinctual ability to mimic.[11] Thomas Jefferson's *Notes on the State of Virginia* (1765) provides us with similar testimony.

Simian simulation, or simply mimicry, itself is the way out that is not freedom.[12] But this mimicry is, for Rotpeter, always already the mimicry of mimicry. His genius is to apprehend that all human behavior is mimicry; his *Ausweg* of the prison house of mimicry is to amplify it, and in so doing reveal mimicry as the basis of human thought. By being able to ape aped human thought, he shows that he has mastered the fundamental rules of the game and can play at being human better than a human being is able to do.

V. Aping Thought Aping

Still attuned to his slave/simian heritage but irrevocably divorced from the experience of "apeness," Rotpeter retraces the steps of his spiritual journey on the way to becoming human. As he becomes human, he does not think his dilemma out: "Ich rechnete nicht so menschlich, aber unter dem Einfluß meiner Umgebung verhielt ich mich so, wie wenn ich gerechnet hätte" (*D* 307) (I did not think it out in the human way, but under the influence of my surroundings I acted as if I had thought it out [*C* 179]). Simian mimicry doubles for cultural mimicry as Rotpeter acts out thought. *He is not confessing to having acted as humans do but to have mimicked how humans think about taking action.* The difference is tangible and crucial. To mimic human activity would in no way separate him from this apeness; he would simply be doing what all slaves/apes do and thus reinforcing the profound purchase of his slave/simian origin. But to be capable of mimicking thought—not the pensive look of someone thinking but thinking itself—is Rotpeter's great achievement. He has performed an act of mimicry that, by its mere existence, undermines human thought entirely by collapsing the difference between man and ape. The slave Rotpeter has planned and is making his escape by hiding in plain sight and acting free. His escape from bondage is the equivalent of that of the slave who surreptitiously learns to write and forges his own travel pass; and his account of coming to the *Ausweg* is his version of the slave narrative's "descriptions of patrols, of failed attempt(s) to escape, of pursuit by men and dogs."

Rotpeter's mimicry enables him to approach the category of the human because human thought is nothing more than mimicry in the first place.[13] Human thought here is the best, yet essentially impoverished, mimicry of "Mother Nature." By mimicking human thought, Rotpeter reproduces the "inessential" relation of language to nature. This is both what allows Rotpeter to close in on the human and what keeps him forever at a distance from his goal. The initial, bestial, instinctual response is translated into linguistic thought, or mind. Mind short-circuits the body's direct, unmediated relation to itself and translates thought back into the body, into action. This action is no longer instinctual, unmediated, and unconscious; it is an interpretation or secondary mimicry of an initial impulse or drive.

In the case of Rotpeter, another step must be added to this process. Before a thought can be retranslated into the body, the act of thinking must be mimicked, or translated. Thus arises a tertiary network of mimicry based upon the aping of a process as opposed to an object or action. The attainment of, or fall into, human freedom thus follows the same structural principles as Rotpeter's erasure of his "original" identity and his interminable transformation into the human. Eventually, Rotpeter does mimic human actions with uncanny accuracy. But the perfect mimicry of the act is impossible without first mimicking the essential Cartesian act of the human—namely, thought. For Rotpeter, Descartes's axiom must be amended to read, I mimic thought mimicking, therefore I am.

This structure is mimicked by yet another in "Ein Bericht," that of becoming artist:

> Was für ein Sieg dann allerdings für ihn wie für mich, als ich eines Abends vor großem Zuschauerkreis—vielleicht war ein Fest, ein Grammophon spielte, ein Offizier erging sich zwischen den Leuten—als ich an diesem Abend, gerade unbeachtet, eine vor meinem Käfig versehentlich stehengelassene Schnapsflasche ergriff, unter steigender Aufmerksamkeit der Gesellschaft sie schulgerecht entkorkte, an den Mund setzte und ohne Zögern, ohne Mundverziehen, als Trinker von Fach, mit rund gewälzten Augen, schwappender Kehle, wirklich und wahrhaftig leer trank; nicht mehr als Verzweifelter, sondern als Künstler die Flasche hinwarf; zwar vergaß den Bauch zu streichen; dafür aber, weil ich nicht anders konnte, weil es mich drängte, weil mir die Sinne rauschten, kurz und gut "Hallo!" ausrief, in Menschenlaut

> ausbrach, mit diesem Ruf in die Menschengemeinschaft sprang und ihr Echo—"Hört nur, er spricht!" wie einen Kuß auf meinem ganzen schweißtriefenden Körper fühlte.
>
> Ich wiederhole: es verlockte mich nicht, die Menschen nachzuahmen; ich ahmte nach, weil ich einen Ausweg suchte, aus keinem anderen Grund. (*D* 310–11)

> What a triumph it was then both for him and for me, when one evening before a large circle of spectators—perhaps there was a celebration of some kind, a gramophone was playing, an officer was circulating among the crew—when on this evening, just as no one was looking, I took hold of the schnapps bottle that had been carelessly left standing before my cage, uncorked it in the best style, while the company began to watch me with mounting attention, set it to my lips without hesitation, with no grimace, like a professional drinker, with rolling eyes and full throat, actually and truly drank it empty; then threw the bottle away, not this time in despair but as an artistic performer; forgot, indeed, to rub my belly; but instead of that, because I could not help it, because my senses were reeling, called a brief and unmistakable "Hallo!" breaking into human speech, and with this outburst broke into the human community, and felt its echo: "Listen, he's talking!" like a caress over the whole of my sweat-drenched body.
>
> I repeat: there was no attraction for me in imitating human beings; I imitated them because I needed a way out, and for no other reason. (*C* 257)

Lost in the throes of intoxication, beside himself with drink, Rotpeter ostensibly makes his final transition from the inhuman to the human. He has completed his "successful attempt(s) to escape, lying by during the day, travelling by night guided by the North Star, reception in a free state by Quakers who offer a lavish breakfast and much genial thee/thou conversation."

For, as Dagmar Lorenz writes, "Rotpeter learns that drinking alcohol and having illicit sex are touchstones of being human. Like privileged fin-de-siècle men, he indulges himself but keeps his embarrassing mistress out of the public eye" (Lorenz 2007, 162). Surrounded by a "circle of spectators" waiting to see an ape act human, Rotpeter offers them something more. His show is not that of the mime or mimic but of mental and physical transformation; he does not mimic the human, he becomes human mimicry.

Aping the attributes of the professional drinker, Rotpeter empties his schnapps bottle and loses control of his senses. He has not lost control of his reason, for, at this point, he has no reason to lose. The effect of the alcohol is to disrupt the cognitive processes, but in an inverted fashion. Where intoxication is normally understood to exacerbate the passions at the cost of reason, it has the opposite effect on Rotpeter. His senses reel; he forgets to rub his belly, the seat of his bestial cognitive powers; he leaves his essential apeness behind. As Equiano might put it, Rotpeter is able "to imbibe their spirit."

Rotpeter has imbibed the European spirit and gives proof of this through a mastery of the master's tongue. Most important, his despair has been usurped by artistry. Replacing genuine emotion is now the sentiments of "an artistic performer," an actor, or, as Erhard Schüttpelz has shown, a writer. Tracing iconographic representations of *Menschenaffen* back to ancient Egyptian mythology—which Kafka was familiar with and employed, as we have seen in *Die Verwandlung*—Schüttpelz concludes that Rotpeter "ist ein vertrackter Nachfolger des ägyptischen Schreibergottes, eine unvorhergesehene Hommage" (is an initiated follower of the Egyptian god of writing, an homage yet to be noticed) (Schüttpelz 2007, 113). Whether or not this is the case, Rotpeter discerns that his activity is essentially the mimicry of mimicry, or the representation of the representation, placing him squarely in the regime of Platonic thinking on art. Given that Rotpeter's mode of engagement is language, as opposed to visual representation of direct musicality, his art is the performance of a text of his own devising.

It is, in any event, not incumbent on the reader to decide between an Egyptian-mythological reading or a Platonic one. As Andreas Kilcher and Detlef Kremer put it, "Der Text erweist sich bei genauerem Hinsehen als ein mehrschichtiges Palimpsest, in dessen Schriftspur unterschiedliche Texte und Diskurse verwoben sind, verbunden in der Bildsemantik um den Komplex 'Mimesis' " (The text, upon close examination, proves to be a multilayered palimpsest, in which are woven the traces of several other texts and sources, and which is bound by the semantics of images determined by a complex "mimesis") (Kilcher and Kremer 2004, 61). The text thus echoes, or repeats, Rotpeter's own aesthetic process; it engages in an allusive game of mimetic, or better described, mimic intertextual discursive reproduction, aping literary artifacts and then weaving them together to form the "Ein Bericht." Rotpeter's *Ausweg* is the practice of his narrative, a fact to which clues are given in the repetitive linguistic structures and word choices he employs. He uses human speech and literary achievement against themselves. As Gerhard Neumann has observed, "Doch geht es Kafka in seinem 'Bericht' nicht nur um die Denkform, also das Wissensparadigma, das beim Verstehen der Verwandlung der Tiers in den Menschen, oder der Natur in die Kultur in Geltung zu setzen ist, sondern auch um eine Kunstform; um die besondere Art eines Textes nämlich, einer Sprachform also, in der eine derart spezifische Figur der präsenzgeborenen Nachträglichkeit sich literarisch verwirklichen lässt" (In Kafka's "Bericht" we find not only the thought-form, the paradigm of knowledge, that reveals itself through the understanding of animal transformation or that of nature into culture, but we also encounter an art-form, specifically the particular nature of a text, a linguistic form, in which a particular figure of arriving too late, born from presence, is embodied) (Neumann 2004, 141).

Indeed, it is at this very moment of Rotpeter's induction, conscription, or kidnapping into writing as *Kunstform* that he enters human speech at all, and "into the human community" in particular. Thus, everything that has preceded this moment in Rotpeter's account has been, as in slave narratives, a "record of the barriers raised against slave literacy and the overwhelming difficulties encountered in learning to read and write."

However, this separation between body and mind, instinct and art, is at this point not quite complete. Although Rotpeter speaks and is spoken to, he receives verbal confirmation of his utterances as physical delectation. The audience's verbal reply is for Rotpeter "wie einen Kuß auf meinem ganzen schweißtriefenden Körper fühlte" (*D* 311) (like a caress over the whole of my sweat-drenched body [*C* 257]). Rotpeter has found his way out, but unlike the authors of slave narratives, he cannot pass entirely through this opening. For whereas the ex-slave who writes her autobiography consolidates her place among "men" through the writing of the autobiography itself as proof of linguistic mastery and mode of self-fashioning, Rotpeter, having already exposed autobiography as a perversion of a life, a swindle, remains forever with one foot in and one foot out of slavery's cage.[14]

Chapter 6

✦

Negro's Martyrdom

I. *Es fuhren die Neger aus dem Gebüsch*

In a fragment from "Oktavheft G," 1917, Kafka dramatizes something like what the manumission and return of Rotpeter to Africa would look like in the figure of an ex-*Ausstellungsneger*: "Der Neger, der von der Weltausstellung nach Hause gebracht wird, und, irrsinnig geworden von Heimweh, mitten in seinem Dorf unter dem Wehklagen des Stammes mit ernstestem Gesicht als Überlieferung und Pflicht die Späße aufführt, welche das europäische Publikum als Sitten und Gebräuche Afrikas entzückten" [*N* 64]) (The Negro, who is brought home from the world exhibition and, having become insane from homesickness, in the middle of his village, surrounded by the mournful wailings of tribesmen and with a serious countenance, performs amusements with a sense of tradition and beauty that entertain the European public as African customs and mores). Once again the *Ausstellungsneger* appears, this time in his "homeland" after a period of exploitation in Europe's *Völkerschauen*. The automatic assumption is that his *Heimweh* is for Africa, but the strict grammatical sense of the sentence does not guarantee that. Indeed, Kafka leaves it an open question as to whether or not *Heimweh* means here longing for Africa or for the Europe that has so influenced the African. To become *irrsinnig* in this context is to live in the ambiguity of this open question, to experience what one critic has called Rotpeter's "racial melancholy" (Garloff 2011). Noticeably, the sadness of the voices surrounding him are described as *Wehklagen*, adding to the atmosphere of martyrdom as well as to the Negro's background of organic dissonant noise, signaling Kafka's own aesthetic process.

The scene is reminiscent of another of Kafka's African fragments, in which he expands on this idea of the inherent dissonant musicality of the Negro in a journal entry of July 6, 1916: "Es fuhren die Neger aus dem Gebüsch. Um den mit silberner Kette umzogenen Holzpflock warfen sie sich im Tanz. Der Priester saß abseits, ein Stäbchen über dem Gong erhoben. Der Himmel war umwölkt, aber regenlos und still" (*T* 794) (The Negroes came out of the thicket. They leaped into a dance which they performed around a wooden stake encircled by a silver chain. The priest sat to one side, a little rod raised above the gong. The sky was overcast and silent; no rain fell [*J* 365]). A priest dramatically pauses before banging a gong as chained Negroes dance in a circle. In a ritual of unknown religious significance, the godhead remains veiled by thick clouds in the sky; and yet the lack of rain and wind indicates a solemn, divine vigilance above what only appears to be controlled chaos. Within the circle, the musical Negro has access to natural phenomena that, through portentous signs, seem to speak in tongues.[1] And yet, Kafka may very well be translating a scene he saw in a variety show.

The two fragments read together give us an initial scene of individual suffering that becomes one of communal self-recognition through the martyr's agonal ritual sacrifice. What the *Neger* eventually performs exists, like him, between two modes of cultural and religious expression, art and martyrdom.

Kafka became fascinated with African ritual and martyrdom upon reading about the Ugandan martyrs, the newspaper clippings of which he included in a letter to Felice—the first time he had ever done such a thing:

> Nun habe ich schon längst den Plan gehabt und nur aus Nachlässigkeit ihn immer wieder auszuführen unterlassen, verschiedene Zeitungsnachrichten, die mir aus irgendeinem Grunde überraschend waren, mir nahegingen und mir persönlich für nicht absehbare Zeit wichtig schienen, meistens waren es für den ersten Blick nur Kleinigkeiten, aus der letzten Zeit z.B. "Seligsprechung der 22 christlichen Negerjünglinge von Uganda" (ich habe es sogar jetzt gefunden und lege es bei) auszuschneiden und zu sammeln. Fast jeden Tag finde ich in der Zeitung eine derartige, förmlich für mich allein bestimmte Nachricht, aber ich habe nicht die Ausdauer, eine solche Sammlung für mich anzufangen, wie erst für mich sie fortsetzen. (*BF* 121)
>
> Seligsprechung der Märtyrer von Uganda (Notiz aus dem "Prager Tagblatt" vom 25. September 1912)
>
> Ein Dekret der Ritenkongregation vom 13. August veröffentlicht die Einleitung des Seligsprechungsprozesses der sogenannten "Märtyrer von Uganda," 22 christliche Negerjünglinge, die als erste Bluzeugen vor 26 Jahren für den Glauben den Verbrennungstod erlitten. Wie aus Rom von der Zentrale der St. Petrus Claver-Sodalität gemeldet wird, waren die Kardinäle, welche die Angelegenheit zu beraten hatten, über den Heldenmut der jugendlichen Märtyrer bis zu Tränen ergriffen. Es herrscht über die Nachricht des eingeleiteten Seligsprechungsverfahrens allenthalben bei den Negern und besonders bei denen von Nord-Viktoria-Nyanza, der Heimat der ersten Märtyrer, der größte Jubel, den sie in Tänzen und Sprüngen zum Ausdruck brachten. (*BF* 763).
>
> For a long time now I have planned, and only my indolence has prevented me repeatedly from carrying it through, to cut out and collect

> from various papers news items that astonished me for some reason, that affected me, that seemed important to me personally for a long time to come; at a glance, they were usually quite insignificant, for instance just recently "The beatification of 22 Christian Negro youths in Uganda"—(which I have just come across and am enclosing. (an article taken from the *Prager Tagblatt* of 25 September 1912). I find something of the kind in the papers nearly every other day. News which seems to be meant only for me, but I haven't got the patience to start the collection for myself, let alone keep it up. (*LF* 61)

> A decree of the Congregation of Rites of 13 August published the initiation of the beatification process of the so-called "Martyrs of Uganda," 22 Christian Negro youths who first suffered martyrdom 26 years ago for the faith, being burned alive. As reported by the Rome seat of the St. Peter Claver Sodality, the Cardinals, who had to discuss the matter, were moved to tears by the heroism of the young martyrs. The beatification process dominates the Negro news, especially in northern Victoria Nyanza, the home of the first martyr, where they express their great joy by dancing and jumping around. (*LF* 615)

Read by Kafka as if they were written solely for him, the news stories and Felice's impending response to them were important enough to him that he later complained to her, "Du schickst mir so wenig Zeitungsausschnitte, und ich schicke Dir da wieder einen so schönen. Du hast doch nicht am Ende den Zeitungsausschnitt über die Seligsprechung der 22 Negerjünglinge von Uganda verloren?" (*BF* 270) (You send me so very few newspaper clippings, and I am sending you such a nice one again. Surely you couldn't have lost the clipping about the beatification of the 22 Negro youths from Uganda? [*LF* 171]). Of all the newspaper clippings that he eventually sends to her, the ones reporting the beatification of martyred Ugandans are those that Kafka singles out for special attention.

And indeed, the story of the Ugandans is compelling. Caught up in a bloody political struggle that was defined in part by competing religious orientations (Roman Catholic, Protestant, and Islamic), twenty-two black Ugandan Catholics were murdered by King Mwanga II of Buganda between 1885 and 1887. Recognizing the Ugandan victims as martyrs, Rome decided in 1912 that they were to be beatified (1920). In the report, the accounts of the lives and deaths of the Ugandan martyrs are accompanied by tears from the Roman Catholic bishops. But the news of the coming beatification is greeted by the Africans' expressions of joy via dancing, "jumping," and presumably singing. The news article juxtaposes European expressions of solemnity with African forms of jubilation. The deaths of twenty-two Africans for the greater glory of God are here understood through transcendence, austerity, and what would have been read by many as lurid expressions of wanton abandon and outright noise.

Figure 2. *Diese Postkarte wurde in Tausenden von Exemplaren hergestellt und versandt* (This postcard was produced and sent in the thousands).

The report evokes, then, two things of great interest to Kafka regarding the Negro. The first is the persecution and murder of the Negro in the name of law and order. We recall his abiding interest in a photo of a lynched Negro among his murderers and, presumably, in a postcard Holitscher reproduces of an artist's rendering of another lynching victim surrounded by his white assailants.[2] The second is, once again, the ritual, unreadable and untoward musicality of the Negro. Murder, martyrdom, and the profane combine in cacophony, generating in and as ritual and illegible aesthetic-cultural text. Kafka's "Ein Hungerkünstler" presents us with a type of martyr and, through the idea of martyrdom in its relation to metaphorical blackness, rethinks the aesthetics of recapitulation through ritual.

II. *Ich bin es, der alte, Dir und vielleicht nur Dir allein wohlgesinnte Menschenfresser*

This combination of Africa, ritual, and death are united, in the pop cultural conceptions of Kafka's ethnographical moment, with European fantasies of rampant black cannibalism and the attendant idea of the unavoidable cannibalism of recapitulative man.[3] Kafka himself in a journal fragment introduced a cannibal into "Ein Hungerkunstler," an old acquaintance of the hunger artist's. The fragment seems to create a point of identification and analogy between the two, as if to establish the cannibal as the representative of the art of hunger as a savage rebellion against the repressive disciplinary apparatuses of family and society. In rehearsing here just a fraction of Gerhard Neumann's brilliant, definitive essay on the subject, this chapter emphasizes the cannibalism of the audience over that of the hunger artist.[4] Awakened by the cannibal come to visit, the hunger artist is greeted with the following:

> "Ja," sagte er, "ich bin es, der alte, Dir und vielleicht nur Dir allein wohlgesinnte Menschenfresser. Einen kleinen Besuch will ich Dir machen, mich erholen an Deinem Anblick, die Nerven ein wenig ausruhn lassen von dem lästigen Volk." (*N* 648–49)

> "Yes," he said. "It is I, the old cannibal who is to you and to you alone well-meaning. I want to pay you a little visit in order to replenish myself in your presence and let my nerves relax a little after having to deal with annoying people.

The cannibal does not embody the semiotic core of all that the hunger artist tries to accomplish; he is the manifestation of the audience's own repressed atavism. This is why, spending most of his time among the audience, the cannibal needs to rest his nerves from the burden the crowd places on him. His relationship to the hunger artist is special in that it is the hunger artist, and the hunger artist alone, who tells the story of his overcoming. For, rather than break bread with the cannibal, Kafka reminds us in a letter to Felix Weltsch of December 1917, "Naturally, you imagine you have nothing against cannibals either, but if they should start crawling about in the night behind every chest and chattering their teeth at you, you surely could not bear them any longer" (*L* 173).

For Kafka, the most honest father was the "cannibal" Kronos. As he writes to his sister Elli in 1921, "Kronos, der seine Sohne auffraß,—der ehrlichste Vater, aber vielleicht hat Kronos seine Methode der sonst Üblichen gerade aus Mitleid mit seinen Kindern vorgezogen" (*B* 345) (Kronos, the most honest of fathers, who devoured his sons; but perhaps Kronos preferred this to the usual methods out of pity for his children [*L* 295]). Whether or not Kronos would do this out of sympathy remains to be seen; the fact persists that a sign of paternal authority is the right, symbolic or otherwise, to devour one's son, to incorporate him in the body of the father, to make him become the father. The statement becomes all the more powerful when set alongside Kafka's letter to his father in which he gives a harrowing account of his father's eating habits and table manners, only to punctuate it by causally associating Hermann Kafka's dietary regime and practice with his ability to command and shape the world of his son as if from up on high. Thus, when the condemned man of “In der Strafkolonie” threatens to cannibalize his superior officer, he threatens to overturn not only the colonial order but also the order of Noahic patriarchal power. Eating, cannibalistic or otherwise, and Noahic paternal power are in Kafka indivisibly linked.

Kafka’s fraught relationship to eating is well documented. With regard to his disgust for meat in particular, he writes in a journal entry of October 30, 1911,

> Dieses Verlangen, das ich fast immer habe, wenn ich einmal meinen Magen gesund fühle, Vorstellungen von schrecklichen Wagnissen mit Speisen in mir zu häufen . . . Sehe ich eine Wurst, die ein Zettel als seine alte harte Hauswurst anzeigt, beiße ich in meiner Einbildung mit ganzem Gebiß hinein und schlucke rasch, regelmässig und rücksichtslos, wie eine Maschine. . . . Die langen Schwarten von Rippenfleisch stoße ich ungebissen in den Mund und ziehe sie dann von hinten, den Magen und die Därme durchreißend, wieder heraus. (*T* 210)

> This craving that I almost always have, when for once I feel my stomach is healthy, to heap up in me the notions of terrible deeds of daring with food . . . If I see a sausage that is labeled as an old, hard sausage; I bite into it in my imagination with all my teeth and swallow quickly, regularly, and thoughtlessly, like a machine. . . . I shove the long slabs of rib meat unbitten into my mouth, and then pull them out again from behind, tearing through stomach and intestines. (*J* 96)

The experience of eating meat is that of embracing the disemboweled, dismembered corpse. It is also that of becoming an eating machine. While eating meat, one becomes mechanized, dehumanized.

This machinelike act of eating meat is described in a letter to Milena in terms reminiscent of the death of the officer at the hands of the execution machine in “In der Strafkolonie.” Kafka writes, “Am wenigsten gern fahre ich in ein Sanatorium. Was soll ich dort? Vom Chefarzt zwischen die Knie genommen werden und an den Fleischklumpen würgen, die er mir mit den Karbolfingern in den Mund stopft und dann entlang der Gurgel hinunterdrückt” (*BM* 280) (The last thing I want to do is go to a sanatorium. What am I supposed to do there? Have the head physician take me between his knees and use his carbolic fingers to stuff meat into my mouth and down my throat until I choke? [*LM* 207]). A finger probes in a similar way to the Harrow, the dying man gurgles one last time. Eating meat transforms the machinelike consumer into an efficiently machinelike animal, which in turn can be consumed in a machinelike way. If there is an art to this, it is that of presenting the body for culinary delectation. To complete this art, one requires an audience of Africanized, recapitulative cannibals.

For in order to be constituted as such, the work of art requires an audience. Karl Roßmann's circus is nothing without a public for which to perform. Georg Bendemann acrobatically jumps to his "death" in the middle of rush hour. Gregor Samsa's transformation is played out not only in front of his family but also before their three lodgers and during a "public" music performance. The officer dies as part of a travesty of communal ritual. And Rotpeter delivers his report. All these characters are thus in their way performance artists. Their relationship to their audience is of course violent and ambiguous. In each case the audience is either antagonistic or indifferent to their art. The disconnect between artist and audience is caused by patriarchal intolerance, even in "In der Strafkolonie," where the Old Commandant and his rule of law still have the power to condemn the officer, and in "Ein Bericht," in which the academy itself, composed of all men (*hohe Herrn*), sits in judgment.

In "Ein Hungerkünstler," the weight of this authority falls on the audience, which, practicing a carnivorous dietary regime, is set over and against the hunger artist. Eating meat is for Kafka linked to Noahic patriarchal power exercised at one remove from cannibalism. What shocks the hunger artist's audience is having to watch a perfectly good meal vanish before it. The audience is hostile Kronos who once appreciated the artist's work but who now, as the world becomes more civilized, is no longer able to. "Es waren andere Zeiten" (we live in a different world now), the narrator of "Ein Hungerkünstler" tells us (*D* 334; *C* 268). The "mythological" or simply primitive time of the hunger artists has passed. The last practitioner of this once seemingly great art is about to bring his last work to completion, removing the only remaining atavistic signifier of a savage past from advanced culture. The primal, mythological, or essential narrative of this work, then, is the overcoming of cannibalism through renunciation. Within the logic of recapitulative cannibalism, the hunger artist's performance tells the tale of how society evolved from a group of cannibals to meat eaters able to renounce this primal instinct, perhaps on the way, teleologically speaking, to becoming vegetarians. Thus, the work of the hunger artist displays the renunciation of savagery through starvation (and not by fasting) and, in this way, removing oneself entirely from the scene of cannibalism.

To continue the performance beyond the point of its semiotic legibility in society, beyond the point at which it becomes a transmissible mythopoetic text recounting an essential moment in the development of society, is to present a work that once meant victory over savagery but that itself is now seen as savage. No longer able to connect with the savagery of this narrative of aversion, the audience becomes averse and ultimately indifferent to it. The tension between the hunger artist's conception of his performance as the representation, for the good of society, of the victory over cannibalism places it in his mind partly in the order of martyrdom. But he also understands that the primitive ritual aspect of what he enacts is lost on his audience. This sets his performance of self-abnegation unto death also in the realm of secular murder. There are, then, two competing yet complementary ways of reading the hunger artist's act: as martyrdom to a higher cause than personal aesthetic achievement and as veiled ritual violence that is murder for the sake of the health and coherence of the community.

For Kafka, then, the relationship between these two ways of understanding the single recapitulative sacrificial event (both secular and sacred) is always already qualified by anthropologically "primitive" Africanicity and thus brought out in the contrast between the Ugandan martyrs and the black men in the images of lynching. While the circumstances of the deaths are divergent, he sees the common root of violent communal spectacle in a recapitulative cultural-racial context. What Kafka is now claiming, though, is that it is the audience that is savage, not the black victim, and that this savagery is revealed in its encounter with the visual record of the violence of how art is made (sitting in a cage, wasting away). In this way, understanding that recidivism and recapitulation are always possible—that the logic of cannibalism persists under a different guise, that of eating animal flesh—the hunger artist's once heroic narrative becomes devastating critique as well as desperate warning.

In the hunger artist and his performance, martyrdom and murder are at stake, mediated by the recidivist logic of cannibalism. This is why his work is not a fast but self-starvation. For although there were actual hunger artists, and their techniques may have been akin to fasting, this is not what the hunger artist in Kafka's story is doing (Oye 2004, 1136–40). His art deals in death, not restitution. As Alan Astro has pointed out, "Kafka never uses the term *fasten* and only employs *hungern*; the sole word in the story that even connotes religion is *Märtyrer*, after which we read, *welcher der Hungerkünstler allerdings war, nur in ganz anderem Sinn* ('a martyr, which the hunger artist indeed was, though in a completely other sense'). Indeed, the story seems to ask what it could possibly mean to choose to go hungry in a modern, de-mystified (*entzauberter)* world 'where religious fasting is impossible.'" (Astro 2004, 164). The hunger artist is a martyr not to a specific religious cause but to a ritualized secular world premised upon recapitulative cannibalism. There is, then, an important distinction made between fasting and self-starvation; for fasting (*fasten*) has a very different goal in mind in comparison with self-starvation. Fasting does not seek to approach death or reproach a cannibalistic dietary regime; it is a form of healthy, sometimes religio-spiritual, purge. Starvation is purely destructive. It rejects the ritual sacrifice and cannibalism upon which society is based.

Attempting to realize this martyrdom through self-starvation in a theoretically African context, a strong interest in which Kafka displays when he goes so far as to cut out the newspaper reports of the Ugandan martyrs and send them to Felice, Kafka's hunger artist locks himself in his *Käfig*, a word that, we recall, is etymologically related to *Käfer*. But whereas Gregor's "keepers" tried to feed him, the hunger artist keeps his overseers awake in order to prove to his audience that he is starving (*hungern*) himself:

> Er war sehr gerne bereit, mit solchen Wächtern die Nacht gänzlich ohne Schlaf zu verbringen; er war bereit, mit ihnen zu scherzen, ihnen Geschichten aus seinem Wanderleben zu erzählen, dann wieder ihre Erzählungen anzuhören, alles nur, um sie wachzuhalten, um ihnen immer wieder zeigen zu können, daß er nichts Eßbares im Käfig hatte und daß er hungerte, wie keiner von ihnen es könnte. (*D* 230)

> He was quite happy at the prospect of spending a sleepless night with such watchers; he was ready to exchange jokes with them, to tell them stories out of his nomadic life, anything at all to keep them awake and demonstrate to them again that he had no eatables in his cage and that he was fasting as not one of them could fast. (*C* 269)

The only way to ensure that a society of cannibals registers the full scope of the hunger artist's, not protest against but annihilation of the logic of cannibalism (which, for Kafka, begins with the relationship between father and son) is to have this constant surveillance and verification of self-starvation (here, *hungern*).[5] This act of self-starvation is always already in an African context via recapitulative cannibalism and contextually reinforced by Kafka's fascination with the Ugandan martyrs.

This martyrdom as bodily transformation through self-starvation is the substance and work of the hunger artist's art. Hunger artistry is performance art; but it is performance as nonperformance. The hunger artist simply does nothing with the exception of displaying his nonworking body in a skintight black body stocking. The body of the hunger artist, *im schwarzen Trikot* (in black tights), is for Kafka a metaphor for the dying black body as aesthetic spectacle, first and most viscerally encountered in *Der Verschollene*. As we have seen, Kafka's use of bodies racially coded black, ornamentally or otherwise, has been to this point extensive, even programmatic. The hunger artist is no different, especially when we recall that there were actual hunger artists, a fact of which Kafka was well aware, and that none of them wore black tights. They performed in street clothes. Breon Mitchell is thus correct in observing that "amazingly enough, almost every detail of 'A Hunger Artist' is historically accurate with regard to the actual profession of fasting for pay, from the beginnings of this strange occupation in 1880, down to 1922" (Mitchell 1987, 238). It is because Kafka was so accurate in his depiction of hunger artistry that the divergence in dress becomes striking. The solution to this riddle is not found if we posit that Kafka had no idea what a hunger artist actually looked like, or that this detail is too insignificant for comment. For these suppositions become untenable if, as Astrid Lange-Kirchheim suggests, "der 1896 in der Wochenzeitung 'Das interessante Blatt' in fünf Fortsetzungen erschienene und mit Fotoserien ausgestattete Bericht über den italienischen Hungerkünstler Giovanni Succi als möglicher Intertext vorgestellt werden soll" (the photo-series and a report about the Italian hunger artist, Giovanni Succi, that appeared in 1896 in the weekly newspaper *Das interessante Blatt*, in five parts, may also be seen as a possible source) (Lange-Kirchheim 1999 "Nachrichten," 11).The report, along with its extensive photo layout, is one Kafka would have been familiar with. But if he missed this opportunity, he had a chance to see a hunger artist in the flesh, in Vienna in 1917. Hannelore Rodlauer writes,

> Wahrscheinlich hat Kafka den hungernden Künstler selbst gesehen, als er im Sommer 1917 mit Rudolf Fuchs das Café "Central" besuchte, sicher aber die Zeitschrift *Der Friede* gelesen, wie wir aus den Briefen wissen. In der Weihnachtsausgabe vom 23. Dezember 1918 erschien dort ein Portrat des "verhungerten Dichters" aus der Feder Polgars und bereits am 6. Dezember ein anonym veröffentlichtes Gedicht *In memoriam Otfried Krzyzanowski* (von Georg Froschel). (Rodlauer 1989, 161)
>
> Kafka probably saw the starving artist with his own eyes when he went to Café Central with Rudolf Fuchs in the summer of 1917. And we know without doubt from his letters that he read the newspaper, *Der Friede*. A portrait by Polgar of the starving artist appeared in the Christmas edition of the newspaper of 23 December 1918 that had already published on 6 December an anonymous poem, "In memoriam of Otfried Krzyzanowski" (by Georg Froschel).

The hunger artist of Kafka's story is in all likelihood a composite figure of actual hunger artists, including Succi, and Krzyzanowski's hungering artist. Unlike these hunger artists, however, Kafka's hunger artist wears a "uniform" that is a black second skin more real to him than his own hide (*Kaf*).[6] The idea that what Kafka's characters are wearing is of trifling importance is a myth that was dispelled some time ago. And when linked to, in "Strafkolonie," the skin-blackening, racially signifying machine as well as all the elements of discursive racial transformation that precede it, including the recapitulation of society's victory over cannibalism represented in the hunger artist's mythopoetic performance, the notion of the hunger artist in a black second skin, in the absence of any historical precedent, warrants serious consideration along the lines of race.[7]

For as serious as it must be to watch a man reduce himself to a pile of skin, in Kafka's story hunger artistry was what "für die Erwachsenen oft nur ein Spaß war, an dem sie der Mode halber teilnahmen, sahen die Kinder staunend, mit offenem Mund, der Sicherheit halber einander bei der Hand haltend" (*D* 334) (for their elders he was often just a joke that happened to be in fashion, but the children stood openmouthed, holding each other's hands for greater security [*C* 268]). Here we witness the same order of gesture as that of the spectators at an execution in the penal colony watching someone's skin be permanently blackened, or the reactions of adults and children at a widely attended lynching.[8] Children join hands, are held, and understand. The spectacle of the work of art communicates on a preverbal or infantile level that in part responds to an emaciated black body. Children can perceive the work's precognitive import, if only as horror.[9] The children hold on to one another, extend their bodies, and affirm their unity in multiplicity, their communal being over and against the dying black body.[10] In this sense, the hunger artist performs his own lynching. Kafka returns to Holitscher's horrific photos in order to explore the communal ritual to which they led and give Karl Roßmann his ending. The Nature Theater of Oklahama becomes a troupe of one.The work of hunger art's public function as lynching affirms communal being through negation. The pain and isolation of the artist and his work mandate a combining and coalescing of the white bodies of spectators. In doing so, the spectators identify with one another as a structurally coherent community of like individuals.[11] This identification was taken to the point of cannibalism at one remove, as a lynching was often either accompanied or followed by communal barbecues, and pieces of the dead (and sometimes living) victim's body were passed around and eventually kept as souvenirs.[12] Photos and postcards, like the ones in Holitscher's book, were either kept as mementos or sent to friends and loved ones as signs of affection and communal belonging. But no identification is possible with the radical alterity of the victim. Because of this, each member of the (white) audience is not subject to transformation into the exogamous black other (Patterson 169–232).

Of course, a martyr is not the same thing, strictly speaking, as a victim of a lynching. And while there is no disputing this, the situation of the hunger artist as martyr and victim is unique and prefigured in Kafka in his thinking on recapitulation, lynching, and the Ugandan martyrs, as shown above, and in Karl Roßmann. Karl willingly identifies with African Americans. He chooses to be black. In his way, the hunger artist does this as well, and in so doing he collapses, for his otherwise idiosyncratic situation, the difference between lynching and martyrdom. Instead of selling his soul for power and clarity, the hunger artist purchases an ideal of racial disenfranchisement and pious imprisonment in his *Käfig*, and in death. Kafka is not making a political statement here in the way later representations of murdered civil rights workers would. And the hunger artist is no saint. With "Ein Hungerkünstler" Kafka is not taking up the Negro cause or making a religious statement. Although he is using blacks to represent antisemitic persecution and postcolonial displacement, in his later writings he is primarily interested in the Negro as the embodied yet emblematic rendering of art's illegibility in the administered and at the same time senselessly violent world. Guided by this aesthetic ideal, the hunger artist's body conforms to a metaphorical, conceptual appropriation of slavery's legacy, just as the officer's body conforms to his ideal of justice. A black skin contingently announces this ideal.

The body of the artist transforms into the black embodiment of an aesthetic principle because it has no other way to identify itself as art. Recapitulative transformation is the expression of the black aesthetic ideal as material fact. Once the transformation of the black body into the aesthetic ideal is completed, it, as aesthetic ideal, returns to its proper realm, that of pure (belly) thought. The black body of the artist as martyr and victim thus belongs a priori to its aesthetic ideal exactly as, and over and against, the manner in which the individual belongs to the crowd. Martyrdom here denotes the dying for, into, and as the art form demanded of the black aesthetic subject that Kafka created five years before writing "Ein Hungerkünstler." What he could not see at the time was that such a death would be both martyrdom and murder, and that it could have no satisfying conclusion. The time of this martyrdom is endless (Becker 2010, 105).[13]

III. *Märtyrer*

Just as in the case of the ex-*Ausstellungsneger* suffering from unnamable *Heimweh*, the hunger artist's *Käfig* displacement marks the drive to dissipate, to waste away, bringing with it a vague sense of melancholy:

> Und wenn sich einmal ein Gutmütiger fand, der ihn bedauerte und ihm erklären wollte, daß seine Traurigkeit wahrscheinlich von dem Hungern käme, konnte es, besonders bei vorgeschrittener Hungerzeit, geschehn, daß der Hungerkünstler mit einem Wutausbruch antwortete und zum Schrecken aller wie ein Tier an dem Gitter zu rütteln begann. (*D* 341)
>
> And if some good-natured person, feeling sorry for him, tried to console him by pointing out that his melancholy was probably caused by fasting, it could happen, especially when he had been fasting for some time, that he reacted with an outburst of fury and to the general alarm began to shake the bars of his cage like a wild animal. (*C* 272)

After the performance, feeling the melancholy most acutely, the hunger artist is sometimes "consoled" by a spectator who opines that the physical effects of starvation cause depression. The hunger artist rejects this interpretation, lashing out in fury at the bars of his cage, rattling them *wie ein Tier*. The suggestion is that the hunger artist's melancholy, and so his dissatisfaction, is caused by the detrimental effects of self-starvation, which bring about a radical change in his demeanor. The moment of the artist's rage marks a readable sign of the conflict inherent in his art (Neumann 1986, 47). Unable to pose the question of their interpretation properly, ritual starvation and rage become responses to the hunger artist's dissatisfaction with discursive cannibalistic meaning. Akin to the madness of the ex-*Ausstellungsneger*, they are means to a black aesthetic end that reveal themselves slowly to the hunger artist during his gradual disappearance. That is to say, melancholy precedes self-starvation. The hunger artist starves himself because he is a melancholic. To place melancholy after the fact of self-starvation is to deny the entire performance in its aesthetic drives, its (un)interpretability, and its origin as critique of and care for the cultural logic of cannibalism—which is precisely what his audience does.

The suggestion of self-starvation as cause of melancholy and not vice versa betrays the fact that the spectator has not seen what she has seen. Named in this is the very reason why the hunger artist's performance is misread and subsequently misunderstood as purely, individually atavistic. The supposition of melancholy after the fact individualizes the hunger artist's act, thus missing the communal narrative his body relates. The historical overcoming of cannibalism is replaced with a case study of a disturbed individual as the audience turns a blind eye to its potentially recidivist cannibalism. The audience, then, has not understood the spectacle as the attempt to sate a greater hunger, a hunger beyond hunger:

> Wenn die Zeugen solcher Szenen ein paar Jahre später daran zurückdachten, wurden sie sich oft selbst unverständlich. Denn inzwischen war jener erwähnte Umschwung eingetreten; fast plötzlich war das geschehen; es mochte tiefere Gründe haben, aber wem lag daran, sie aufzufinden; jedenfalls sah sich eines Tages der verwöhnte Hungerkünstler von der vergnügungssüchtigen Menge verlassen, die lieber zu anderen Schaustellungen strömte. (*D* 342)

> A few years later when the witnesses of such scenes called them to mind, they often failed to understand themselves at all. For meanwhile the aforementioned change in public interest had set in; it seemed to happen almost overnight; there may have been profound causes for it, but who was going to bother about that; at any rate the pampered hunger artist suddenly found himself deserted one fine day by the amusement-seekers, who went streaming past him to other more-favored attractions. (C 273)

Thus the hunger artist also has a filial relation to Gregor Samsa, in that the nourishment that he yearns for cannot be obtained by eating. Indeed, the refusal to eat is the means by which to attain nourishment in the greater sense while simultaneously rejecting Noahic authority. The act of self-starvation is the by-product of hunger. The hunger artist, then, is an artist in the sense that he starves himself and in so doing makes a work of art out of his body in the performance (or nonperformance) of self-starvation. Hunger and melancholy are *the* creative drives and as such exist outside the realm of Noahic power and bourgeois hermeneutic control (the logic of cannibalism). Any true art will always suffer the fate of being misread, misrecognized, and ultimately ignored, because it exists outside the field of a given audience's critical-aesthetic vision, *which is its appetite or desire to be subject to Noahic authority*.

In this sense, every true artist is in effect a hunger artist. It is this hunger that qualifies the artist as such in terms of that which drives her to create. The animal fury of the artist comes from the essential misunderstanding of the work itself, not from the creative drive. Recapitulative bestial fury (the hunger artist's rage) is the inner strength required to execute the work, to transform the body and in so doing pass through blackness; and it is created and fueled by the audience's necessary misinterpretation, or misreading, of the performance. This misreading is essential to the completion of the work as recapitulative transformation, because without it the artist cannot muster the strength in rage to go on. When the hunger artist loses his audience's suspicion, doubt, and even ridicule, his work as transformation grinds to a halt in that the effects of its critique are no longer felt.[14]

This unbearable dissatisfaction with the melancholic, isolated self leads to the desire, or hunger, to become other—a process of subjective transformation realized through and as the disappearing black body and objectively validated by a community as it rejects, or lynches, the new being. The ex-*Ausstellungsneger*'s attempt to reintegrate fails because of the "performer's" now mixed cultural disposition. The hunger artist is also denied this communal integration, leaving him to face either untransfigured death or to remain mere bestial bare life. The curse of Noah cannot be broken. Or, as Jahraus writes,

> Die Tragik des Hungerkünstlers besteht darin, die körperliche Beglaubigung seiner Kunst nicht mehr sozial vermitteln zu können. Die Folge ist ein Auseinanderdriften der Sphären. Je mehr er hungert, umso weniger Aufmerksamkeit findet er, umso mehr wird er zum Tier. . . . Es ist also das Tier, das diesen extremen Endpunkt einer ästhetischen, einer körperlichen und einer sozialen Entwicklung zum Ausdruck bringt. (Jahraus 2008, 539)

> The tragedy of the hunger artist consists in the bodily belief in the impossibility of being still able to transmit his art socially. The result is separation of these two spheres. The more he starves, the less attention he finds and the more he becomes an animal (. . .) It is thus the animal that is expressed by this extreme terminus of an aesthetic, an embodiment and a social development.

Instead of embracing the radical otherness of the work of art, as did Roßmann, Bendemann, and Samsa, the officer, Rotpeter, and the hunger artist wish to be acknowledged as great artists. But by the very radical otherness of race and art that allows them to transform and gain an audience, their aesthetic projects are doomed to failure.[15] Melancholy ensues again. The choice that they are left with is either to repeat the process or perish.

To die as such is to die "like a dog," as Josef K. did, or as a beast caught between states of becoming, furious.[16] The fury of the animal is the violence of melancholy; yet it is ultimately impotent violence (he shakes his cage, not the body of the spectator), which acknowledges, formally, failure and so gives rise to the new attempt. The animal in its cage marks the stage after having become Negro and the starting point of every doomed attempt to complete the work as transformation and Noahic critique, a vicious cycle that can only end, no longer as disappearance, but in death. Thus here we find that the presence of the cannibalistically determined and so uncomprehending spectator is in fact a creative drive and a death sentence; it is the ultimate hindrance to the successful completion of the work and a necessary element of the work's initial and final movement as critique of the cultural logic of cannibalism. For the work to end, if not succeed, the spectator must understand the work of art in all its aspects. This being impossible, the audience leaves.

Eventually, no one returns for the new performance. In the earlier years of his performances, when some comprehension of the communal stakes still abided, the spectators at least returned at the end of the fast to cast a judgment:

> In der ersten Zeit hatte er die Vorstellungspausen kaum erwarten können; entzückt hatte er der sich heranwälzenden Menge entgegengesehn, bis er sich nur zu bald—auch die hartnäckigste, fast bewußte Selbsttäuschung hielt den Erfahrungen nicht stand—davon überzeugte, daß es zumeist der Absicht nach, immer wieder, ausnahmslos, lauter Stallbesucher waren. Und dieser Anblick von der Ferne blieb noch immer der schönste. Denn wenn sie bis zu ihm herangekommen waren, umtobte ihn sofort Geschrei und Schimpfen der ununterbrochen neu sich bildenden Parteien, jener, welche—sie wurde dem Hungerkünstler bald die peinlichere—ihn bequem ansehen wollte, nicht etwa aus Verständnis, sondern aus Laune und Trotz, und jener zweiten, die zunächst nur nach den Ställen verlangte. War der große Haufe vorüber, dann kamen die Nachzügler, und diese allerdings, denen es nicht mehr verwehrt war, stehenzubleiben, solange sie nur Lust hatten, eilten mit langen Schritten, fast ohne Seitenblick, vorüber, um rechtzeitig zu den Tieren zu kommen. (*D* 345)

> At first he could hardly wait for the intervals; it was exhilarating to watch the crowds come streaming his way, until only too soon—not even the most obstinate self-deception, clung to almost consciously, could hold out against the fact—the conviction was borne in upon

> him that these people, most of them, to judge from their actions, again and again, without exception, were all on their way to the menagerie. And the first sight of them from the distance remained the best. For when they reached his cage he was at once deafened by the storm of shouting and abuse that arose from the two contending factions, which renewed themselves continuously, of those who wanted to stop and stare at him—he soon began to dislike them more than the others—not out of real interest but only out of obstinate self-assertiveness, and those who wanted to go straight to the animals. (C 274–75)

Overcoming suspicion and horror, the spectator returns to the scene of the self-starvation to close the subject of the hunger artist, to bring closure to the trauma of his presence, but not to that of her own communal, cannibalistic past. In doing so, the spectator, just as Kafka's country doctor, is called upon to suture a wound that cannot be closed. The spectator attempts to force a fitting end to an ongoing process, thus unleashing animal rage. Representing the stages of recapitulation now simultaneously, Kafka's animal and insatiable hunger artist are now identical, fused with narratives of outrages against blacks. The presence of the animal posits a quasi-evolutionary scale that marks off various stages of hunger transformation as perpetual, simultaneous racial recapitulation.

All this passes, barely perceptible, before the spectator; and when, after an epochal shift brought about by her lack of understanding, the spectator no longer comes, the hunger artist in his cage is rightfully put close to the animals. The hunger artist finds himself where he belongs: in and as a *Völkerschau*. Indeed, his body itself has come to embody the very idea of the *Völkerschau*. In this way, the story poses, as Günter Saße writes, the topical question, "Ist die Kunst eine autonome Sphäre, die vom Leben abgelost ist, oder verbindet sie sich auf spezifische Weise mit dem Leben, und wenn ja, welche Voraussetzungen muss die Kunst erfüllen, damit sie für die Menschen bedeutsam werden kann?" (Is art an autonomous sphere that has been totally separated from life, or does art combine in a certain way with life and if it does, what are the conditions that art must meet in order for it to become meaningful for human beings?) (Saße 2007, 246). Knowing the correct answer is to be found in the latter half of the question but unable to devise the proper *Voraussetzungen* that would make the work of art intelligible to his audience, the hunger artist chooses the *Völkerschau* as that fusion of life and art. No longer the main attraction, the work of the hunger artist begins to be an autonomous one-man *Völkerschau*. By letting go of any concern for the world, for the audience, the hunger artist is "free" to be an indigenous yet displaced tribal society, as well as the prehistory of that society, unto himself. The hunger artist eschews human freedom as illusion and embraces the *Ausweg* of Rotpeter—who was also a one-man *Völkerschau*—a choice made possible by a process of recapitulation that passes through a stage of being Negro as *Ausstellungsneger*. Abandoning the judgment of the spectator as the instigation of the rage necessary to do the work of transformation (recapitulation), the hunger artist fatefully seeks acknowledgment using animal instinct. This is why his art in the new order is perceived as bestial: because it is purely instinctual and oriented solely toward its own survival in a human zoo.

CONCLUSION

While describing his oppression at the table due to his father's strict rules and, hypocritically, unseemly eating habits, Kafka paints a picture of the three worlds that became his reality as an effect of Hermann Kafka's dominant personality:

> Dadurch wurde die Welt für mich in drei Teile geteilt, in einen, wo ich, der Sklave, lebte, unter Gesetzen, die nur für mich erfunden waren und denen ich überdies, ich wußte nicht warum, niemals völlig entsprechen konnte, dann in eine zweite Welt, die unendlich von meiner entfernt war, in der Du lebtest, beschäftigt mit der Regierung, mit dem Ausgeben der Befehle und mit dem Ärger wegen deren Nichtbefolgung, und schließlich in eine dritte Welt, wo die übrigen Leute glücklich und frei von Befehlen und Gehorchen lebten. (*BV* 12–13)

> Hence the world was for me divided into three parts: one in which I, the slave, lived under laws that had been invented only for me and which I could, I did not know why, never completely comply with; then a second world, which was infinitely remote from mine, in which you lived, concerned with government, with the issuing of orders and with the annoyance about their not being obeyed; and finally a third world where everybody else lived happily and free from orders and from having to obey. (*LTF* 183)

This model of Kafka's universe is in effect exactly what this study has mapped. Indeed, there is no clearer image of Hamic crisis than Kafka's three worlds, with Noahic patriarchal power as the gravitational center and the slave cursed to be beholden to its pull while at the same time pushing back. Others are free to live self-directed lives, but the slave son is caught in the impossible situation. "Slave" (*Sklave*) has been figuratively transformed into the triadic model of Hamic crisis Kafka lays out for us in his work; it signifies the son cursed Africanicity for seeing something he ought not to have—in this case, his father's hypocrisy laid bare. Spiritually blackened to match his swarthy skin, the son is condemned in perpetuity to a life dictated by the whims of Noahic authority. In other words, Kafka put this very scheme, this scene of slavery realized at the table, into aesthetic praxis. Through the figurative appropriation of blacks considered as the progenitors of slaves and the carriers of a patriarchal malediction, Kafka constructs an aesthetic of racial transformation premised upon and undermining black stereotypes. It is a reflection that first fully displays its "Negergesicht," to quote Felice, as Karl Roßmann voices the parameters of his racial pantomime, his black performance.

Jack Greenberg has suggested that "nothing explicit is made of the name (the incomplete or partially lost text is fragmentary) but for someone in search of connections, Karl Roßmann's unhappy travels raise the image of American racial experience, which in many ways is Kafkaesque. It is likely, of course, that Kafka, personally affected by anti-Semitism and deeply interested in Zionism, readily equated the two groups" (Greenberg 2008, 368). Greenberg voices the most current critical understanding of Kafka's use of the word "Negro" in *Der Verschollene*. This argument sees the appearance of "Negro" as Kafka making a connection between the racial injustices suffered by African Americans and those experienced by Jews, and projects coming racial misery for Karl Roßmann (Zilcosky 2003). While this is undoubtedly the instigation for Kafka's initial appropriation of the term and of the racial discourse of not just American but also European antiblack racism, it does not define what this appropriation became in Kafka's writings. Greenberg takes "Negro" seriously but, like contemporary criticism surrounding the figure, takes it only so far. So while Greenberg makes important connections to American legal-racial history, he limits the scope of all possible connections between Kafka and blackness by fixing them impressively and entirely in the American context.

While this way of reading Negro in *Der Verschollene* is correct and even obligatory, it should not obfuscate Kafka's wider claims on blackness. What I hoped to have shown with this book is that these connections, or correspondences, are far more wide-ranging and complex in Kafka's oeuvre and cannot be so easily localized. This localization is also at work when Negro is viewed at bottom as a stand-in for Jewishness. The dual tendency to equate racial discourse in Kafka exclusively with antisemitism and to limit the role of Negro, blacks, and blackness in Kafka to a subsidiary of this important concern is understandable but also incomplete.

Indeed, blackness took on a life of its own for Kafka from the very early stages of his writing. The initial connection Kafka makes to blackness is no doubt as, if not an analogical, then a homological discourse to that of antisemitism. But blackness quickly becomes for Kafka a way of expressing artistic aspiration and the ontological ground of the artist in its own right while attempting, metaphorically, to construe and configure the artist's position in a society inimical to what he felt the artist essentially was. Negro is the unveiling of this discursive task, but it is not its beginning. "Das Urteil" already considers the legacy of Noah's curse—a tropological element present in "Beschreibung eines Kampfes." And Negro names *Die Verwandlung*'s *Käfer* in Prague German—*Die Verwandlung* being the very work he broke off writing *Der Verschollene* to begin. "In der Strafkolonie" is defined by the colonial encounter inherent in deportation. The *Menschenaffe* Rotpeter is an embodied epitaph for Africans. His story is as much a schematic take on a slave's narrative as it is a kidnapped *Völkerschau* African's journey. And "Ein Hungerkünstler" is at its core a profound meditation on black cannibalism and atavism at the heart of so-called civilization.

These connections extend well beyond the borders of *Amerika*. As noted above, Zilcosky's reading of Negro within the context of lynching, while perhaps too much at variance with *Der Verschollene*'s overall tone, is the trajectory followed by Negro as he travels throughout Kafka's oeuvre. The stakes and implications of Kafka's choice to align his aesthetic with this racial disposition form a foregone conclusion. Whereas Kafka in his earlier works does not seem to have fully integrated the various outcomes inhering in Negro, by the time of "In der Strafkolonie" it is clear that art as Negro in the world is bound for a violent end. Kafka's innovation is to transform this "fate" into a choice, a martyrdom. In doing so, Kafka's Negro transcends the site of his original manifestation and surpasses any localized reading of his place in Kafka's world. Negro is not merely an American phenomenon in Kafka's work. Having gone underground, Negro resurfaces time and again under various guises, and is always present, shaping an aesthetic that relies on concepts of race as a means of evading them. In this sense, what Negro calls on us to do as readers is to see blackness in the shadows of an entire body of work. Negro is more than a joke or an irresponsible invocation of American communal racial violence and scapegoating; and he is more than a mask donned as another way to perform Jewishness. He exists for himself, in himself, in Kafka's work in any context the writer deemed fit. The critical task in addressing this figuration throughout Kafka's work begins with our openness to the possibility of Negro as a defining characteristic of his aesthetic.

Clayton Koelb has recently written that "there are just too many Kafkas to be encompassed in a single editorial perspective. The 'real' Franz Kafka is never going to stand up" (Koelb 2006, 31). The question forms the heart of his introduction to *A Companion to the Works of Franz Kafka* (Rolleston 2002). The collection of essays brings together the finest Kafka scholars, each dealing with themes that have been the most important to the field over the past twenty years or so. What is striking about these essays aside from how good they are is precisely what Koelb gets at in his question. Essays this convincing can be not only at odds with one another but also not the final word. Of course, one knows better than to listen for the final word when in critical dialogue with any artist's work. But Kafka's oeuvre defies even something like basic critical consensus.

I began this book with a defense of postcolonial approaches to Kafka, asserting that several different ways of reading his work could happily coexist in a single essay or monograph. To expand on this, I would suggest that

Kafka's texts demand an open methodology and a varied theoretical palette. In suggesting this it may seem that I believe that through even more interdisciplinary work we will get to the "real Kafka" and that monochromatic critical appraisals have prevented this. In fact, there is no real Kafka to get to. If decades and thousands of essays and books on Kafka have us still posing Koelb's question, the truth of the matter is that there is no definitive truth of the matter. There are, however, local truths. And it would seem that as soon as we uncover one such truth, another territory opens up for us to deterritorialize. The future of Kafka studies is the proliferation of Kafkas, each one rising and falling in its truth on the bases of the constant reappraisal of the objective evidence at hand and the force of critical blindness and insight. Stanley Corngold's and Ruth V. Gross's 2011 edited volume *Kafka for the Twenty-First Century* might give us a glimpse of the Kafkas to come. The volume's essays, all of the highest caliber, are diverse in their approach, each representing an approach to Kafka that is considered new and promising. But a critical volume is always in itself a testament to an established field. And just as each essay follows its particular critical trajectory, what we don't find in the volume are essays that are studies of Kafka studies. In essence, this is what introductions are for; but they do not treat the volume they introduce critically, and rightfully so. Such is not the point of such collections, which exist to present an objective overview of a body of contributions to public knowledge. This is not to criticize the particular volume in question, which is interdisciplinary and self-reflexive in the sense that the essays taken as a whole present a wide range of critical perspectives, all of which are conscious of their publication setting. Nor is it to call for a proliferation of *Jahr-* and *Handbücher*, despite how invaluable they are. Instead I am thinking about the extent to which Kafka studies would profit from establishing a subfield devoted entirely to the study of Kafka studies. By this I do not mean the occasional essay and introduction on the state of the art. In an ideal critical engagement, such a subfield would rigorously keep track of the various, rapidly expanding Kafkas being reproduced and periodically synthesize them into something like a coherent, unified being. What this body of work, in dialogue with itself as much as with the larger field of Kafka studies, would also do is show us the extent to which a unified field theory of Kafka is impossible.

In so doing, the base critical consensus would become not simply that this consensus is not possible but also that we are always already operating under tacit assumptions about Kafka that in fact do form a base consensus that presumes a "real" Kafka. My point here is that while there is no definitive Kafka worked out in fine, there is nevertheless a set of assumptions about him and his work to which Kafka studies adhere. And while I am not proposing that a self-analysis open Kafka studies to anarchy, if we are to have a Kafka studies "for the twenty-first century" beyond mere facticity and in the true, "new" sense of that rhetorical gesture, then it is going to require a rethinking of not only who Kafka was and what he wrote about but also of who we are as critics and what we will allow Kafka to have written about.

If Corngold and Gross's volume is any indication of what to expect, then we are obviously moving in the right direction. For the question is not only, who was the real Kafka? It is also, whose Kafka is it? It goes without saying that Kafka himself defies not just the answer to this question but also the very notion that it should be asked. This may seem polemical. But any book that presents the reader with "the black Kafka" is bound to engage, simply by the fact of what it is, in polemic. But my intention here is simply to note that, while it is impractical and indeed impossible to imagine a fully integrated Kafka, we can counterbalance this shortcoming by proliferating ever new Kafkas.

NOTES

Introduction

1. See, for example, John Zilcosky, *Kafka's Travels: Exoticism, Colonialism, and the Traffic of Writing* (New York: Palgrave, 2003); Rolf J. Goebel, "Kafka and Postcolonial Critique: *Der Verschollene*, 'In der Strafkolonie,' 'Beim Bau der chinesischen Mauer,'" in *A Companion to the Works of Franz Kafka*, ed. James *Rolleston*, 187–212 (Rochester, N.Y.: Camden House, 2002), and his *Constructing China: Kafka's Orientalist Discourse* (Columbia, S.C.: Camden House, 1997); and Gerhard Neumann, *Verfehlte Anfänge und offenes Ende: Franz Kafkas poetische Anthropologie* (Munich: Siemens Stiftung, 2011).

2. See Peter Becher, Steffen Höhne, and Marek Nekula, eds., *Kafka und Prag: Literatur-, kultur-, sozial- und sprachhistorische Kontexte* (Cologne: Böhlau, 2012). See also Stanley Corngold, Jack Greenberg, and Benno Wagner, eds., *Franz Kafka: The Office Writings* (Princeton, N.J.: Princeton University Press, 2008).

3. On Pound, Eliot, and black dialect, see *Michael North, The Dialect of Modernism: Race, Language and Twentieth-Century Literature* (New York: Oxford University Press, 1994). For Apollinaire and primitivism, see Katia Samaltanos, *Apollinaire, Catalyst for Primitivism, Picabia, and Duchamp* (Ann Arbor, Mich.: UMI Research Press, 1984).

4. Robert C. Toll, *Blacking Up: The Minstrel Show in Nineteenth-Century America* (New York: Oxford University Press, 1974).

5. Eric Lott, *Love and Theft: Blackface Minstrelsy and the American Working Class* (New York: Oxford University Press, 1995); Karen Sotiropoulos, *Staging Race: Black Performers in Turn of the Century America* (Cambridge, Mass.: Harvard University Press, 2006); and Marc A. Bauch, *"Gentlemen, Be Seated!": The Rise and Fall of the Minstrel Show* (Munich: Grin, 2012).

6. Tricia Rose, Black Noise: Rap Music and Black Culture in Contemporary America (Hanover, N.H.: University Press of New England / Wesleyan University Press, 1984).

7. Gabi Eißenberger, *Entführt, verspottet und gestorben: Lateinamerikanische Völkerschauen in deutschen Zoos* (Frankfurt: IKO, 1996); Hilke Thode-Arora, *Für fünfzig Pfennig um die Welt: Die Hagenbeckschen Völkerschauen* (Frankfurt: Campus, 1989); Günther H. W. Niemeyer, *Hagenbeck: Geschichte und Geschichten* (Hamburg: Christians, 1972).

8. Werner Michael Schwarz, *Anthropologische Spektakel: Zur Schaustellung "exotischer" Menschen, Wien 1870–1910* (Vienna: Turia and Kant, 2001).

9. Nicolas Bancel, Pascal Blanchard, and Sandrine Lemaire, "Menschenzoos als Instrument der Kolonialpropaganda," *Le Monde diplomatique*, August 11, 2000, 16–17; Sibylle Benninghoff-Lühl, "Die Ausstellung der Kolonialisierten:

Völkerschauen 1874–1932," in *Andenken an den Kolonialismus: Eine Ausstellung des Völkerkundlichen Instituts der Universität Tübingen*, ed. Volker Harms, 52–65 (Tübingen: Attempto, 1984); Bernhard Gißibl, "Imagination and Beyond: Cultures and Geographies of Imperialism in Germany, 1848–1918," in *European Empires and the People: Popular Responses to Imperialism in France, Britain, the Netherlands, Belgium, Germany and Italy*, ed. John MacKenzie, 158–98 (Manchester: Manchester University Press, 2001); Utz Anhalt, "Tiere und Menschen als Exoten: Exotisierende Sichtweisen auf das 'Andere' in der Gründungs- und Entwicklungsphase der Zoos" (Ph.D. diss., Leibniz Universität Hannover, 2007); Anne Dreesbach, *Gezähmte Wilde: Die Zurschaustellung "exotischer" Menschen in Deutschland 1870–1940* (Frankfurt: Campus, 2005); Angelika Friederici, *Völker der Welt auf Castans Bühnen*, no. 10 (D3) of *Castan's Panopticum: Ein Medium wird besichtigt* (Berlin: Verlag Karl-Robert Schütze, 2011); Susann Lewerenz, "Völkerschauen und die Konstituierung rassifizierter Körper," in *Marginalisierte Körper: Beiträge zur Soziologie und Geschichte des anderen Körpers*, ed. Torsten Junge and Imke Schmincke, 135–53 (Münster: Unrast, 2007).

10. See Anne Fausto-Sterling, "Gender, Race, and Nation: The Comparative Anatomy of 'Hottentot' Women in Europe, 1815–1817," in *Deviant Bodies: Critical Perspectives on Difference in Science and Popular Culture*, ed. Jennifer Terry and Jacqueline Urla, 19–48 (Bloomington: Indiana University Press, 1995); Sander L. Gilman, "Black Bodies, White Bodies: Toward an Iconography of Female Sexuality in Late Nineteenth-Century Art, Medicine, and Literature," in *"Race," Writing, and Difference*, ed. Henry Louis Gates Jr. and Kwame Anthony Appiah, 223–61 (Chicago: University of Chicago Press, 1985); Z. S. Strother, "Display of the Body Hottentot," in *Africans on Stage: Studies in Ethnological Show Business*, ed. Bernth Lindfors, 1–61 (Bloomington: Indiana University Press, 1999). See also Patricia Hill Collins, *Black Sexual Politics: African Americans, Gender, and the New Racism* (New York: Routledge, 2005).

11. For a full account of Kafka and the Yiddish theater, see Evelyn Torton Beck, *Kafka and the Yiddish Theater: Its Impact on His Work* (Madison: University of Wisconsin Press, 1971).

12. See Sander L. Gilman, *Franz Kafka, the Jewish Patient* (New York: Routledge, 1995), 101–68.

13. For more of the second great corrsponence, see Malte Kleinwort, *Kafkas Verfahren: Literatur, Individuum und Gesellschaft im Umkreis von Kafkas Briefen an Milena* (Würzburg: Königshausen and Neumann, 2004).

14. Herbert Spencer, *The Principles of Psychology* (London: Longman, Brown, Green and Longmans, 1855).

Chapter 1

1. On Kafka and the association of sexuality with filth, see Frank Möbus, *Sünden-Fälle: Die Geschlechtlichkeit in Erzählungen Franz Kafkas* (Göttingen: Wallstein, 1994) 7–9; for a general reading of Kafka and the erotics of writing, see Detlef Kremer, *Kafka: Die Erotik des Schreibens; Schreiben als Lebensentzug* (Frankfurt: Athenäum, 1989).

2. As Peter Brandes notes, "Es ist nicht zufällig das Glück des Schreibens, das mit dem Versprechen des Eheglücks koinzidiert. Das Gute und das höchste Gut

der Literatur liegen einmal mehr in der Selbstbeziehung, in der Imagination des phantasierenden und schreibenden Subjekts" (It is no coincidence that the joy of writing coincides with the promise of marital bliss. The good and the highest Good of literature lies more in the relationship to the self, in the imagination of the fantasizing and writing subject) (Brandes 2008, 101).

3. A legitimate form of writing would be one sanctioned by bourgeois culture. "It is a culture," Berman writes, "in which self-interest has become congruent with betrayal: Georg's betrayal of his friend and the memory of his mother, as well as his disregard for his father. It is however above all a culture characterized by a degraded mode of writing . . . we learn that [Georg] is quite satisfied to generate texts intentionally devoid of substance and that he attempts to use language strategically in order to manipulate the reader" (Berman 2002, 97).

4. For an overview of the body in Kafka criticism, see Robert Sell, "Körper und Körperlichkeit bei Kafka im Spiegel der Forschung," in *Bewegung und Beugung des Sinns: Zur Poetologie des menschlichen Körpers in den Romanen Franz Kafkas*, 26–70 (Stuttgart: Metzler 2002); for a detailed analysis of the relationship between writing as the expression of the body and writing as expressive of the body, see Elisabeth Lack, *Kafkas bewegte Körper: Die Tagebücher und Briefe als Laboratorien von Bewegung* (Munich: Fink, 2009).

5. On the interplay of women and familial structure in "Urteil," see Karl-Bernhard Bödeker, *Frau und Familie im erzählerischen Werk Franz Kafkas* (Bern: Lang, 1974), 42–45.

6. On Kafka and power, see also Heinz-Peter Flocken, "Der 'Lüstling des Entsetzens': Franz Kafkas Protokolle der Macht" (Ph.D. diss., Heinrich Heine University, Düsseldorf, 1991).

7. For Kafka's literary appropriation of the Bible, see Bertram Rohde, "Kafkas Bibel," in *"Und blätterte ein wenig in der Bibel": Studien zu Franz Kafkas Bibellektüre und ihre Auswirkungen auf sein Werk*, 20–31 (Würzburg: Königshausen and Neumann, 2002).

8. See Ritchie Robertson, "Kafka as Anti-Christian: 'Das Urteil,' 'Die Verwandlung,' and the Aphorisms," in *A Companion to the Works of Franz Kafka*, ed. James Rolleston, 101–22 (Rochester, N.Y.: Camden House, 2002), in particular 104–7. For a more general exposition of Kafka's relation to Judaism and Zionism, see Ritchie Robertson, *Kafka: Judaism, Politics, and Literature* (Oxford: Clarendon Press, 1985); Karl Erich Grözinger, Stéphane Mosès, and Hans Dieter Zimmermann, eds., *Franz Kafka und das Judentum: Colloquium, das die Hebräische Universität Jerusalem und die Johann-Wolfgang-Goethe-Universität, Frankfurt im Dezember 1986 in Frankfurt veranstalteten* (Frankfurt: Jüdischer Verlag bei Athenäum, 1987); Karl Erich Grözinger, *Kafka und die Kabbala: Das Jüdische in Werk und Denken von Franz Kafka* (Frankfurt: Eichborn, 1992); Walter A. Strauss, *On the Threshold of a New Kabbalah: Kafka's Later Tales* (New York: Lang, 1988); Giuliano Baioni, *Kafka: Literatur und Judentum*, trans. into German by Gertrud Billen and Josef Billen (Stuttgart: Metzler, 1994); Gilman, *Jewish Patient*; Mark H. Gelber, *Kafka, Zionism, and Beyond* (Tübingen: Niemeyer, 2004); and Manfred Voigts, *Kafka und die jüdisch-zionistische Frau: Diskussionen um Erotik und Sexualität im Prager Zionismus; Mit Text-Materialien* (Würzburg: Königshausen and Neumann, 2007). The list could go on and on.

9. See Rolf J. Goebel, *Kritik und Revision: Kafkas Rezeption mythologischer, biblischer und historischer Traditionen* (Frankfurt: Lang, 1986).

10. For a discussion of hidden backgrounds in "Urteil," see Christian Eschweiler, *Kafkas Erzählungen und ihr verborgener Hintergrund* (Bonn: Bouvier, 1991), 19–38. Oddly, Noah is not mentioned.

11. On the "curse of Ham" and New World slavery, see Werner Sollors's definitive "The Curse of Ham; or, From 'Generation' to 'Race,'" in *Neither Black nor White Yet Both*, 78–111 (New York: Oxford University Press, 1997). See also David M. Goldenberg, *The Curse of Ham: Race and Slavery in Early Judaism, Christianity, and Islam* (Princeton, N.J.: Princeton University Press, 2005), 168–77, and, on the importance of skin color in the designation of slaves, 79–130.

12. Though I will not follow this line here, it should be noted that the friend in Russia is also an element of the story's exoticism. As Christine Kanz writes, "Der ferne, fremdartige, gelbgesichtige, vollbärtige, in Rußland lebende Freund verkörpert einerseits Abenteuer, Freiheit, Exotik. . . . Er repräsentiert also ein Bild 'wilder' und ursprünglicher Männlichkeit. Andererseits aber verweist sein Erscheinungsbild auf eine kranke und damit anti-typische Männlichkeit" (The distant, foreign, yellow-faced, full-bearded, friend living in Russia embodies on the one hand adventure, freedom and the exotic . . . he represents thus a picture of a wild and original masculinity. On the other hand, the character of his appearance shows at the same time a sick and abnormal masculinity) (Kanz 2002, 167). The friend is also linked to writing. As Paul Reitter reminds, "The friend is himself a story-teller, an Erzähler. Nonplussed by his father's unwillingness to acknowledge the existence of the friend, Georg reminds his father of the stories the friend told of life in Russia" (Reitter 2002, 135). In the friend, writing and exoticism combine.

13. In a journal entry of February 11, 1913, Kafka first describes the importance of the friend in Russia:

> Der Freund ist die Verbindung zwischen Vater und Sohn, er ist ihre größte Gemeinsamkeit. Allein bei seinem Fenster sitzend wühlt Georg in diesem Gemeinsamen mit Wollust, glaubt den Vater in sich zuhaben und hält alles bis auf eine flüchtige traurige Nachdenklichkeit für friedlich. Die Entwicklung der Geschichte zeigt nun, wie aus dem Gemeinsamen, dem Freund, der Vater hervorsteigt und sich als Gegensatz Georg gegenüber aufstellt, verstärkt durch andere kleinere Gemeinsamkeiten nämlich durch die Liebe, Anhänglichkeit der Mutter durch die treue Erinnerung an sie und durch die Kundschaft, die ja der Vater doch ursprünglich für das Geschäft erworben hat. (*T* 491–92)

> The friend is the link between father and son, he is their strongest common bond. Sitting alone at his window, Georg rummages voluptuously in this consciousness of what they have in common, believes he has his father within him, and would be at peace with everything if it were not for a fleeting, sad thoughtfulness. In the course of the story the father, with the strengthened position that the other, lesser things they share in common give him—love, devotion to the mother, loyalty to her memory, the clientele that he (the father) had been the first to acquire for the business. (*J* 214)

Here it would seem that the friend plays the decisive role in the text. However, Kafka later addressed the character of the friend in a letter to Felice of June 10, 1913, "der Freund ist kaum eine wirkliche Person, er ist vielleicht eher das, was dem Vater und Georg gemeinsam ist. Die Geschichte ist vielleicht ein Rundgang um Vater und Sohn, und die wechselnde Gestalt des Freundes ist vielleicht der perspektivische Wechsel der Beziehungen zwischen Vater und Sohn" (*BF* 397) (The friend is hardly a real person, perhaps he is more whatever the father and Georg have in common. The story may be a journey around father and son, and the friend's changing shape may be a change in perspective in the relationship between father and son [*LF* 267]).

The part played by the friend is no longer definitive. Kafka writes that the friend is "perhaps" this. Indeed, to press the point of uncertainty as to the role of the friend, he uses the word "vielleicht" here no fewer than three times. Certainly, the friend is of great importance to the struggle between father and son. But an author's own commentary on his work is no key to it, especially not in this case, where there is no certainty.

14. For the role of the father as God in Kafka, see Arno A. Gassmann, *Lieber Vater, lieber Gott? Der Vater-Sohn-Konflikt bei den Autoren des engeren Prager Kreises* (Oldenburg: Igel, 2002), 97–183.

15. Georg's father is invested with the same supreme authority Kafka gave to Hermann Kafka: "Für mich als Kind war aber alles, was Du mir zuriefst, geradezu Himmelsgebot, ich vergaß es nie, es blieb mir das wichtigste Mittel zur Beurteilung der Welt" (*BV* 12) (But for me as a child everything you called out at me was positively a heavenly commandment, I never forgot it, it remained for me the most important means of forming a judgment of the world [*LTF* 183]). Never able to forget that his father's word is the Law, Kafka continues as an adult to evaluate and judge the world according to "a heavenly commandment."

16. For a full interpretation of Kafka's correspondence with Felice, see Elias Canetti, *Der andere Prozeß: Kafkas Briefe an Felice* (Munich: Hanser, 1984).

17. The name Frieda Brandenfeld itself can be linked to that of Felice Bauer, Kafka's own fiancée with a "Negergesicht." For the connection between the names, see Elizabeth M. Rajec, *Namen und ihre Bedeutungen im Werke Franz Kafkas: Ein interpretatorischer Versuch* (Bern: Lang, 1977), 266–69.

18. The mode and movement of this chain are determined, as one critic has put it, by "the metalogical terms of identity, difference, and their synthesis, and correlatively around the rhetorical terms of metaphor, metonymy, and their fusion, respectively," and the "association of metaphor and metonymy with, respectively, condensation and displacement" (Librett 2007, 514). While language here is indeed productive of identity, I would say that "the rhetorical terms of metaphor, metonumy, and their fusion" happens first and foremost in the story as a fusion of bodies, which is what makes "Das Urteil" "perverse."

19. For a comprehensive study of Kafka's link between writing, birth, and the demonic, see Manfred Voigts, "Schreiben als Geburt," in *Geburt und Teufelsdienst: Franz Kafka als Schriftsteller und als Jude*, 47–74 (Würzburg: Königshausen and Neumann, 2008).

20. On death in "Urteil" as the only way out of an incomprehensible, aporetic situation, see Josef Hermann Mense, *Die Bedeutung des Todes im Werk Franz Kafkas* (Frankfurt: Lang, 1978), 42.

21. On the relationship between transcendence and death in "Urteil," see Hans Walther, *Franz Kafka: Die Forderung der Transzendenz* (Bonn: Bouvier, 1977), 48–53, 56–57.

Chapter 2

1. For a sustained study on the theater's role in the novel, see Alfred Borchardt, *Kafkas zweites Gesicht: Der Unbekannte; Das große Theater von Oklahoma* (Nuremberg: Glock and Lutz, 1960), and, for "die Negro-Episode," 154–63, 198.

2. James Creelman, "Dvořák's Negro Symphony," *Pall Mall Budget*, June 21, 1894.

3. I will retain the misspelling "Oklahama" throughout the text in referring to this theater.

4. On otherness and the other in Kafka in an African context, see Patrice Djoufack, *Der Selbe und der Andere: Formen und Strategien der Erfahrung der Fremde bei Franz Kafka* (Wiesbaden: Deutscher Universitäts-Verlag, 2005).

5. On writing and aesthetics with regard to "Negro" in Kafka's first novel, see Jörg Wolfradt, *Der Roman bin ich: Schreiben und Schrift in Kafkas "Der Verschollene"* (Würzburg: Königshausen and Neumann, 1996), 57, 152–54.

6. On ethnicity as social construction, see Joan Ferrante and Prince Browne Jr., *The Social Construction of Race and Ethnicity in the United States* (New York: Pearson, 2000); Arash Abizadeh, "Ethnicity, Race, and a Possible Humanity," *World Order* 33, no. 1 (2001): 23–34.

7. For the most comprehensive reading of the *Heizer* beginning of *Verschollene*, see Neumann, *Verfehlte Anfänge*, 42–50.

8. On Benjamin reading Kafka, see Sven Kramer, *Rätselfragen und wolkige Stellen: Zu Benjamins Kafka-Essay* (Lüneburg: Zu Klampen, 1991).

9. For more on *Wunsch, Indianer zu werden* and its relation to *Verschollene*, see Peter Henisch, *Vom Wunsch, Indianer zu werden: Wie Franz Kafka Karl May traf und trotzdem nicht in Amerika landete* (Salzburg: Residenz, 1994).

10. For more on this subject, see Mark Anderson, "Kafka and New York: Notes on a Traveling Narrative," in *Modernity and the Text: Revisions of German Modernism*, ed. Andreas Huyssen and David Bathrick, 142–61 (New York: Columbia University Press, 1989).

Chapter 3

1. Perhaps the most complete guide to *Die Verwandlung*'s inception, publication, and critical history is Hartmut Binder, *Kafkas "Verwandlung": Entstehung, Deutung, Wirkung* (Frankfurt: Stroemfeld, 2004). For a reading of Kafka's desire that an image of Gregor Samsa not be created as a form of negative theology, see Michael Schreiber, *"Ihr sollt euch kein Bild— . . .": Untersuchungen zur Denkform der negativen Theologie im Werk Franz Kafkas* (Frankfurt: Lang, 1986).

2. Another translation for *Mistkäfer* is "scarab," a creature rich in antique and non-Western mythological significance. As Michael Ryan shows, "Kafka knowingly utilized the insect which in Egyptian lore is the symbol for resurrection" (Ryan 1999, 147). For more on Kafka's Egyptian connection in *Verwandlung*, see Harald Bost, *Die Schrift mit den Augen: Kafkas ägyptische Rätsel* (Sulzbach: Kirsch, 2006), 19, 22. Thinking of the figure of the dung beetle in classical literature, Lewis Leadbeater opines, "the answer, perhaps, lies in the fact that the dung

beetle, especially as it appears in classical literature, has always been a creature of two dimensions. That is, the gross, ugly, and repulsive side of its physical nature is usually counterbalanced by a quasi-divine association, with the result that its entomological *katabasis* is, in a way, compensated for by a spiritual *anabasis* (Leadbeater 1986, 170).

3. For a Marxist reading, see Walter H. Sokel, "Von Marx zum Mythos: Das Problem der Selbstentfremdung in Kafkas 'Verwandlung,'" *Monatshefte* 73, no. 1 (1981): 6–22; on Kafka and existentialism, see Walter Kaufmann, *Existentialism from Dostoevsky to Sartre* (New York: Penguin, 1975), 142–51, and for Gregor Samsa as an insect in a strictly entomological sense, see Vladimir Nabokov, *Lectures on Literature* (New York: Mariner Books, 2002), 251–84.

4. For the thinking of the "father of racism," see Arthur Gobineau, *The Inequality of Human Races* (1853; repr., New York: Fertig, 1999); for scientific racism see Ernst Haeckel, *Anthropogenie; oder, Entwickelungsgeschichte des menschen* (Leipzig: Engelmann, 1874); for ethnological theories of sacrifice, sovereignty, and marginal figures, see James Frazer, *The Golden Bough: A Study in Magic and Religion* (London, 1890), and René Girard, *La violence et le sacré* (Paris: Grasset, 1972).

5. I am thinking again here of the previously referenced passages in Gilman.

6. For an analysis of the relationship between *Verwandlung* and *Venus im Pelz*, see Holger Rudloff, *Gregor Samsa und seine Brüder: Kafka, Sacher-Masoch, Thomas Mann* (Würzburg: Königshausen and Neumann, 1997), 15–35.

7. The father in this crisis instance is described as behaving like a *Wilder* and in this sense is akin to "savage" Gregor. The "savage one" for Kafka is a being who dwells in us all and who awakens out of dormancy in the moment of crisis, a concept he may have developed through seeing the Yiddish play by Yakov Gorin, *The Savage One*, starring Yitzhak Löwy. In the play, one character questions, "What—where is this savage one? A savage who observes our behavior and our ways is buried deep within each of us. . . . When we improve ourselves, when the spirit in us wakens, when our souls reign over our bodies, then the savage one within us sleeps. But when we strive only for material goals, when we have no ideals, when our spirit sleeps, then the savage one awakens and forces us to go against civilization, against the laws of humanity" (Beck 1971, 145).

In *Die Verwandlung*, the family crisis awakens the father-savage, but the savage here is a quality that the father will lose as the story progresses, as he improves himself and is brought into harmony with the laws of bourgeois social existence. Inversely, this savage inheritance is exactly what will become dominant in Gregor, insofar as he loses all the qualities the father will come to repossess.

The perception of the father as savage is not unheard of in Kafka's writings. One need only remember Kafka's description of his own father, Hermann, eating bones in *Brief an den Vater*:

> Was auf den Tisch kam, mußte aufgegessen, über die Güte des Essens durfte nicht gesprochen werden—Du aber fandest das Essen oft ungenießbar; nanntest es "das Fressen"—das "Vieh" (die Köchin) hatte es verdorben. Weil Du entsprechend Deinem kräftigen Hunger und Deiner besonderen Vorliebe alles schnell, heiß und in großen Bissen gegessen hast, mußte sich das Kind beeilen, düstere Stille war bei

Tisch, unterbrochen von Ermahnungen: "zuerst iß, dann sprich" oder "schneller, schneller, schneller" oder "siehst Du, ich habe schon längst aufgegessen." Knochen durfte man nicht zerreißen, Du ja. Essig durfte man nicht schlürfen, Du ja. Die Hauptsache war, daß man das Brot gerade schnitt; daß Du das aber mit einem von Sauce triefenden Messer tatest, war gleichgültig. Man mußte achtgeben, daß keine Speisereste auf den Boden fielen, unter Dir lag schließlich am meisten. Bei Tisch durfte man sich nur mit Essen beschäftigen, Du aber putztest und schnittest Dir die Nägel, spitztest Bleistifte, reinigtest mit dem Zahnstocher die Ohren. Bitte, Vater, verstehe mich recht, das wären an sich vollständig unbedeutende Einzelheiten gewesen, niederdrückend wurden sie für mich erst dadurch, daß Du, der für mich so ungeheuer maßgebende Mensch, Dich selbst an die Gebote nicht hieltest, die Du mir auferlegtest. Dadurch wurde die Welt für mich in drei Teile geteilt, in einen, wo ich, der Sklave, lebte, unter Gesetzen, die nur für mich erfunden waren und denen ich überdies, ich wußte nicht warum, niemals völlig entsprechen konnte, dann in eine zweite Welt, die unendlich von meiner entfernt war, in der Du lebtest, beschäftigt mit der Regierung, mit dem Ausgeben der Befehle und mit dem Ärger wegen deren Nichtbefolgung, und schließlich in eine dritte Welt, wo die übrigen Leute glücklich und frei von Befehlen und Gehorchen lebten. Ich war immerfort in Schande, entweder befolgte ich Deine Befehle, das war Schande, denn sie galten ja nur für mich; oder ich war trotzig, das war auch Schande, denn wie durfte ich Dir gegenüber trotzig sein, oder ich konnte nicht folgen, weil ich zum Beispiel nicht Deine Kraft, nicht Deinen Appetit, nicht Deine Geschicklichkeit hatte, trotzdem Du es als etwas Selbstverständliches von mir verlangtest; das war allerdings die größte Schande. (*BV* 12–13)

What was brought to the table had to be eaten, the quality of the food was not to be discussed—but you yourself often found the food inedible, called it "this swill," said "that beast" (the cook) had ruined it. Because in accordance with your strong appetite and your particular predeliction you ate everything fast, hot, and in big mouthfuls, the child had to hurry; there was a somber silence at the table, interrupted by admonitions: "Eat first, talk afterwards," or "faster, faster, faster," or "there you are, you see, I finished the eggs ages ago." Bones musn't be cracked with the teeth, but you could. The main thing was that the bread should be cut straight. But it didn't matter that you did it with a knife dripping with gravy. Care had to be taken that no scraps fell on the floor. In the end it was under your chair that there were the most scraps. At table one wasn't allowed to do anything but eat, but you cleaned and cut your fingernails, sharpened pencils, cleaned your ears with a toothpick. Please, Father, understand me correctly: in themselves these would have been utterly insignificant details, they only became depressing for me because you, so tremendously the authoritative man, did not keep the commandments you imposed on me. Hence the world was for me divided into three parts: one in which I, the slave, lived under laws that had been invented only for me and which I could, I did

> not know why, never completely comply with; then a second world, which was infinitely remote from mine, in which you lived, concerned with government, with the issuing of orders and with the annoyance about their not being obeyed; and finally a third world where everybody else lived happily and free form orders and from having to obey. I was continually in disgrace; either I obeyed your orders, and that was a disgrace, for they applied, after all, only to me; or I was defiant, and that was a disgrace too, for how could I presume to defy you; or I could not obey because I did not, for instance, have your strength, your appetite, your skill, although you expected it of me as a matter of course; this was the greatest disgrace of all. (*LTF* 182–83)

I will return to this quote in the conclusion. For more on the influence of Gordin's *The Savage One* on *Verwandlung*, see Evelyn Torton Beck, *Kafka and the Yiddish Theater: Its Impact on His Work* (Madison: University of Wisconsin Press, 1971), 135–46.

8. On writing as "a replacement for living, that was actually a mourning for not having lived," see Peter Mailloux, *A Hesitation before Birth: The Life of Franz Kafka* (Newark: University of Delaware Press, 1989), 509.

9. The seduction is powerful, overcoming any concern for the family's situation and the violence that was done to him the last time he ventured out of his prison. Gregor is, in any event, beyond such cares. The music is his nourishment. Yet Ingeborg Henel writes, "Keine von Kafkas drei Figuren findet die unbekannte Nahrung: Gregor und der Hungerkünstler sterben, und der Hund ist nahe daran zu verhungern. Aber alle drei erleben eine Art Ekstase, ein Außersichsein. . . . Die Frage ist, ob man die Idee von der unbekannten Nahrung nicht zu wörtlich genommen hat. Kafka hat ihr niemals konkrete Form gegeben, er handelt immer nur von der Sehnsucht oder dem Hunger nach ihr" (Not one of Kafka's three figures finds the unknown nourishment. Gregor and the Hunger Artist die, and the dog is very close to starvation. But all three experience a kind of art ecstasy, a feeling of being outside of themselves. The question is, if one takes the idea of the unknown nourishment too literally. Kafka never gave this nourishment concrete form. He indicated it always through longing or hunger) (Henel 74). Henel's point is well taken, with the proviso that the ecstasy that all three characters experience is indissolubly linked to a *black* aesthetic event. It is not only that they hunger for the idea of an unknown mode of nourishment but also that they understand this idea as bound to an aesthetic ideal that is conditioned by blackness.

10. For Nietzsche's influence on Kafka's *Amerika*, see Patrick Bridgwater, *Kafka and Nietzsche* (Bonn: Bouvier, 1987), 64.

11. On primitivism and European aesthetics, see Frances S. Connelly, *The Sleep of Reason: Primitivism in Modern European Art and Aesthetics, 1725–1907* (University Park: Pennsylvania State University Press, 1999).

12. For a history of ragtime, see Edward A. Berlin, *Ragtime: A Musical and Cultural History* (Los Angeles: University of California Press, 1980). For the early history of jazz, see Gunther Schuller, *Early Jazz: Its Roots and Musical Development* (New York: Oxford University Press, 1998).

13. For studies on blackface, see Eric Lott, *Love and Theft: Blackface Minstrelsy and the American Working Class* (New York: Oxford University Press,

1995); Annemarie Bean, James V. Hatch, and Brooks McNamara, eds., *Inside the Minstrel Mask: Readings in Nineteenth-Century Blackface Minstrelsy* (Hanover, N.H.: University Press of New England / Wesleyan University Press, 1996). On black music and the African American presence in Europe, see Heike Raphael-Hernandez, *Blackening Europe: The African American Presence* (New York: Routledge, 2004). For studies on the first exported American cultural product, see Michael Rogin, "Nowhere Left to Stand: The Burnt Cork Roots of Popular Culture," *Cineaste* 26, no. 2 (2001): 15; Ken Emerson, *Doo-Dah! Stephen Foster and the Rise of American Popular Culture* (New York: Da Capo Press, 1997).

14. See Jaromír Kazda and Josef Kotek, *Smích Èervené sedmy* (Prague: Československý spisovatel, 1981).

15. Gregor would be seeking something like art as a way of life, much like Kafka was. For an account of Kafka's understanding of writing as a way of life, see Joachim Unseld, *Franz Kafka: A Writer's Life*, trans. Paul F. Dvorak (Riverside, Calif.: Ariadne, 1997), 13–38.

Chapter 4

1. It is not beside the point to bear in mind that, as of 1914, Kafka himself began to feel like a prisoner because of his engagement to Felice, again giving a thematic connection between developments in Kafka's writing and shifts in his relationship to his fiancée. In a journal entry of June 6, 1914, just after celebrating his engagement to Felice in Berlin, Kafka writes that being engaged to be married felt to him as if he were "gebunden wie ein Verbrecher. Hätte man mich mit wirklichen Ketten in einen Winkel gesetzt und Gendarmen vor mich gestellt und mich nur auf diese Weise zuschauen lassen, es wäre nicht ärger gewesen" (*T* 528–29) (tied hand and foot like a criminal. Had they sat me down in a corner bound in real chains, placed policemen in front of me, and let me look on simply like that, it could not have been worse [*J* 275]). Given that 1914 is also the year in which Kafka wrote "In der Strafkolonie," it is tempting to see in the story an allegory for how he felt during the *Verlobungszeit*. Indeed, marriage seems to have loomed over Kafka's life as a spiritual death sentence. Writing to Greta Bloch in a letter of February 19, 1914, Kafka relates, "Mein letzter näherer, unverheirateter und unverlobter Freund (Felix Weltsch) hat sich verlobt; daß es zu dieser Verlobung kommen wird, wußte ich seit drei Jahren (es gehörte für den Unbeteiligten kein großer Scharfsinn dazu), er und sie aber erst seit 14 Tagen. Dadurch verliere ich allerdings gewissermaßen einen Freund, denn ein verheirateter ist keiner" (*BF* 503) [The last of my closer, unmarried, unengaged friends (Felix Weltsch) has got engaged; while I have foreseen this engagement for three years (for the outsider, no great perspicacity was required), he and she have known of it for a mere fortnight. Thus to some extent I am losing a friend, for a married friend isn't a true friend (*LF* 349)].

The interjection of the friend here recalls the friend in Russia, whose status as single was one of the many strikes against him in attempting to gain success in bourgeois society. But that success is exactly what Kafka has his artist characters, to say the least, avoid at all costs, as it is emblematic of one's inescapable imprisonment in the general economy of Noahic patriarchal power. One of the ways Kafka's artists avoid marriage is by revealing their utter unsuitability to the societal demands of the task. They are degenerate, perverse, Negro. Because of this, the artists are cast out or take flight into an uncertain "freedom."

2. On Kafka and punctuation, see Malcolm Pasley, "Zu Kafkas Interpunktion," in "*Die Schrift ist unveränderlich . . .": Essays zu Kafka*, 121–44 (Frankfurt: Fischer, 1995).

3. On crime and custom in "savage" society, see Bronislaw Malinowski, *Crime and Custom in Savage Society* (New York: Harcourt, Brace, 1926).

4. On doubles and fragmented subjectivity in Kafka's "Strafkolonie," see Andreas Töns, *"Nur mir gegenübergestellt": Ich-Fragmente im Figurenfeld; Reduktionsstufen des Doppelgängermotivs in Kafkas Erzählprosa* (Bern: Lang, 1998), 134–35.

5. For a canonical example of nineteenth-century criminology and its racial (racist) underpinnings, see Cesare Lombroso, *Crime: Its Causes and Remedies* (Boston: Little, Brown, 1911).

6. For a summation and rebuttal of this belief, see Walter Francis Willcox, "Negro Criminality," (Boston: G.H. Ellis,1899).

7. For a general study of Kafka and alienation and foreignness in a sociological-historical setting (as opposed to a mainly theoretical-philosophical one), see Uwe Jahnke, *Die Erfahrung von Entfremdung: Sozialgeschichtliche Studien zum Werk Franz Kafkas* (Stuttgart: Heinz, 1988).

8. On writing and the written as sacred in "Strafkolonie," see Christian Schärf, *Franz Kafka: Poetischer Text und heilige Schrift* (Göttingen: Vandenhoeck and Ruprecht, 2000), 96–107.

9. One could go so far as to suggest that Kafka saw the only end to the work of art as illegible yet irrefutable punishment. Attempting to explain the story to its publisher, Kurt Wolff, Kafka capitulates, writing on October 11, 1916, "Zur Erklärung dieser letzten Erzählung füge ich nur hinzu, daß nicht nur sie peinlich ist, daß vielmehr unsere allgemeine und meine besondere Zeit gleichfalls sehr peinlich war und ist und meine besondere sogar noch länger peinlich als die allgemeine" (*B* 150) (By way of clarifying this last story, I need only add that the painfulness is not peculiar to it alone but that our times in general and my own time as well have also been painful and continue to be, and my own even more consistently than the times [*L* 127]).

The passage, which seems to indicate dissatisfaction with and even embarrassment over the story, is mannerist in style, relying on repetition. The word *peinlich* is repeated three times, as if to drive the stake home. But aside from "embarrassing," *peinlich*, from *peinigen*, also carries the signification of "punish." "Allgemeine" and "besondere" are also repeated, creating a tension between the general and the specific, as if to say, either in a general or specific sense, the story means only punishment.

10. The end product, a dead, partially blackened body instead of a disappearance, thematizes the inability to finish a work of art. It is here that "Kafka lässt wissen, das seine solche Schrift nie unerreichbar von der 'Totschlägerreihe' aus sein kann" (Mladek 2006, 119). The work of art is now defined in part by its impossibility to be completed even and especially unto death. See Mladek, 119. For the process of transformation that engenders the work of art and that previously ended in death as metaphor for escape now disappears in death understood as finitude's sole horizon. Because there is no disappearance in apparent death, and no messianic afterlife, the work of art becomes impossible.

11. For a more general account of the shift in Kafka's poetics between *Der Proceß* and *Das Schloß*, and in particular in "Strafkolonie," see Waldemar Fromm,

Artistisches Schreiben: Franz Kafkas Poetik zwischen "Proceß" und "Schloß" (Munich: Fink, 1998), 29–37.

12. The ritual of the machine's writing is artistic process. This means that the work of art and the artist are fused in and as a dead black body. The photo of a lynched Negro reproduced in Holitscher that so impressed Kafka becomes generative of an incomprehensible but undeniable narrative (Kruse 1987, 248–49). The machine writes the story of judgment, which is in itself the judgment. To write is to judge, but outside any known or comprehensible system of law. It is a high-tech lynching.

Chapter 5

1. There are seemingly countless studies of animals in Kafka. For the seminal study of Kafka, in which Rotpeter is simply one animal figure among others, see Karl-Heinz Fingerhut, *Die Funktion der Tierfiguren im Werke Franz Kafkas: Offene Erzählgerüste und Figurenspiele* (Bonn: Bouvier, 1969), 27.

2. Haeckel, *Anthropogenie*; see also Ernst Haeckel, *Über unsere gegenwärtige Kenntnis vom Ursprung des Menschen*, *Deutsche Rundschau* 25 (2: 179–84), 1898). On Kafka and anthropological reflection in "Bericht," see Michael L. Rettinger, *Kafkas Berichterstatter: Anthropologische Reflexionen zwischen Irritation und Reaktion, Wirklichkeit und Perspektive* (Frankfurt: Lang, 2003), 21–51.

3. For recent histories of New World slavery, see David Brion Davis, *Inhuman Bondage: The Rise and Fall of Slavery in the New World* (New York: Oxford University Press, 2006); Seymour Drescher, *Abolition: A History of Slavery and Antislavery* (Cambridge: Cambridge University Press, 2009).

4. On the life of slaves in America, see the classic study by Kenneth M. Stampp, *The Peculiar Institution: Slavery in the Ante-Bellum South* (New York: Knopf, 1956).

5. For Kafka's relationship to film and movie going, see Hanns Zischler, *Kafka geht ins Kino* (Reinbek: Rowohlt, 1999); Dany Scholten, *Kafka und das Kino* (Munich: Grin, 2011); Peter-André Alt, *Kafka und der Film: Über kinematographisches Erzählen* (Munich: Beck, 2009).

6. Hugh S. R. Elliot and A. G. Thacker, trans., *Beasts and Men: Being Carl Hagenbeck's Experiences for Half a Century Among Wild Animals* (London: Longmans, Green, 1912); for a study of Hagenbeck, see Eric Ames, *Carl Hagenbeck's Empire of Entertainments* (Seattle: University of Washington Press, 2009).

7. Equiano's ethnographic picture of Africa has recently come under scrutiny, leading at least one major Equiano scholar, Vincent Carretta, to argue convincingly that the writer and activist falsified the account of his life in Africa. While Kafka could have had no knowledge of this debate, the point is that even in the slave narrative where a description of Africa is given with a seemingly meticulous exactitude, questions remain as to what the slave, violently removed from the scene of her African childhood, could consciously remember of this early existence. Such questions were snidely brought to bear in Equiano's day by slavery's advocates. On the questions of Equiano's African birth, see the following works by Vincent Carretta: *Equiano, the African: Biography of a Self-Made Man* (Athens: University of Georgia Press, 2005); "Why Equiano Matters," *Historically Speaking* 7, no. 3 (2006): 2–7; "Olaudah Equiano or Gustavus Vassa? New Light

on an Eighteenth-Century Question of Identity," *Slavery and Abolition* 20, no. 3 (1999): 96–105; "More New Light on the Identity of Olaudah Equiano or Gustavus Vassa," in *The Global Eighteenth Century*, ed. Felicity Nussbaum, 226–35 (Baltimore: Johns Hopkins University Press, 2003).

8. On Kafka and the "truth" as art, see Christian Eschweiler, *Kafkas Wahrheit als Kunst: Lichtblicke im Dunkel* (Bonn: Bouvier, 1996).

9. Although I mention the "talking book" here, I do not mean Gates's conception of it as a mode of textual doublespeak that defines the African American literary tradition. I indicate with the term only the slave's coming to awareness of the potentially freeing power of literacy. See Robert Stepto, "I Rose and Found My Voice: Narration, Authentication, and Authorial Control in Four Slave Narratives," in *The Slave's Narrative*, ed. Charles T. Davis and Henry Louis Gates Jr., 225–41 (New York: Oxford University Press, 1985).

10. For a general evaluation of freedom in Kafka, see Felix Gress, *Die gefährdete Freiheit: Franz Kafkas späte Texte* (Würzburg: Königshausen and Neumann, 1994).

11. See Henry Louis Gates Jr., *The Trial of Phillis Wheatley: America's First Black Poet and Her Encounters with the Founding Fathers* (New York: Basic Civitas Books, 2003).

12. For Kafka and mimicry, see Hartmut Binder, *Kafka in neuer Sicht: Mimik, Gestik u. Personengefüge als Darstellungsformen d. Autobiographischen* (Stuttgart: Metzler, 1976). On mimicry in postcolonial discourse, see Homi K. Bhabha, "Of Mimicry and Man: The Ambivalence of Colonial Discourse," in *The Location of Culture*, 121–31 (London: Routledge, 1994).

13. One should take pause when Sokel writes,

> Rotpeter setzt dabei richtig voraus, daß diese Gesellschaft nicht von rassistischem Vorurteile gehemmt ist. Sie ist bereit, ihre eigene beschützte Freiheit auszudehnen auf diejenigen, die den Willen und die Fähigkeit aufweisen, sich ihr anzupassen, was immer sie auch der Herkunft und Abstammung nach sein mögen. . . . Er macht seine totale Isolierung zum Sprungbrett rapider Entwicklung in ein neues, befreites und nach den Maßstäben eines anthropozentrischen Evolutionsideals höheres Wesen. (Sokel 2005, 253)

> Rotpeter takes it as a given that this society is not hindered by racist assumptions. It is prepared to extend its protected freedom to those who have shown the will and the ability to belong to it, regardless of family background and racial origin. . . . He makes out of his total isolation a springboard for the rapid development of a new, free and, following the precepts of the ideal of anthropological evolution, higher Being.

The opposite of this almost laughable suggestion that the academy's opinions are in no way determined by racist stereotypes is in fact the case. Rotpeter explicitly rejects human freedom and in no way views "the human" as a higher nature. Defined by self-delusion and swindle, the human is as debased as the ape; indeed, the two modes of being are ontologically reciprocal. Finally, Rotpeter does not see his new society as free of racism; he knows that his audience is defined by it in the way that a white abolitionist could vehemently oppose slavery and still be a virulent racist. Over and against this he actively seeks to recall, to mimic his old ape mimicry as his mode of self-genesis and fashioning.

14. Thus, it is not possible to agree with one critic who suggests, "Im Werk Kafkas ist dies das einzige Beispiel eines gelungenen Ausbrechens aus der Macht der bestehenden Ordnung. *Der Bericht* kann deshalb als die einzige Verwandlungsgeschichte gelesen werden, deren Verwandlung durch die noch näher zu bestimmenden Rituale der Befriedung Frieden zwischen der Welt und den Menschen suggeriert" (von Jagow 598–99). For Rotpeter, trapped between the states of Negro and ape, the exact opposite is the case. There is, here, no escape from the existing power structure, only endless vacillation between the structure's two defining points. This constant, unconscious motion is Rotpeter's *Ausweg*, not his freedom.

Chapter 6

1. For an analysis of silence and tautological experience in Kafka's journals, see Sandra Markewitz, *Das Schweigen: Tautologizität in Kafkas Tagebüchern* (Munich: Fink, 2006).

2. On Kafka and photography, and in particular the photographs reproduced in Holitscher, see Carolin Duttlinger, *Kafka and Photography* (Oxford: Oxford University Press, 2007), 65–78, 98.

3. For the definitive account of how colonized people were stigmatized with cannibalism in order to present them as inferior, see W. Arens, *The Man-Eating Myth: Anthropology and Anthropophagy* (New York: Oxford University Press, 1979).

4. Gerhard Neumann, "Hungerkünstler und Menschenfresser: Zum Verhältnis von Kunst und kulturellem Ritual im Werk Franz Kafkas," *Archiv für Kulturgeschichte* 66, no. 2 (1984): 347–89. See also Alexander Honold, "Menschenfresser/Hungerkünstler: Kafkas literarische Schaustellungen des Fremden," in *Maskeraden des (Post-)Kolonialismus: Verschattete Repräsentationen 'der Anderen' in der dt.-sprachigen Literatur und im Film*, ed. Ortrud Gutjahr and Stefan Hermes, 123–48 (Würzburg: Königshausen and Neumann, 2012).

5. Likewise, the hunger artist is not engaging in a diet. Heather Benbow reminds us that "Kafka's celebration of a feminized diet and his revulsion for meat are an embracing of his status as outsider; slightly built, devoid of masculine appetite, lacking the masculine traits of father Hermann Kafka, he seeks to elude the three-way association of meat-masculinity-power by eating milk and vegetable products, in short, 'women's food'" (Benbow 2006, 359). While this is absolutely an accurate assessment of at least one aspect of Kafka's relationship to nourishment, it does not account for the decision to starve oneself. The hunger artist is not on a diet.

6. Kafka's deformation of the body was in line with the expressionism of his milieu. See, for example, Walter Falk, *Franz Kafka und die Expressionisten im Ende der Neuzeit* (Frankfurt: Lang, 1990), 16; Hans-Peter Kunisch, *Gefährdete Spiegel: Körper in Texten der frühen Moderne, 1890–1930; Musil, Schnitzler, Kafka* (Frankfurt: Lang, 1996).

7. Furthermore, we recall that in the global history of slavery, skin color, and skin color alone, was the primary factor in determining whether or not one was a slave.

8. As Leon Litwack has written on lynching as public ritual, "The ordinary modes of execution and punishment were deemed insufficient; they no longer satisfied the emotional appetite of the crowd. To kill the victim was not enough; the execution needed to be turned into a public ritual, a collective experience, and the victim needed to be subjected to extraordinary torture and mutilation" (Litwack 1998, 285).

9. The import they perceive is that of the representation of the founding of communal being and civilization, premised over and against cannibalism. Seen here as martyrdom and lynching, sacrifice resolves incongruities in the foundational logic of society as is denied over time. Thus, as Orlando Patterson (1998) observes in the context of lynching, "Ritual of sacrifice violently emphasized and dissociated the incongruity, in the process first isolating and then reconstructing the only acceptable association of qualities: freedom = manhood = white status. . . . Psychologically, the 'fiendish eagerness' with which Afro-Americans were stabbed and killed, and the 'delight in suffering' they went through, not only vented all the rage of the Euro-American Southern male over the loss of his beloved dulotic way of life but projected all his chronic violence upon the Afro-American. Spiritually, the degenerate, masterless slave who dared to assert his manhood or freedom became the ideal sacrificial victim. As ex-slave, he symbolized the human wickedness and sin that haunted the fundamentalist souls of his executioners. And as 'black beasts,' he could be horribly sacrificed, without any sense of guilt, to a wrathful, vengeful God as a prime offering of blood and human flesh and as the soul of his enemy, Satan" (212).

10. Litwack (1998) reminds us that "neither crazed fiends nor the dregs of white society, the bulk of the lynchers tended to be ordinary and respectable people, animated by a self-righteousness that justified their atrocities in the name of maintaining the social and racial order and the purity of the Anglo-Saxon race" (294).

11. Lynching as a form of sacrifice is, as Susan Mizruchi writes, "necessary to the maintenance of social order, the achievement of a certain level of culture, and the perpetuation of a certain kind of economy" (Mizruchi 1998, 22–23).

12. See Amy Louise Wood, *Lynching and Spectacle: Witnessing Racial Violence in America, 1890–1940* (Chapel Hill: University of North Carolina Press, 2011), 71–112; 108.

13. Death would mean the termination of the work as transformation and, as Rolleston (1995) suggests, "an enigmatic historical shift, reducing to nonexistence the values that defined the artist's identity" (136). The liquidation and ultimate nonexistence of the body in transformation must not be a death or a historical shift but an endless, unbroken self-destruction.

14. As Del Caro (1989) rightly concludes, "However imperfectly the public may interpret or receive an artist's work, rarely must an artist remain in doubt about the public's acceptance of him as an artist. This most basic question in the relation between artist and public implies that Kafka is not merely using the hunger artist as a symbol for traditional art; rather, he is attempting to define philosophically the precondition of art and the state of art with regard to being" (41).

The very audience, then, that the hunger artist disdains is precisely that which, negatively and objectively, defines him as an artist. This entails the fundamental problem of "Ein Hungerkünstler." The hunger artist's work is incomplete without a spectator to appraise it as such. Thus, the problem of art is that of sacrifice and martyrdom; it is its reception, its visibility and its recognition.

15. Thus, Melchionne (2007) misrepresents the hunger artist's intentions when he writes, "The pious celebration of the artist's painstaking devotion to his craft is revealed as the rationalization of a less noble motivation, the artist's need for attention" (147). The hunger artist will exist, whether or not he has an audience. But without an audience he cannot be recognized as an artist as such, and to be acknowledged as an artist means to be cast out. The art of hunger is not driven by a craving for acceptance and applause but by an essential need for rejection, under the guise of which Noah's curse returns. This is not to say that the artist does not "need attention" but that this requirement is not a subjective desire; it is the objective precondition of the hunger artist's art. Without Noah's curse as exile, rejection, disappearance, and so on, there can be no art.

16. This is of course how Josef K. dies in *Der Proceß*, signifying a type of animal transformation, if only in the manner in which one meets one's death.

BIBLIOGRAPHY

Works by Franz Kafka

Amerika. Translated by Willa and Edwin Muir. New York: Schocken Books, 1996. (*AM*)

Amerika (The Man Who Disappeared). Translated by Michael Hofmann. New York: New Directions, 2004. (*AH*)

Brief an den Vater. Frankfurt: Fischer, 2011. (*BV*)

Briefe an Felice und andere Korrespondenz aus der Verlobungszeit. Edited by Erich Heller and Jürgen Born. Frankfurt: Fischer, 1967. (*BF*)

Briefe an Milena. Edited by Jürgen Born and Michael Müller. Frankfurt: Fischer, 1983. (*BM*)

Briefe 1902–1924. Edited by Max Brod. Frankfurt: Fischer, 1958. (*B*)

The Complete Stories. Edited by Nahum N. Glatzer. New York: Schocken Books, 1995. (*C*)

Das Ehepaar und andere Schriften aus dem Nachlaß. Edited by Hans-Gerd Koch. Frankfurt: Fischer, 1994.

Das Schloß. Edited by Jürgen Born, Gerhard Neumann, Sir Malcolm Pasley, and Jost Schillemeit. Frankfurt: Fischer, 1994.

Der Proceß. Edited by Jürgen Born, Gerhard Neumann, Sir Malcolm Pasley, and Jost Schillemeit. Frankfurt: Fischer, 1994.

Der Verschollene (Amerika). Edited by Jürgen Born, Gerhard Neumann, Sir Malcolm Pasley, and Jost Schillemeit. Frankfurt: Fischer, 1994. (*V*)

The Diaries. Translated by Joseph Kresh and Martin Greenberg. New York: Schocken Books, 1975. (*J*)

Drucke zu Lebzeiten: Kritische Ausgabe. Edited by Wolf Kittler, Hans-Gerd Koch, and Gerhard Neumann. Frankfurt: Fischer, 1994. (*D*)

"Letter to His Father." In *Kafka's "The Metamorphosis" and Other Writings*, edited by Helmuth Kiesel, translated by Ernst Kaiser and Eithne Wilkins, 175–229. New York: Continuum, 2002. (*LTF*)

Kritische Ausgabe. Edited by Jürgen Born, Gerhard Neumann, Sir Malcolm Pasley, and Jost Schillemeit. Frankfurt: Fischer, 1994. (*KA*)

Letters to Felice. Edited by Erich Heller and Jürgen Born.Translated by James Stern and Elisabeth Duckworth. New York: Schocken Books, 1973. (*LF*)

Letters to Friends, Family, and Editors. Translated by Richard and Clara Winston. New York: Schocken Books, 1977. (*L*)

Letters to Milena. Translated by Philip Boehm. New York: Schocken Books, 1990. (*LM*)

Nachgelassene Schriften und Fragmente: Kritische Ausgabe. Edited by Jürgen Born, Gerhard Neumann, Malcolm Pasley, and Jost Schillemeit. 2 vols. Frankfurt: Fischer, 1992–93. (*N*)

Tagebücher. Edited by Hans-Gerd Koch, Michael Müller, and Malcolm Pasley. Frankfurt: Fischer, 1990. (*T*)

Other Sources

Adorno, T.W. "Music and Language: A Fragment." In *Quasi Una Fantasia: Essays on Modern Music*, translated by Rodney Livingstone, 1–6. New York: Verso, 1998 [1956].

Albert, Claudia, and Andreas Disselnkötter. "'Inmitten der Strafkolonie steht keine Schreibmaschine': Eine Re-Lektüre von Kafkas Erzählung." *Internationales Archiv für Sozialgeschichte der deutschen Literatur* 27 (2002): 168–84.

Andermatt, Michael. *Haus und Zimmer im Roman: Die Genese des erzählten Raums bei E. Marlitt, Th. Fontane und F. Kafka*. Bern: Lang, 1987.

Anderson, Mark. "Kafka and New York: Notes on a Traveling Narrative." In *Modernity and the Text: Revisions of German Modernism*, edited by Andreas Huyssen and David Bathrick, 142–61. New York: Columbia University Press, 1989.

———. *Kafka's Clothes: Ornament and Aestheticism in the Habsburg Fin de Siècle*. Oxford: Clarendon, 1992.

———. "Kafka's Unsigned Letters: A Reinterpretation of the Correspondence with Milena." *MLN* 98, no. 3 (1983): 384–98.

———. "The Ornaments of Writing: Kafka, Loos and the Jugendstil." *New German Critique* 43 (1988): 125–45.

———. *Reading Kafka: Prague, Politics, and the Fin de Siècle*. New York: Schocken Books, 1989.

Andrews, William L., and Henry Louis Gates Jr., eds. *Slave Narratives*. New York: Library of America, 2000.

Anhalt, Utz. "Tiere und Menschen als Exoten: Exotisierende Sichtweisen auf das 'Andere' in der Gründungs- und Entwicklungsphase der Zoos." Ph.D. diss., Leibniz Universität Hannover, 2007.

Apollinaire, Guillaume. *Alcools: Poèmes 1898–1913*. Paris: Folio, 2013.

Astro, Alan. Review of *La Renaissance culturelle juive: Europe centrale et orientale 1897–1930*, by Delphine Bechtel. *Shofar* 22, no. 3 (2004): 162–64.

Baioni, Giuliano. *Kafka: Literatur und Judentum*. Translated into German by Gertrud Billen and Josef Billen. Stuttgart: Metzler, 1994.

Bauch, Marc A. *"Gentlemen, Be Seated!": The Rise and Fall of the Minstrel Show*. Munich: Grin, 2012.

Bay, Hansjörg. "Das eigene Fremde der Kultur: Travestien der ethnographischen Situation bei Kafka." *Deutsche Vierteljahrsschrift für Literaturwissenschaft und Geistesgeschichte* 83, no. 2 (2009): 287–309.

Bean, Annemarie, James V. Hatch, and Brooks McNamara, eds. *Inside the Minstrel Mask: Readings in Nineteenth-Century Blackface Minstrelsy*. Hanover, N.H.: University Press of New England / Wesleyan University Press, 1996.

Becher, Peter, Steffen Höhne, and Marek Nekula, eds. *Kafka und Prag: Literatur-, kultur-, sozial- und sprachhistorische Kontexte*. Cologne: Böhlau, 2012.

Beck, Evelyn Torton. *Kafka and the Yiddish Theater: Its Impact on His Work*. Madison: University of Wisconsin Press, 1971.

Becker, John. "Making the Incomprehensible Incomprehensible: The Trickery of Kafka's 'A Hunger Artist.'" In *The Trickster*, edited by Blake Hobby, 101–120. New York: Bloom's Literary Criticism, 2010.

Benbow, Heather Merle. "'Was auf den Tisch kam, mußte aufgegessen werden': Food, Gender, and Power in Kafka's Letters and Stories." *German Quarterly* 79, no. 3 (2006): 347–65.

Ben-Ephraim, Gavriel. "Making and Breaking Meaning: Deconstruction, Four-Level Allegory, and 'The Metamorphosis.'" *Midwest Quarterly* 35, no. 4 (1994): 450–67.

Benjamin, Walter. "Franz Kafka: On the Tenth Anniversary of His Death." In *Illuminations: Essays and Reflections*, edited by Hannah Arendt, translated by Harry Zohn, 111–40. New York: Schocken Books, 1969 [1934].

Benninghoff-Lühl, Sibylle. "Die Ausstellung der Kolonialisierten: Völkerschauen von 1874–1932." In *Andenken an den Kolonialismus: Eine Ausstellung des Völkerkundlichen Instituts der Universität Tübingen*, edited by Volker Harms, 52–65. Tübingen: Attempto, 1984.

Bensmaïa, Réda. "Foreword: The Kafka Effect." Translated by Terry Cochran. In Deleuze and Guattari, *Kafka*, ix–xxi.

Berlin, Edward A. *Ragtime: A Musical and Cultural History*. Los Angeles: University of California Press, 1980.

Berman, Russell A. *Enlightenment or Empire: Colonial Discourse in German Culture*. Lincoln: University of Nebraska Press, 1998.

———. "Tradition and Betrayal in 'Das Urteil.'" In Rolleston, *Companion to the Works of Franz Kafka*, 85–99.

Bernd, Christian Samuel Theodor. *Die deutsche Sprache in dem Großherzogthume Posen und einem Theile des angrenzenden Königreiches Polen, mit Vergleichungen sowol der Mundarten, als auch anderer Sprachen, und mit eigenen Forschungen*. Bonn: Weber, 1820.

Binder, Hartmut, ed. *Franz Kafka und die Prager deutsche Literatur: Deutungen und Wirkungen; Die Vorträge der 3. literarischen Fachtagung der Kulturstiftung der deutschen Vertriebenen vom 3.-4. Juni 1988 in Königswinter*. Bonn: Kulturstiftung der deutschen Vertriebenen, 1988.

———. *Kafka in neuer Sicht: Mimik, Gestik u. Personengefüge als Darstellungsformen d. Autobiographischen*. Stuttgart: Metzler, 1976.

———. *Kafka-Kommentar zu den Romanen, Rezensionen, Aphorismen und zum Brief an den Vater*. Munich: Winkler, 1976.

———. *Kafkas "Verwandlung": Entstehung, Deutung, Wirkung*. Frankfurt: Stroemfeld, 2004.

Bödeker, Karl-Bernhard. *Frau und Familie im erzählerischen Werk Franz Kafkas*. Bern: Lang, 1974.

Borchardt, Alfred. *Kafkas zweites Gesicht: Der Unbekannte; Das große Theater von Oklahoma*. Nuremberg: Glock and Lutz, 1960.

Bost, Harald. *Die Schrift mit den Augen: Kafkas ägyptische Rätsel*. Sulzbach: Kirsch, 2006.

Brandes, Peter. "Falsche Freunde: Zu Kafkas 'Urteil.'" In *An den Rändern Moral*, edited by Ulrich Kinzel, 89–102. Würzburg: Königshausen and Neumann, 2008.

Bridgwater, Patrick. *Kafka and Nietzsche*. Bonn: Bouvier, 1987.

Brod, Max. *Franz Kafka: A Biography*. Translated by G. Humphreys Roberts and Richard Winston. New York: Schocken Books, 1963 [1937].

Burian, Emil František. "Tanec v novém světle." *České divadlo* 5 (1981): 30–33.

Canetti, Elias. *Der andere Prozeß: Kafkas Briefe an Felice*. Munich: Hanser, 1984.

Cervo, Nathan. "Kafka's 'A Hunger Artist.'" *Explicator* 50, no. 2 (1992): 99–100.

Connelly, Frances S. *The Sleep of Reason: Primitivism in Modern European Art and Aesthetics, 1725–1907*. University Park: Pennsylvania State University Press, 1999.

Corngold, Stanley. "Allotria and Excreta in "In the Penal Colony." *Modernism/Modernity* 8, no. 2 (2001): 281–93.

———. *The Commentators' Despair: The Interpretation of Kafkas "Metamorphosis."* Port Washington, N.Y.: Kennikat Press, 1973.

———. "In the Circle of Kafka's 'Das Urteil.'" *Skrift* (Oslo) 12, no. 24 (2000): 39–62.

———. "Kafka and the Dialect of Minor Literature." *College Literature* 21, no. 1 (1994): 89–101.

———. "Kafka and Sex." *Daedalus* 136, no. 2 (2007): 79–87.

Corngold, Stanley, Jack Greenberg, and Benno Wagner, eds. *Franz Kafka: The Office Writings*. Princeton, N.J.: Princeton University Press, 2008.

Corngold, Stanley, Ruth V.Gross, eds. *Kafka for the Twenty-First Century*. Rochester, N.Y.: Camden House, 2011.

Dawe, Tracey. "Kafka's *The Penal Colony*: Reflections of German Colonialism and National Identity." In *Reflections: New Directions in Modern Languages and Cultures*, edited by Sarah Buxton, Laura Campbell, Tracy Dawe, and Elise Hugueny-Léger, 129–43. Newcastle upon Tyne, U.K.: Cambridge Scholars, 2008..

De Bruyker, Melissa. "Who Identified the Animal? The Rhetoric Behind the Hybrid in Kafka's 'The Metamorphosis' and *Amerika* (*The Man Who Disappeared*)." In *Kafka's Creatures: Animals, Hybrids, and Other Fantastic Beings*, edited by Marc Lucht and Donna Yarri, 191–210. Lanham, Md.: Lexington Books, 2010.

Deladurantaye, Leland. "Kafka's Reality and Nabokov's Fantasy: On Dwarves, Saints, Beetles, Symbolism, and Genius." *Comparative Literature* 59, no. 4 (2007): 315–31.

Del Caro, Adrian. "Denial versus Affirmation: Kafka's 'Ein Hungerkünstler' as a Paradigm of Freedom." *Modern Austrian Literature* 22, no. 1 (1989): 35–55.

Deleuze, Gilles, and Félix Guattari.. *Kafka: Toward a Minor Literature*. Translated by Dana Polan. Minneapolis: University of Minnesota Press, 1986 [1975].

Djoufack, Patrice. *Der Selbe und der Andere: Formen und Strategien der Erfahrung der Fremde bei Franz Kafka*. Wiesbaden: Deutscher Universitäts-Verlag, 2005.

Dodd, William J. "Kafka and Freud: A Note on 'In der Strafkolonie.'" *Monatshefte* 70, no. 2 (1978): 129–37.

Dreesbach, Anne. *Gezähmte Wilde: Die Zurschaustellung "exotischer" Menschen in Deutschland 1870–1940*. Frankfurt: Campus, 2005.

Duttlinger, Carolin. *Kafka and Photography*. Oxford: Oxford University Press, 2007.

Eißenberger, Gabi. *Entführt, verspottet und gestorben: Lateinamerikanische Völkerschauen in deutschen Zoos*. Frankfurt: IKO, 1996.

Elmarsafy, Ziad. "Aping the Ape: Kafka's 'Report to an Academy.'" *Studies in 20th Century Literature* 19, no. 20 (1995): 159–70.

Emrich, Wilhelm, William W. Langebartel, and Irene Zuk. "Franz Kafka and Literary Nihilism." *Journal of Modern Literature* 6, no. 3 (1977): 366–79.

Eschweiler, Christian. *Kafkas Erzählungen und ihr verborgener Hintergrund*. Bonn: Bouvier, 1991.

———. *Kafkas Wahrheit als Kunst: Lichtblicke im Dunkel*. Bonn: Bouvier, 1996.

Falk, Walter. *Franz Kafka und die Expressionisten im Ende der Neuzeit*. Frankfurt: Lang, 1990.

Fausto-Sterling, Anne. "Gender, Race, and Nation: The Comparative Anatomy of 'Hottentot' Women in Europe, 1815–1817." In *Deviant Bodies: Critical Perspectives on Difference in Science and Popular Culture*, edited by Jennifer Terry and Jacqueline Urla, 19–48. Bloomington: Indiana University Press, 1995.

Fickert, Kurt J. "The Failed Epiphany in Kafka's 'In der Strafkolonie.'" *Germanic Notes and Reviews* 32, no. 2 (2001): 153–59.

Fingerhut, Karl-Heinz. *Die Funktion der Tierfiguren im Werke Franz Kafkas: Offene Erzählgerüste und Figurenspiele*. Bonn: Bouvier, 1969.

Flocken, Heinz-Peter. "Der 'Lüstling des Entsetzens': Franz Kafkas Protokolle der Macht." Ph.D. diss., Heinrich Heine University, Düsseldorf, 1991.

Foster, Frances Smith. *Witnessing Slavery: The Development of Ante-bellum Slave Narratives*. Westport, Conn.: Greenwood Press, 1979.

Freud, Sigmund. *Totem und Tabu: Einige Übereinstimmungen im Seelenleben der Wilden und der Neurotiker*. Vol. 9 of *Gesammelte Werke in Einzelbänden*. Frankfurt: Fischer, 1952.

Friederici, Angelika. *Völker der Welt auf Castans Bühnen*. No. 10 (D3) of *Castan's Panopticum: Ein Medium wird besichtigt*. Berlin: Verlag Karl-Robert Scütze, 2011.

Friedrich, Lars. "Die Topophobie der Handschrift: Zu Franz Kafkas 'Ein Bericht für die Akademie.'" In *Tiere, Texte, Spuren*, edited by Norbert Otto Eke and Eva Geulen. Special issue, *Zeitschrift für deutsche Philologie* 126 (2007): 195–220.

Fromm, Waldemar. *Artistisches Schreiben: Franz Kafkas Poetik zwischen "Prozeß" und "Schloß."* Munich: Fink, 1998.

Fuchs, Anne. "A Psychoanalytic Reading of *The Man Who Disappeared*." In *The Cambridge Companion to Kafka*, edited by Julian Preece, 25–41. Cambridge: Cambridge University Press. 2002.

Gailus, Andreas. "Lessons of the Cryptograph: Revelation and the Mechanical in Kafka's 'In the Penal Colony.'" *Modernism/Modernity* 8, no. 2 (2001): 295–302.

Garloff, Katja. "Kafka's Racial Melancholy: 'A Report to an Academy.'" In *Kafka for the Twenty-First Century*, edited by Stanley Corngold and Ruth V. Gross, 89–104. Rochester, N.Y.: Camden House, 2011.

Gassmann, Arno A. *Lieber Vater, lieber Gott? Der Vater-Sohn-Konflikt bei den Autoren des engeren Prager Kreises*. Oldenburg: Igel, 2002.

Gelber, Mark H., ed. *Kafka, Zionism, and Beyond*. Tübingen: Niemeyer, 2004.

Gilman, Sander L. "Black Bodies, White Bodies: Toward an Iconography of Female Sexuality in Late Nineteenth-Century Art, Medicine, and Literature." In *"Race," Writing, and Difference*, edited by Henry Louis Gates Jr. and Kwame Anthony Appiah, 223–61. Chicago: University of Chicago Press, 1985.

———. *Franz Kafka, the Jewish Patient*. New York: Routledge, 1995.

Gißibl, Bernhard. "Imagination and Beyond: Cultures and Geographies of Imperialism in Germany, 1848–1918." In *European Empires and the People: Popular Responses to Imperialism in France, Britain, the Netherlands, Belgium, Germany and Italy*, edited by John MacKenzie, 158–98. Manchester: Manchester University Press, 2001.

Goebel, Rolf J. *Constructing China: Kafka's Orientalist Discourse*. Columbia, S.C.: Camden House, 1997.

———. "Kafka and Postcolonial Critique: *Der Verschollene*, 'In der Strafkolonie,' 'Beim Bau der chinesischen Mauer.'" In Rolleston, *Companion to the Works of Franz Kafka*, 187–212.

———. *Kritik und Revision: Kafkas Rezeption mythologischer, biblischer und historischer Traditionen*. Frankfurt: Lang, 1986.

Gray, Richard T. *Constructive Destruction: Kafka's Aphorisms; Literary Tradition and Literary Transformation*. Tübingen: Niemeyer, 1987.

Greenberg, Jack. "Wraparound: From Kafka to Kafkaesque." In Corngold, Greenberg, and Wagner, *Office Writings*, 355–72.

Gress, Felix. *Die gefährdete Freiheit: Franz Kafkas späte Texte*. Würzburg: Königshausen and Neumann, 1994.

Grözinger, Karl Erich. *Kafka und die Kabbala: Das Jüdische im Werk und Denken von Franz Kafka*. Frankfurt: Eichborn, 1992.

Grözinger, Karl Erich, Stéphane Mosès, and Hans Dieter Zimmermann, eds. *Franz Kafka und das Judentum: Colloquium, das die Hebräische Universität Jerusalem und die Johann-Wolfgang-Goethe-Universität Frankfurt im Dezember 1986 in Frankfurt veranstalteten*. Frankfurt: Jüdischer Verlag bei Athenäum, 1987.

Haeckel, Ernst. *Anthropogenie*. Leipzig: Engelmann, 1879.

———. *Generelle Morphologie der Organismen*. Berlin: Reimer, 1867.

Harel, Naama. "De-allegorizing Kafka's Ape: Two Animalistic Contexts." In *Kafka's Creatures: Animals, Hybrids, and Other Fantastic Beings*, edited by Marc Lucht and Donna Yarri, 53–66. Lanham, Md.: Lexington Books, 2010. 53–66.

Hartman, Tom. "Kafka's *The Metamorphosis*." *Explicator* 43, no. 2 (1985): 32–34.

Henel, Ingeborg. 'Ein Hungerkunstler.' *Deutsche Vierteljahresschrift* 38 (1964): 230–47.

Henisch, Peter. *Vom Wunsch, Indianer zu werden: Wie Franz Kafka Karl May traf und trotzdem nicht in Amerika landete*. Salzburg: Residenz, 1994.

Hippolytus. "The Extant Works and Fragments of Hippolytus: Dogmatical and Historical." In *The Fathers of the Third Century: Hippolytus, Cyprian, Caius, Novatian*. Vol. 5 of *The Ante-Nicene Fathers*. Edited by Alexander Roberts and James Donaldson, revised by A. Cleveland Coxe, 163–204. New York: Christian Literature Publishing, 1886.

Holitscher, Arthur. *Amerika, Heute und Morgen*. 1912. Reprint, Berlin: Fischer 1919.

Holland, Norman N. "Realism and Unrealism: Kafka's 'Metamorphosis.'" In *Rebirth and Renewal*, edited by Blake Hobby, 169–80. New York: Bloom's Literary Criticism, 2009.

Honold, Alexander. "Menschenfresser/Hungerkünstler: Kafkas literarische Schaustellungen des Fremden." In *Maskeraden des (Post-)Kolonialismus:*

Verschattete Repräsentationen 'der Anderen' in der dt.-sprachigen Literatur und im Film, edited by Ortrud Gutjahr and Stefan Hermes, 123–48. Würzburg: Königshausen and Neumann, 2012.

Hornung, Maria, and Sigmar Grüner. *Wörterbuch der Wiener Mundart*. Vienna: öbvhpt, 2002.

Irenaeus. "Against Heresies." In *The Apostolic Fathers: Justin Martyr, Irenaeus*. Vol. 1 of *The Ante-Nicene Fathers*. Edited by Alexander Roberts and James Donaldson, revised by A. Cleveland Coxe, 309–568. New York: Scribner's, 1903.

Ireton, Sean. "Die Transformation zweier Gregors: Thomas Manns 'Der Erwählte' und Kafkas 'Die Verwandlung.'" *Monatshefte* 90, no. 1 (1998): 34–48.

Jahn, Wolfgang. *Kafkas Roman "Der Verschollene" ("Amerika")*. Stuttgart: Metzler, 1965.

Jahnke, Uwe. *Die Erfahrung von Entfremdung: Sozialgeschichtliche Studien zum Werk Franz Kafkas*. Stuttgart: Heinz, 1988.

Jahraus, Oliver. "Das Urteil." In *Kafka-Handbuch*, edited by Bettina von Jagow and Oliver Jahraus, 409–20. Göttingen: Vandenhoeck and Ruprecht, 2008.

———. *Kafka: Leben, Schreiben, Machtapparate*. Stuttgart: Reclam, 2006.

———. "Zeichen-Verschiebungen: Vom Brief zum Urteil, von Georg zum Freund; Kafkas 'Das Urteil' aus poststrukturalistischer/dekonstruktivistischer Sicht." In *Kafkas "Urteil" und die Literaturtheorie: Zehn Modellanalysen*, edited by Oliver Jahraus and Stefan Neuhaus, 241–62. Stuttgart: Reclam, 2002.

Jahraus, Oliver, and Bettina von Jagow. "Kafkas Tier- und Künstlergeschichten." In *Kafka-Handbuch*, edited by Bettina von Jagow and Oliver Jahraus, 530–52. Göttingen: Vandenhoeck and Ruprecht, 2008.

Janz, Rolf-Peter. "Schwindelnde Männer oder die Liebe zum Betrug: Krull, Schwejk, Gunten, 'Rotpeter.'" In *Schwindelerfahrungen: Zur kulturhistorischen Diagnose eines vieldeutigen Symptoms*, edited by Rolf-Peter Janz, Fabian Stoermer, and Andreas Hiepko, 99–116. Amsterdam: Rodopi, 2003.

Kanz, Christine. "Differente Mannlichkeiten: Kafkas 'Das Urteil' aus gendertheoretischer Perspektive." In *Interpretationsmethoden am Beispiel von Franz Kafkas "Das Urteil,"* edited by Oliver Jahraus and Stefan Neuhaus, 152–75. Stuttgart: Reclam, 2002.

Kazda, Jaromír, and Josef Kotek. *Smích Červené sedmy*. Prague: Československý spisovatel, 1981.

Kilcher, Andreas B., and Detlef Kremer. "Die Genealogie der Schrift: Eine transtextuelle Lektüre von Kafkas 'Bericht für eine Akademie.'" In *Textverkehr: Kafka und die Tradition*, edited by Claudia Liebrand and Franziska Schößler, 45–72. Würzburg: Königshausen and Neumann, 2004.

Kittler, Friedrich A. *Grammophon, Film, Typewriter*. Berlin: Brinkmann and Bose, 1986.

Kittler, Wolf. "In dubio pro reo: Kafkas 'Strafkolonie.'" In *Kafkas Institutionen*, edited by Arne Höcker and Oliver Simons. Bielefeld: Transcript, 2007.

Kleinwort, Malte. *Kafkas Verfahren: Literatur, Individuum und Gesellschaft im Umkreis von Kafkas Briefen an Milena*. Würzburg: Königshausen and Neumann, 2004.

Kluge, Friedrich, and Elmar Seebold. *Etymologisches Wörterbuch der deutschen Sprache*. Berlin: De Gruyter, 2002.

Koch, Hans-Gerd. "Ein Bericht für eine Akademie." In *Interpretationen: Franz Kafka; Romane und Erzählungen*, edited by Michael Müller, 173–96. Stuttgart: Reclam, 2005.

Koelb, Clayton. "Critical Editions II: Will the Real Franz Kafka Please Stand Up?" In *A Companion to the Works of Franz Kafka*, edited by James Rolleston, 27–33. Rochester, N.Y.: Camden House, 2006.

———. "'In Der Strafkolonie': Kafka and the Scene of Reading." *German Quarterly* 55, no. 4 (1982): 511–25.

Kotek, Josef. *Dějiny české populární hudby a jazzu (1918–1968)*. Prague: Akademia, 1998.

———. *Kronika české synkopy: Půlstoletí českého jazzu a moderní populární hudby v obrazech a svědectví současníků (1903–1938)*. Prague: Supraphon, 1975.

Kramer, Sven. *Rätselfragen und wolkige Stellen: Zu Benjamins Kafka-Essay*. Lüneburg: Zu Klampen, 1991.

Kremer, Detlef. *Kafka: Die Erotik des Schreibens; Schreiben als Lebensentzug*. Frankfurt: Athenäum, 1989.

Kruse, Jens. "Lukács' 'Theorie des Romans' und Kafkas 'In der Strafkolonie': Eine Konstellation im Jahre 1914." *German Studies Review* 10, no. 2 (1987): 237–53.

Kunisch, Hans-Peter. *Gefährdete Spiegel: Körper in Texten der frühen Moderne, 1890–1930; Musil, Schnitzler, Kafka*. Frankfurt: Lang, 1996.

Lack, Elisabeth. *Kafkas bewegte Körper: Die Tagebücher und Briefe als Laboratorien von Bewegung*. Munich: Fink, 2009.

Lange-Kirchheim, Astrid. "Das fotografierte Hungern: Neues Material zu Franz Kafkas Erzählung 'Ein Hungerkünstler.'" *Hofmannsthal-Jahrbuch* 17 (2009): 7–56.

———. "Franz Kafka, 'Ein Hungerkünstler': Zum Zusammenhang von Eßstörung, Größenphantasie und Geschlechterdifferenz (mit einem Blick auf neues Quellenmaterial)." In *Grössenphantasien*, vol. 18 of *Freiburger literaturpsychologische Gespräche: Jahrbuch für Literatur und Psychoanalyse*, edited by Johannes Cremerius, 291–313. Würzburg: Königshausen and Neumann, 1999.

———. "Nachrichten vom italienischen Hungerkünstler Giovanni Succi: Neue Materialien zu Kafkas 'Hungerkünstler.'" In *Grössenphantasien*, vol. 18 of *Freiburger literaturpsychologische Gespräche: Jahrbuch für Literatur und Psychoanalyse*, edited by Johannes Cremerius, 315–40. Würzburg: Königshausen and Neumann, 1999.

Langer, František. *Byli a bylo*. Prague: Akropolis, 2003.

Leadbeater, Lewis W. "Aristophanes and Kafka: The Dung Beetle Connection." *Studies in Short Fiction* 23 (1986): 169–78.

Lemon, Robert. "Cargo Colonies and Penal Cults: Ethnology and Ethnocentrism in Kafka's 'In der Strafkolonie.'" *Colloquia Germanica* 40, no. 3/4 (2007): 279–95.

Lewerenz, Susann. "Völkerschauen und die Konstituierung rassifizierter Körper." In *Marginalisierte Körper: Beiträge zur Soziologie und Geschichte des anderen Körpers*, edited by Torsten Junge and Imke Schmincke, 135–53. Münster: Unrast, 2007.

Librett, Jeffrey S. "'With These Repulsive Things Indissolubly Bound': Kafka as Primal Scene." *American Imago* 64, no. 4 (2007): 513–33.

Litwack, Leon F. *Trouble in Mind: Black Southerners in the Age of Jim Crow.* New York: Knopf, 1998.

Loose, Gerhard. *Franz Kafka und Amerika.* Frankfurt: Klostermann, 1968.

Lorenz, Dagmar C. G. "Transatlantic Perspectives on Men, Women, and Other Primates: The Ape Motif in Kafka, Canetti, and Cooper's and Jackson's *King Kong* Films." *Women in German Yearbook* 23 (2007): 156–78.

Lothe, Jakob. "The Narrative Beginning of Kafka's 'In der Strafkolonie.'" In *Franz Kafka: Narration, Rhetoric, and Reading*, edited by Jakob Lothe, Beatrice Sandberg, and Ronald Speirs, 149–69. Columbus: Ohio State University Press, 2011.

Lott, Eric. *Love and Theft: Blackface Minstrelsy and the American Working Class.* New York: Oxford University Press, 1995.

Machosky, Brenda. "Fasting at the Feast of Literature." *Comparative Literature Studies* 42, no. 2 (2005): 288–305.

Maier, Thomas. "Das anorexische Ich, oder Der Künstler als sein eigener Zuschauer: Überlegungen zu Kafkas Erzählung 'Ein Hungerkünstler.'" In *Wege in und aus der Moderne*, edited by Werner Jung et al., 199–217. Bielefeld: Aisthesis, 2006.

Markewitz, Sandra. *Das Schweigen: Tautologizität in Kafkas Tagebüchern.* Munich: Fink, 2006.

Matzner, Antonín, Ivan Poledňák, and Igor Wasserberger, eds. *Encyklopedie jazzu a moderní populární hudby.* Prague: Supraphon, 1983.

Medeiros, Paulo. "Cannibalism and Starvation: The Parameters of Eating Disorders in Literature." In *Disorderly Eaters*, edited by Lilian R. Furst and Peter W. Graham, 11–28. University Park: Pennsylvania State University Press, 1992.

Melchionne, Kevin. "Why Artists Starve." *Philosophy and Literature* 31, no. 1 (2007): 142–48.

Meltzer, Edmund S. "Gregor Samsa the Scarab: An Additional Note." *German Quarterly* 73, no. 1 (2000): 84.

Menninghaus, Winfried. *Ekel: Theorie und Geschichte einer starken Empfindung.* Frankfurt: Suhrkamp, 2002.

Mense, Josef Hermann. *Die Bedeutung des Todes im Werk Franz Kafkas.* Frankfurt: Lang, 1978.

Mitchell, Breon. "Kafka and the Hunger Artists." In *Kafka and the Contemporary Critical Performance*, edited by Alan Udoff, 236–55. Bloomington: Indiana University Press, 1987).

Mizruchi, Susan L. *The Science of Sacrifice: American Literature and Modern Social Theory.* Princeton, N.J.: Princeton University Press, 1998.

Mladek, Klaus. "'Ein eigentümlicher Apparat': Franz Kafkas 'In der Strafkolonie.'" In *Text und Kritik: Sonderband Franz Kafka*, edited by Heinz Ludwig Arnold, 115–42. Munich: Text und Kritik, 2006.

Möbus, Frank. *Sünden-Fälle: Die Geschlechtlichkeit in Erzählungen Franz Kafkas.* Göttingen: Wallstein, 1994.

Müller-Seidel, Walter. *Die Deportation des Menschen: Kafkas Erzählung "In der Strafkolonie" im europäischen Kontext.* Franfurt: Fischer, 1986.

Nerad, Sonja. "Das teufelische Früchtchen und die widerliche Gans: Wer ist wer in Kafkas Erzählung 'Das Urteil'? *Literatur für Leser* 26 (2003): 63–81.

Neumann, Gerhard. "Der Affe als Ethnologe: Kafkas Bericht über den Ursprung der Kultur und dessen kulturhistorischer Hintergrund." In *Für Alle und Keinen: Lektüre, Schrift und Leben bei Nietzsche und Kafka*, edited by Friedrich Balke, Joseph Vogl, and Benno Wagner, 79–97. Zurich: Diaphanes, 2008.

———. "'Ein Bericht für eine Akademie': Kafkas Theorie vom Ursprung der Kultur." In *Franz Kafka: Ein Landarzt; Interpretationen*, edited by Elmar Locher and Isolde Schiffermüller, 275–93. Innsbruck: Studien, 2004.

———. "Hungerkünstler und Menschenfresser: Zum Problem der Kunst im Werk Franz Kafkas." In *Jenseits der Gleichnisse*, edited by Luc Lamberechts and Jaak de Vos, 45–76. Bern: Lang, 1986.

———. "Hungerkünstler und singende Maus: Franz Kafkas Konzept der 'kleinen Literaturen.'" In *Metamorphosen des Dichters*, edited by Gunter E. Grimm, 228–47. Frankfurt: Fischer, 1992.

———. "Kafka als Ethnologe." In *Odradeks Lachen: Fremdheit bei Kafka*, edited by Hansjörg Bay and Christof Hamann, 325–45. Freiburg: Rombach, 2006.

———. "Script, Work and Published Form: Franz Kafka's Incomplete Text." *Studies in Bibliography* 41 (1988): 77–99.

———. *Verfehlte Anfänge und offenes Ende: Franz Kafkas poetische Anthropologie*. Munich: Siemens, 2011.

Neumann, Gerhard, and Barbara Vinken. "Kulturelle Mimikry: Zur Affenfigur bei Flaubert und Kafka." In *Tiere, Texte, Spuren*, edited by Norbert Otto Eke and Eva Geulen. Special issue, *Zeitschrift für deutsche Philologie* 126 (2007): 126–42.

Neumeyer, Harald. "'Das Land der Paradoxa': Franz Kafkas 'In der Strafkolonie' und die Deportationsdebatte um 1900." In *Textverkehr: Kafka und die Tradition*, edited by Claudia Liebrand and Franziska Schößler, 291–334. Würzburg: Königshausen and Neumann, 2004..

Nicolai, Ralf R. *Kafkas Amerika-Roman "Der Verschollene: Motive und Gestalten*. Würzburg: Königshausen and Neumann, 1981.

Niehaus, Michael. "Entgründung: Auch ein Kommentar zu Kafkas 'Das Urteil.'" *Weimarer Beiträge* 48, no. 3 (2002): 344–63.

Niemeyer, Günter H. W. *Hagenbeck: Geschichte und Geschichten*. Hamburg: Christians, 1972.

Nietzsche, Friedrich. *The Birth of Tragedy* and *The Case of Wagner*. Translated by Walter Kaufmann. New York: Vintage, 1967.

Nordau, Max. *Entartung*. Berlin: Duncker, 1892–93.

Norris, Margot. "Kafka's Hybrids: Thinking Animals and Mirrored Humans." In *Kafka's Creatures: Animals, Hybrids, and Other Fantastic Beings*, edited by Marc Lucht and Donna Yarri, 17–32. Lanham, Md.: Lexington Books, 2010.

———. "Sadism and Masochism in Two Kafka Stories: 'In der Strafkolonie' and 'Ein Hungerkünstler.'" *MLN* 93, no. 3 (1978): 430–47.

North, Michael. *The Dialect of Modernism: Race, Language and Twentieth-Century Literature*. New York: Oxford University Press, 1994.

Northey, Anthony D. "Kafka's American Connection." Franz Kafka special number, *Journal of Modern Literature* 6, no. 3 (1977): 448–54.

Olney, James. "'I Was Born': Slave Narratives, Their Status as Autobiography and as Literature." In *The Slave's Narrative*, edited by Charles T. Davis and Henry Louis Gates Jr., 148–75. New York: Oxford University Press, 1985.

Oye, Thorsten. “Hungerkünstler gibt es wirklich: Zu einer Erzählung Franz Kafkas.” *Merkur* 58 (2004): 1136–40.

Pasley, Malcolm. *“Die Schrift ist unveränderlich . . .”: Essays zu Kafka*. Frankfurt: Fischer, 1995.

Patterson, Orlando. *Rituals of Blood: Consequences of Slavery in Two American Centuries*. Washington, D.C.: Civitas/Counterpoint, 1998.

Peters, Paul. “Kolonie als Strafe: Kafkas ‘Strafkolonie.’ ” In *Kolonialismus als Kultur*, edited by Alexander Honold and Oliver Simons, 59–84. Tübingen: Francke, 2002.

———. “Witness to the Execution: Kafka and Colonialism.” *Monatshefte* 93, no. 4 (2001): 401–25.

Petersen, Wolfgang. “Franz Kafka.” *Monatshefte für deutschen Unterricht* 29, no. 8 (1937): 373–88.

Pfeiffer, Herbert. *Das große Schimpfwörterbuch: Über 10.000 Schimpf-, Spott- und Neckwörter zur Bezeichnung von Personen*. Frankfurt: Eichborn, 1996.

Polaschegg, Andrea. “Maschinen (nicht) verstehen: Das kollabierte Paradox in Franz Kafkas Erzählung ‘In der Strafkolonie.’ ” *Deutsche Vierteljahrsschrift für Literaturwissenschaft und Geistesgeschichte* 82 (2008): 654–80.

Politzer, Heinz. *Franz Kafka: Parable and Paradox*. Ithaca, N.Y.: Cornell University Press, 1966.

Polubojarinova, Larissa N. “Kafka und Sacher-Masoch: ‘In der Strafkolonie’ und ‘Der Hungerkünstler.’ ” *Österreichische Literatur und Kultur* 21 (2003): 195–201.

Poulain, Elfie. *Kafka: Einbahnstrasse zur Hölle; Oder die unmögliche Selbstrechtfertigung des Daseins*. Stuttgart: Metzler, 2003.

Rajec, Elizabeth M. *Namen und ihre Bedeutungen im Werke Franz Kafkas: Ein interpretatorischer Versuch*. Bern: Lang, 1977.

Raphael-Hernandez, Heike, ed. *Blackening Europe: The African American Presence*. New York: Routledge, 2004.

Reiss, Hans. “Kafka on the Writer’s Task.” *Modern Language Review* 66, no. 1 (1971): 113–24.

———. Review of *Die Deportation des Menschen: Kafkas Erzählung ‘In der Strafkolonie’ im europäischen Kontext*, by Walter Müller-Seidel. *Modern Language Review* 83, no. 3 (1988): 798–800.

Reitter, Paul. “Bad Writing in Franz Kafka’s ‘Das Urteil.’ ” *Seminar* 38, no. 2 (2002): 134–41.

Rettinger, Michael L. *Kafkas Berichterstatter: Anthropologische Reflexionen zwischen Irritation und Reaktion, Wirklichkeit und Perspektive*. Frankfurt: Lang, 2003.

Richter, Fritz K. “ ‘Verwandlungen’ bei Kafka und Stehr.” *Monatshefte* 63, no. 2 (1971): 141–46.

Roberts, Alexander, and James Donaldson, eds. *The Apostolic Fathers: Justin Martyr, Irenaeus*. Vol. 1 of *The Ante-Nicene Fathers*. Revised by A. Cleveland Coxe. New York: Scribner’s, 1903.

Robertson, Ritchie. “Der Künstler und das Volk: Kafkas ‘Ein Hungerkünstler.’ ” In *Text und Kritik: Sonderband Franz Kafka*, edited by Heinz Ludwig Arnold, 180–91. Munich: Text und Kritik, 2006.

———. "Edwin Muir as Critic of Kafka." *Modern Language Review* 79, no. 3 (1984): 638–52.

———. *Kafka: Judaism, Politics, and Literature*. Oxford: Clarendon Press, 1985.

———. "Kafka as Anti-Christian: 'Das Urteil,' 'Die Verwandlung,' and the Aphorisms." In Rolleston, *Companion to the Works of Franz Kafka*, 101–22.

Rodlauer, Hannelore. "Zwischen Wien und Berlin: Stichproben zur Präsenz der Prager Literatur aus der Sicht der Briefe Franz Kafkas, mit einem Exkurs zum 'Hungerkünstler.' " In *Prager deutschsprachige Literatur zur Zeit Kafkas*, edited by Hannelore Rodlauer, 153–64. Vienna: Braumüller, 1989.

Rohde, Bertram. *"Und blätterte ein wenig in der Bibel": Studien zu Franz Kafkas Bibellektüre und ihre Auswirkungen auf sein Werk*. Würzburg: Königshausen and Neumann, 2002.

Rolleston, James, ed. *A Companion to the Works of Franz Kafka*. Rochester, N.Y.: Camden House, 2002.

———. "Purification unto Death: 'A Hunger Artist' as Allegory of Modernism." In *Approaches to Teaching Kafka's Short Ficion*, edited by Richard T. Gray, 135–42. New York: Modern Language Association of America, 1995.

Rösch, Gertrud Maria. "Rotpeters Vorfahren: Zur Tradition und Funktion der Affendarstellung bei Johann Gottfried Schnabel, Alfred Kubin und Franz Kafka." In *Tiere, Texte, Spuren*, edited by Norbert Otto Eke and Eva Geulen. Special issue, *Zeitschrift für deutsche Philologie* 126 (2007): 98–109.

Rudloff, Holger. *Gregor Samsa und seine Brüder: Kafka, Sacher-Masoch, Thomas Mann*. Würzburg: Königshausen and Neumann, 1997.

Ruhleder, Karl H. "Franz Kafka's 'Das Urteil': An Interpretation." *Monatshefte* 55, no. 1 (1963): 13–22

Rutherford, Danilyn. "The Foreignness of Power: Alterity and Subversion in Kafka's 'In the Penal Colony' and Beyond." *Modernism/Modernity* 8, no. 2 (2001): 303–13.

Ryan, Michael P. "The Aggregate Character in Kafka's 'In der Strafkolonie.' " *Symposium* 55, no. 4 (2002): 213–27.

———. "Kafka's *Die Söhne*: The Range and Scope of Metaphor." *Monatshefte* 93, no. 1 (2001): 73–86.

———. "Samsa and *Samsara*: Suffering, Death, and Rebirth in 'The Metamorphosis.' " *German Quarterly* 72, no. 2 (1999): 133–52.

Ryan, Simon. "Franz Kafka's Die Verwandlung : Transformation, Metaphor, and the Perils of Assimilation." *Seminar: A Journal of Germanic Studies* 43, no. 1 (2007): 1–18.

Samaltanos, Katia. *Apollinaire, Catalyst for Primitivism, Picabia, and Duchamp*. Ann Arbor, Mich.: UMI Research Press, 1984.

Santner, Eric L., and David J. Levin. "Kafka Symposium: Introduction." *Modernism/Modernity* 8, no. 2 (2001): 277–79.

Saße, Günter. "Aporien der Kunst: Kafkas Künstlererzählungen 'Josefine, die Sängerin' und 'Ein Hungerkünstler.' " In *Literarische Moderne*, edited by Sabina Becker and Helmuth Kiesel, 245–55. Berlin: De Gruyter, 2007

Schärf, Christian. *Franz Kafka: Poetischer Text und heilige Schrift*. Göttingen: Vandenhoeck and Ruprecht, 2000.

Scholz, Ingeborg. *Franz Kafka: "Das Urteil," "Die Verwandlung," "Ein Hungerkünstler."* Hollfeld: Bayer, 1993.

Schreiber, Michael. *"Ihr sollt euch kein Bild— . . .": Untersuchungen zur Denkform der negativen Theologie im Werk Franz Kafkas*. Frankfurt: Lang, 1986.

Schuller, Gunther. *Early Jazz: Its Roots and Musical Development*. New York: Oxford University Press, 1998.

Schulz-Behrend, G. "Kafka's 'Ein Bericht für eine Akademie': An Interpretation." *Monatshefte* 55, no. 1 (1963): 1–6.

Schumacher, Eckhard. "Die Kunst der Trunkenheit: Franz Kafkas 'Ein Bericht für eine Akademie.'" In *Trunkenheit: Kulturen des Rausches*, edited by Thomas Strässle and Simon Zumsteg, 175–90. Amsterdam: Rodopi, 2008.

Schüttpelz, Erhard. "Eine Berichtigung für eine Akademie." In *Kafkas Institutionen*, edited by Arne Höcker and Oliver Simons, 97–124. Bielefeld: Transcript, 2007.

Schwartz, Regina M. *The Curse of Cain: The Violent Legacy of Monotheism*. Chicago: University of Chicago Press, 1998

Schwarz, Werner Michael. *Anthropologische Spektakel: Zur Schaustellung "exotischer" Menschen, Wien 1870–1910*. Vienna: Turia and Kant, 2001.

Selg, Peter. *Rainer Maria Rilke und Franz Kafka: Lebensweg und Krankheitsschicksal im 20. Jahrhundert*. Dornach: Pforte, 2007.

Sell, Robert. *Bewegung und Beugung des Sinns: Zur Poetologie des menschlichen Körpers in den Romanen Franz Kafkas*. Stuttgart: Metzler, 2002.

Shahar, Galili. "Fragments and Wounded Bodies: Kafka after Kleist." *German Quarterly* 80, no. 4 (2007): 449–67.

Sheppard, Richard W. "Kafka's *Ein Hungerkünstler*: A Reconsideration." *German Quarterly* 46, no. 2 (1973): 219–33.

Sokel, Walter H. "Identität und Individuum oder Vergangenheit und Zukunft: Zum Identitätsproblem in Franz Kafkas 'Ein Bericht an [*sic*] eine Akademie' in psychoanalytischem und zeithistorischem Kontext." In *Die Vielfalt in Kafkas Leben und Werk*, edited by Wendelin Schmidt-Dengler and Norbert Winkler, 245–57. Prague: Vitalis, 2005.

———. "Von Marx zum Mythos: Das Problem der Selbstentfremdung in Kafkas 'Verwandlung.'" *Monatshefte* 73, no. 1 (1981): 6–22.

Sotiropoulos, Karen. *Staging Race: Black Performers in Turn of the Century America*. Cambridge, Mass.: Harvard University Press, 2006.

Spector, Scott. *Prague Territories: National Conflict and Cultural Innovation in Franz Kafka's Fin de Siècle*. Berkeley: University of California Press, 2000.

Speirs, Ronald. "The Dynamics of Narration in Betrachtung, 'Das Urteil,' and Kafka's Reflections on Writing. In *Franz Kafka: Narration, Rhetoric, and Reading*, edited by Jakob Lothe, Beatrice Sandberg, and Ronald Speirs, 196–231. Columbus: Ohio State University Press, 2011.

Stein, Gertrude. "Melanctha." In *Three Lives*, 47–141. 1909. Reprint, New York: Dover, 1994.

Stepto, Robert. "I Rose and Found My Voice: Narration, Authentication, and Authorial Control in Four Slave Narratives." In *The Slave's Narrative*, edited by Charles T. Davis and Henry Louis Gates Jr., 225–41. New York: Oxford University Press, 1985.

Stern, J. P. "Franz Kafka's 'Das Urteil': An Interpretation." *German Quarterly* 45, no. 1 (1972): 114–29.

Sternstein, Malynne. "Laughter, Gesture, and Flesh: Kafka's 'In the Penal Colony.'" *Modernism/Modernity* 8, no. 2 (2001): 315–23.

Stillmark, Hans-Christian. "Zu Kafkas Erzählung 'In der Strafkolonie.'" *Studien zur Germanistik* 8 (2002): 223–41.

Strauss, Walter A. *On the Threshold of a New Kabbalah: Kafka's Later Tales.* New York: Lang, 1988.

Strother, Z. S. "Display of the Body Hottentot." In *Africans on Stage: Studies in Ethnological Show Business*, edited by Bernth Lindfors, 1–61. Bloomington: Indiana University Press, 1999.

Sweeney, Kevin W. "Competing Theories of Identity in Kafka's *The Metamorphosis.*" *Mosaic* 23, no. 4 (1990): 23–35.

Swinford, Dean. "The Portrait of an Armor-Plated Sign: Reimagining Samsa's Exoskeleton." In *Kafka's Creatures: Animals, Hybrids, and Other Fantastic Beings*, edited by Marc Lucht and Donna Yarri, 211–18. Lanham, Md.: Lexington Books, 2010.

Theisen, Bianca. "Naturtheater: Kafkas Evolutionsphantasien." In *Textverkehr: Kafka und die Tradition*, edited by Claudia Liebrand and Franziska Schößler, 273–90. Würzburg: Königshausen and Neumann, 2004.

Thode-Arora, Hilke. *Für fünfzig Pfennig um die Welt: Die Hagenbeckschen Völkerschauen.* Frankfurt: Campus, 1989.

Toll, Robert C. *Blacking Up: The Minstrel Show in Nineteenth-Century America.* New York: Oxford University Press, 1974.

Töns, Andreas. *"Nur mir gegenübergestellt": Ich-Fragmente im Figurenfeld; Reduktionsstufen des Doppelgängermotivs in Kafkas Erzählprosa.* Bern: Lang, 1998.

Válek, Jiří. "Pokrokové tradice české moderní taneční hudby." In *Taneční hudba a jazz 1960: Sborník statí a příspěvků k otázkám jazzu a moderní taneční hudby*, edited by Lubomír Dorůžka, Jaromír Horek, and Josef Kotek, 15–17. Prague: Státní hudební vydavatelství, 1960.

Voigts, Manfred. *Geburt und Teufelsdienst: Franz Kafka als Schriftsteller und als Jude.* Würzburg: Königshausen and Neumann, 2008.

———. *Kafka und die jüdisch-zionistische Frau: Diskussionen um Erotik und Sexualität im Prager Zionismus; Mit Text-Materialien.* Würzburg: Königshausen and Neumann, 2007.

Von Jagow, Bettina. "Rotpeters Rituale der Befriedung: Ein zweifelhafter 'Menschenausweg.' Franz Kafkas 'Bericht für eine Akademie' aus eth(n)ologischer Perspektive." *Zeitschrift für Germanistik* n.s. 12, no. 3 (2002): 597–607.

Voskovec, Jiří. *Klobouk ve křoví.* Prague: Mladá fronta, 1996.

Wagner, Benno. "'. . . in der Fremde, aus der Sie kommen . . .': Die Geburt des Schreibens aus der Statistik des Selbstmords." In *Odradeks Lachen: Fremdheit bei Kafka*, edited by Hansjörg Bay and Christof Hamann, 193–228. Freiburg: Rombach, 2006.

Waldeck, Peter B. "Kafka's 'Die Verwandlung' and 'Ein Hungerkünstler' as Influenced by Leopold von Sacher-Masoch." *Monatshefte* 64, no. 2 (1972): 147–52.

Walther, Hans. *Franz Kafka: Die Forderung der Transzendenz.* Bonn: Bouvier, 1977.

Weininger, Otto. *Geschlecht und Charakter: Eine prinzipielle Untersuchung.* Vienna: Braumüller, 1903.

Weitin, Thomas. "Revolution und Routine: Die Verfahrensdarstellung in Kafkas 'Strafkolonie.'" In *Kafkas Institutionen*, edited by Arne Höcker and Oliver Simons, 255–68. Bielefeld: Transcript, 2007.

William, Jennifer Marston. "'Gut Zugedeckt?' Metaphors for Memory in *Das Urteil* and *Die Verwandlung*." *Journal of the Kafka Society of America* 26, no. 1/2 (2002): 58–66.
Wolfradt, Jörg. *Der Roman bin ich: Schreiben und Schrift in Kafkas "Der Verschollene."* Würzburg: Königshausen and Neumann, 1996.
Wood, Amy Louise. *Lynching and Spectacle: Witnessing Racial Violence in America, 1890–1940*. Chapel Hill: University of North Carolina Press, 2011.
Zantop, Susanne. *Colonial Fantasies: Conquest, Family, and Nation in Precolonial Germany, 1770–1870*. Durham: Duke University Press, 1997.
Zilcosky, John. *Kafka's Travels: Exoticism, Colonialism, and the Traffic of Writing*. New York: Palgrave, 2003.
———. "Wildes Reisen: Kolonialer Sadismus und Masochismus in Kafkas 'Strafkolonie.'" *Weimarer Beiträge* 50 (2004): 33–54.
Zimmermann, Hans Dieter. "Die aufbauende Zerstörung der Welt: Zu Franz Kafkas 'Der Hungerkünstler.'" In *Kafka und Prag*, edited by Kurt Krolop and Hans Dieter Zimmermann, 167–74. Berlin: De Gruyter, 1994.

INDEX